T0322390

SON OF GRACE

FRANK WORRELL
A BIOGRAPHY

VANEISA BAKSH

fairfield books

SON OF GRACE

FRANK WORRELL
A BIOGRAPHY

First published by Fairfield Books in 2023

fairfield books

Fairfield Books
Bedser Stand
Kia Oval
London
SE11 5SS

Typeset in Garamond and Proxima Nova
Typesetting by Rob Whitehouse
Photography by Getty Images unless stated

This book is printed on paper certified
by the Forest Stewardship Council

Every effort has been made to trace copyright and any oversight
will be rectified in future editions at the earliest opportunity

The views and opinions expressed in this book are those of the author
and do not necessarily reflect the views of the publishers

ISBN 978-1-915237-30-9

A CIP catalogue record for is available from the British Library

Printed by CPI Group (UK) Ltd

For Arnold Rampersad, Jackie Hinkson,
and the dream of a West Indian nation

CONTENTS

Part Four

Part Five

INTRODUCTION

It was not through cricket that I first encountered Frank Worrell, not directly anyway. It was by way of a comic book, more directly related to the addiction to reading that has haunted me since I was three. The title, *SIR FRANK WORRELL*, in pale yellow boxy capital letters backed by a black shadow, stood enticingly on a sky-blue background. Underneath, five drawings presented a montage: a full-faced portrait surrounded by Worrell batting; bowling; striding, bat in one hand, blue cap in the other; and the final one, in a suit, obviously presenting the Frank Worrell Trophy in 1961. I'd planned to write about it in this biography: how it had come to me as a child, and its impact. In the West Indies, it was a novelty to find something written for children about a Caribbean icon.

I tried to locate a copy with no success. Only a couple of people knew of its existence, but none had it. Then, one Saturday evening in late August 2016, I attended a lecture at Trinidad and Tobago's National Museum, and the friend who had organised it came up to me excitedly, proffering a large white envelope. 'It's a present,' he said, as I stood looking bemused in front of the already-seated audience. 'Open it.'

Inside, was a slightly dog-eared copy of the comic. How he came to acquire it is yet another of the serendipitous moments that have favoured this biography. All he would say was that he was driving along one day, when he spotted it lying at the side of the road. What were the chances that someone who knew of my quest would see it and recognise it, posing as a piece of litter on some arbitrary roadway? I still don't believe it.

But the story of the incredible acquisition of this comic book is not the end. The copy he'd found was the one from my childhood, with a logo on the cover saying *Express Caribbean Comics* (I have written for the *Trinidad Express* over many years). The price was 85 cents, and it was touted as Issue No 1.

There was no publication date, and its only credit was the statement that it was drawn by Hugh Cumberbatch from a short biography by Undine Giuseppi. Earlier, when I had sought information from the Express library, they could not tell me the publication date and had no copies in their archives, but they had mentioned that the author was Sean Aberdeen. I found a listing on Amazon for a January 1987 book of unknown binding, and no image, by Sean Aberdeen, called *Sir Frank Worrell, National Heritage Series of Caribbean Heroes*. The publisher was Imprint Caribbean, a subsidiary of the Express Newspapers, but the publication date confused me.

Giuseppi's book had been published in 1969; I had deduced that this comic had been issued in the early Seventies, because I knew I was still in primary school when I read it. I contacted the librarian at Trinidad and Tobago's National Library, asking if she could find any background. She sent me an image of the cover of the comic in their holdings, which was almost identical, except for the colours: the title was in white, and the blue cap had been coloured a purplish maroon. The library stamp said it cost $5 and that the author was Sean Ramdus. I had not noticed the different logos on the cover, and I struggled to figure out who was the actual author of the comic in front of me, and why its publication date was 1987, when I would have been 21.

Eventually it dawned on me that it must have been re-issued in 1987, and the comic I had held in my childhood hands was possibly not to be found in the archives or any other public record that I had checked. It had simply disappeared. If I had not been so obsessively tracking it, I might never have noticed that the cover had been slightly altered, like a spot-the-difference puzzle. But it still leaves behind the mystery of who authored that first edition. The 1987 one on Amazon credited Sean Aberdeen, but the National Library credits it to Sean Ramdus. It was certainly an error in the filing.

This comic tale illustrates one of the challenges facing researchers within the West Indies, and I daresay, in many other locales. The process of archiving has been fitful and arbitrary; often facilitated by happenstance. Whatever personal records have been kept by way of scrapbooks and other memorabilia, are often tossed out by relatives during spring cleaning. The dusty accumulation of clutter exasperates inheritors of faded souvenirs of lives gone by. In many instances, without appropriate storage, documents had deteriorated, or were damaged and lost through fires and floods. It meant that research would not be as simple as obtaining access to collections of papers – very few left such legacies to posterity.

When I was persuaded to write a biography of Frank Worrell, I could not have imagined just how skeletal was the material outside of his cricket. It appeared that the only way to find out what his life was like would be to talk to people who knew him, and the urgency of the project loomed more anxiously. It had been more than 50 years since his death; nearly a hundred since his birth in 1924, so who would still be around and able to talk?

The quest was daunting; more often than not, memories would not deliver despite the generosity of intentions. It became important to record some of these encounters as a way of documenting the biographer's journey; such was the nature of these excursions. It meant weaving into the narrative what might otherwise have been kept as notes as a way of demonstrating the process, and to reveal something of the personalities involved.

Perhaps this extra dredging has added another dimension to research, especially on Caribbean lives. How much of the legwork does one share with readers? In spaces where historical records are sparse, too much room has been left for speculation and it has become vital to fill in as many blanks as we can. This work has been an attempt at portraiture, to spread out before the reader a canvas that depicts the life of a man whose name is still summoned frequently, but who remains essentially an enigma.

It is not that Worrell had not been presented in biographies before, four of varying depth and scope exist; plus, his autobiographical work, *Cricket Punch*, and countless journal, magazine and newspaper articles. But except for Ivo Tennant's biography, they were primarily adulatory summaries of his cricket. There was little to give a sense of the essence of the man whose contribution to West Indian identity was a remarkable one. The substantive question for me was: who was the man, Frank Worrell?

He was a dominant cricketing figure in the 1950s; along with Clyde Walcott and Everton Weekes, the dashing Barbadian trio immortalised as the Three Ws. A whimsical comparison of their personalities and styles might invoke the elements of earth, wind and fire.

Worrell, the eldest, would be the wind – sometimes cool and refreshing, sometimes gusty and fierce, but always defined by a delicate and impalpable force. His batting was unanimously heralded for its style and grace: this was a man of finesse who relished the artistry of the game. His late cuts were his trademark. One report of his batting during the 1950 Lord's Test was eloquent. 'Strokes of exquisite delicacy played so late that one thought he had allowed the ball to go through, when he stroked it imperiously almost out of Evans' hungry gloves. Even the English players applauded his late cuts.'

Walcott, the giant, was fire: pure power and stamina that rendered him often impossible to extinguish. On song, he raged imperiously, heating up any ground.

Weekes, the youngest and shortest of the three, was no less powerful, but he was not given to lofty explosions, instead he relied on masterful technique, and an astute brain to read the ball early. Sixes were not his preference, rather he scored along the ground. In temperament, he was a man of the earth, grounded in an upbringing that kept him close to the philosophy of his grassroots heritage.

What set Worrell apart was his natural air of authority. He did not need to be in a leadership position to manifest it, and this characteristic defined his life. Australian captain, Richie Benaud, hailed him as a great captain. 'Frank Worrell turned West Indies from being the most magnificent group of individual cricketers in the world into a close-knit team. No one else could have done it.'

In the Sixties, until his death in 1967, he was more of an icon as a West Indian leader, whose qualities of grace and wisdom framed him as the ideal representative of a society still constructing its identity.

Yet, for much of his career he was plagued by insecurities, and haunted by traumas, embittered by inequities within the social structures that dominated regional life. He was not one for outbursts, but he was firm in his stances, quietly making his positions known so that people came to know his boundaries. He was a backroom diplomat. His outlook was egalitarian; he was committed to teamwork; he was affable and people were easily drawn into his aura of intimacy. He was a noted drinker, philanderer and party man, adroit at eliciting astonishing discretion from his contemporaries. Nobody would willingly breathe a word about the dalliances he chose to keep under the radar; such was the respect and fierce loyalty he charmingly commanded. A man of extremes, he was as passionate about life as he was about the cricket that fed him. Cricket was his passport, not his destination. To understand his complexity, one had to dig deep into the forces that shaped him: the childhood years that are often overlooked as significant foundations in the development of an adult. Despite moments of despair as I struggled to unearth the tenor of those formative years, I was determined to keep at it because I was convinced that therein was the making of the man. When his sister, Grace, rebuffed me after initially agreeing to talk, I felt her manner represented something typical throughout the region, particularly Barbados, and thought that the story of the encounter was worth including.

Worrell had never been given to discussions about his family; he guarded their privacy scrupulously. Barely anything was known about his domestic life. Because he was not given to public utterances, several inaccuracies still exist, unchallenged, in the public domain. As with often repeated tales, they have solidified into facts about him and his career choices.

Were it not for another act of serendipity, I would not have had access to a stash of documents that went a long way towards clearing up some of these myths. In the course of an entirely different thread of research, on cocoa estates in Trinidad, I met Charles Merry, the son of Cyril Merry who had been the secretary of the West Indies Cricket Board of Control (WICBC) during the 1950s. Cyril, a rare archivist, had kept his collection of papers for that period, and Charles generously lent them to me.

Inside that box of papers contained correspondence that gave an insight into the way the Board functioned. Despite its well-known high-handed ethos, there were surprising episodes of genuine concern over the welfare of cricketers. As patriarchal as they might have been, sometimes annoyingly condescending, Board members were conscious of the youthful naïveté, and in the case of the non-whites, often impecunious states of the players, and regularly discussed ways of improving their circumstances.

Numerous enquiries have led me to believe that it is highly unlikely that these Board records exist in any comprehensive way elsewhere. It presented another challenge, the easiest part of which was knowing that they should be made available for public access once I had scoured them. (Charles has agreed that they should be donated to Trinidad and Tobago's National Library, NALIS.) It is generally the practice in referencing sources of material to direct readers to the originals. Without evidence that these documents existed elsewhere, where would I send the curious? The WICBC had lost all its archival material for that period in a fire years ago, and attempts to locate personal records from those who were members then had yielded nothing.

It was a factor that reconfigured the approach to writing. I chose to quote heavily from these documents, and in some cases, to reproduce them in their entirety in the Notes section. I did not wish to intrude on the narrative of the chapters with reference notes, but I have tried to cite everything as fully as possible in notes to each chapter at the back of the book. Where I have quoted letters and minutes of meetings at length, it is to provide a sense of the tone and manner in which these communications took place.

In some cases, I allowed myself some latitude in what might appear as digressions from the body of the biography. It seemed important to provide context for the central events, especially when misconceptions have prevailed. For instance, whereas C.L.R. James has been credited for being the most instrumental voice in Worrell's appointment as captain of the West Indies team for the 1960-61 tour of Australia, there were several other factors involved. Worrell had been offered the captaincy twice before and had turned it down in favour of pursuing his degree programme at the University of Manchester. The discussions among Board members show that they were unanimously in favour of his captaincy prior to that and, as Gerry Alexander would say, the real shame was that he (Gerry) was chosen over Walcott and Weekes.

Another little known fact surrounds Worrell's plan to tour South Africa in 1959, despite the conditions of apartheid. For almost a year, fierce debates raged over the political wisdom of such a visit, with C.L.R. James encouraging it, and Learie Constantine stridently opposed. The WICBC had refused a previous invitation and sought to dissuade Worrell from accepting. While he seemed to waver at times, he had decided to go, but the tour was cancelled at the South African end.

The arguments over this visit would be later echoed during the early 1980s when the 'rebel tours' actually came off and resulted in lifetime bans for the West Indian players who took part.

The documents contained in that little cardboard box from Charles (and Cyril) Merry provided information about the WICBC's activities, but also served as a pointer to further investigation, leading to new avenues of exploration. It was indeed a find.

Worrell's staff files while he was employed at The University of the West Indies contained numerous requests for leave to visit cricket clubs and associations throughout the islands. He had often been credited as the one to encourage inclusion of the smaller island groups – the Leewards and Windwards – but while he himself had publicly said this, these training and coaching stints offered evidence of the frequency and commitment he showed towards nurturing this ideal. It was typical of the energy with which he pursued his goals and seemed worthy of including the detail surrounding those visits.

As an aside, West Indian cricket has accumulated a large corpus of literature. Biographies, autobiographies, tour diaries, fiction, calypsos, poetry – a considerable amount covers a span of more than a hundred years. The ghostwritten autobiographies seemed to have become popular from the end of the Fifties and into the Sixties, which suggests that this was when the stature of West Indian cricket had been finally recognised – the entry into the comity of nations that C.L.R. James had heralded. The flurry of biographical books published in the Sixties alone is a testament to the marketability that had been gained as a result of the remarkable Australia series at the start of the decade.

These texts, in one way or the other, shaped many of the cricket descriptions that are an inevitable aspect of this biography. All of it was supported by interviews, many done in several stages as participants often tired quickly. In the case of Sir Everton Weekes, perseverance was key, not because his memory was fading, but it took time to ease past his reserved manner.

At the end of the research, I reviewed the notes I had made at the beginning, crossing off the 'facts' that had thrown themselves carelessly across the pages of history, and hoped that at the very least, some inaccuracies would have been cleared up.

Frank Worrell had been consistently described in superlative terms. They were fitting, but what had often been missing was analysis of the complicated nature of his being. He was as much one thing as the other, a man of extremes. Most of what was known was what he wanted the world to see. In this regard he was fastidious, almost obsessive. People saw many sides, depending on their perspective.

Yet, everything I had read, everyone I had spoken to, had invariably invoked the word grace to describe him. It was there in his bearing, both on and off the cricket field. Mindful of his manner, regal in his carriage, and sensitive about his image, he carried so many of the traits of his mother, Grace, that it seemed natural that the title of this book should recognise his lineage and the legacy he left.

PROLOGUE
1963

At 10.30 on the night of 12 June 1963, the BBC Home Service broadcast its regular half-hour interview programme, *People Today*. On that Wednesday, the host was Rex Alston; the guest, Frank Worrell, captain of the touring West Indian team that had just won the first Test match at Old Trafford by ten wickets.

The interview was recorded just before the first Test in June. Worrell and his team had begun their five-month tour of England in late April, with a match at Eastbourne against L.C. Stevens' XI, a mixed group captained by Peter Richardson and including Richie Benaud, but featuring several West Indian players. They lost that match, despite Worrell's 73, on account of solid scores by Garry Sobers, Conrad Hunte and Joe Solomon, who were playing for the Stevens' XI.

It was a packed summer schedule, with 38 fixtures, including the five Tests. By the first Test, beginning on June 6, they had already played 12 games, winning seven and drawing three. Worrell played in most of the matches; his best performance coming in that first Test in Manchester, with a knock of 74 not out that was described by *Wisden* as the 'most graceful exhibition of late-cutting in the last fifty years.'

Just three years before, in 1960, Frank Worrell had become the first black man to be officially appointed captain of the West Indies team for a series, and it was known that this one in England would be his last. He was an international icon, celebrated not only for his outstanding cricket, but for his grace, intelligence and remarkable finesse as a Caribbean statesman. Striding confidently through life, leaving a monumental legacy through his mentorship, his final Test series was simply the beginning of a new phase, offering a horizon of unlimited promise.

The interview was meant to focus on his sparkling career and to give BBC listeners a chance to hear the thoughts of one of cricket's iconographic figures. Just one month before, another of its icons, C.L.R. James, had published his masterpiece, *Beyond a Boundary*, which he called the twelfth man for the West Indies. Dedicated to W.G. Grace, Learie Constantine and Worrell, he unstintingly praised Worrell in the chapter, 'The Proof of the Pudding,' and in his epilogue. The final sentence of the book is a paean to Frank.

A biography by Ernest Eytle was also published after the series, with contributions from Worrell. Madame Tussauds was crafting his likeness into wax – acknowledging his eminence. He was a celebrity. The cricket world would be eagerly awaiting his words.

Rex Alston was a Cambridge Blue for athletics (in 1923, before Worrell was born) and a sportsman of considerable ability – he had played cricket and rugby as well. One of the leading sports commentators for the BBC, he had worked with E.W. Swanton and John Arlott on Test-match commentary.

He would have followed Worrell's career from when he was a gangly youth, slim and unassuming, with ears that attached themselves like cup handles to his narrow face, closely cropped hair with a centre parting, and a moustache that was more a hint of a line being goaded into existence. Twenty years later Worrell had filled out; there was nothing lanky left. A press photograph taken in May, the month before – labelled 'West Indies "retiring captain"' – shows him staring serenely somewhere into a distance, the left eye slightly off-centre. The ears are less obtrusive because his face has grown outward and gathered them in. The hair is still cut low, neatly edged, and is now parted on the left – the parting had been fashionably shifting over the years. The moustache has responded to assiduous grooming and has become one of his defining features for its impeccable symmetry; marking a peak that begins precisely under the tip of his nose and extends outwards at an angle of 160 degrees precisely to the tips of his lips. The rest of his face is as clean shaven as it has appeared in public for all of his life.

Although he had rounded out, he was still evidently fit and the conversation went heartily along, reviewing the past and exploring the possibilities ahead. It is why, in hindsight, the interview ends so poignantly.

'But what about the future? When you're aged 50, what do you think you'll be doing?'

'I've got no idea. Actually I'm a fatalist. I keep on drifting in the breeze, so to speak.'

The final question was an odd one to ask a man two months short of 39. It is the kind of inquiry one makes of someone maybe

30 years older. Perhaps it emanated from the knowledge that he was retiring, but still, it seemed premature.

'Have you any regrets in the way that your life has gone so far?'

'None at all. I'd love to live it all over again.'

That description of himself as a fatalist contradicted all the evidence that demonstrated how he had ended up sitting in that chair as captain of the West Indies team; as a director of student affairs at The University of the West Indies; as one of the Three Ws, who had mesmerised the cricket world for over a decade, and as the man whose very presence was a catalyst for momentous changes in both West Indian and international cricket.

Worrell was known to be a planner, a man who meticulously guided colleagues along their career paths. He had constructed his own life with an unwavering focus on developing himself – towards cricket, during cricket, and outside the cricket days – so his response to that question was incongruous.

From adolescence, when his parents wanted their three children to join them in Brooklyn, he had already determined that being in the United States of America would not allow him to explore the possibilities that were open to him as a West Indian cricketer, and he chose to stay in Barbados with his grandmother.

During the war years, Worrell was establishing his prowess in the region during inter-colonial matches. By the end of the war, he was already recognised as one of the leading cricketers in the region, making his Test debut in 1948. The year before, he had chosen to emigrate to Jamaica, and it was from there he had accepted the offer to play for Radcliffe CC in the Central Lancashire League.

All of his major moves were made after careful consideration and consultation. He left nothing to fate or whim, however nonchalant he may have appeared.

His emigration to England was a clear step towards opening up the opportunities for his international career, and of escaping the oppressive constraints of Barbadian society. The life he envisaged was going to include fortune and fame, and he focused on putting together their accoutrements.

He married Velda Brewster within weeks of his arrival in England, where he had no supportive network. Velda, his Barbadian sweetheart, had the bearing, liveliness, charm and resourcefulness to be an appropriate partner for the life he planned to have, so he sent for her, and she came.

His decision to study for a degree came after consultation, and was part of his preparation for the life he wanted after cricket. Initially, around 1950, he had begun a course of study in Optics, but found its demands too onerous and in conflict with the cricket that was paying his bills and building his stature. Although he stopped the programme after a year, by the mid-Fifties, already a superstar, he applied to the University of Manchester and was warmly accepted as a mature student in 1956 to read for a Bachelor of Arts in Economics, though he switched to the Bachelor of Arts degree in Administration in the second year, graduating in 1959.

This enabled him to qualify for the position he would occupy in 1961, as a Warden at The University of the West Indies, where he served in various capacities until his death. He was intent on continuing to provide the lifestyle that he and his family had grown accustomed to while he was an active player, and so, when he was twice offered the captaincy of the West Indies in 1957 and 1958, he declined. Knowing that his playing days were coming to an end, he chose to complete his studies instead of accepting the pioneering role. Still, by 1959, he had found time to publish an autobiography of sorts, *Cricket Punch*, amid all his hectic activities.

He had joined a Masonic Lodge in 1954 because he knew it would help to develop his social networks and provide him with the access and privileges associated with members globally. He remained a freemason until his death.

After he had completed his degree programme in 1959, he was prepared to accept the captaincy for the memorable tour of Australia in the 1960-61 season. By then, he had said a farewell of sorts to England and returned to Jamaica. His career had been a glittering one, further embellished by the success in Australia. Although they lost the series, Worrell and his team won sporting hearts internationally. In 1962, he was invited to be a senator in Jamaica, a position he held until 1964, the same year he was knighted by Queen Elizabeth II.

Nothing had come by chance. This was not a man who 'drifted in the breeze'. This was someone who carried from childhood an extreme measure of confidence in his ability; someone who knew what he wanted out of life. He had a fastidious mind, an eye for detail – there was no way he was going to leave anything to providential winds.

Embedded in that strategic approach was an extreme attention to his image. Adeptly, he curated his professional identity. This 1963 BBC interview conveys a sense of how meticulously he distilled what information should be put into the public space.

For instance, it had been commonly misreported that Worrell graduated with an economics degree at Manchester University; it was actually in Public Administration. However, the syllabus for the BA in Administration was very mixed and included politics, economics, sociology and social anthropology.

Yet, when asked, Worrell told Alston, 'I read a degree in economics actually, but I specialised in social anthropology and sociology.' It could hardly have been a mistake, but it might have been that an economics degree carried a more desirable weight to him as he presented himself to the British public.

His years in England had influenced him profoundly – in *Cricket Punch*, he spoke of 'we lovers of Britain and all that is British'. The country had been kind to him, he said, 'never once have I regretted my decision to leave the West Indies and try my luck in England'.

He told Alston that he was hoping that later that year his daughter, Lana, would return to England to attend a boarding school.

'I attach a lot of importance to the finishing touches and our formal education at home is as good as you'd probably find over here, but then I find that the sort of social graces aren't as in evidence at home as I would love to see it. As a young lady I would like to see her educated here.'

Lana would turn 14 the following month, and eventually did attend a boarding school in England, the Lucie Clayton Secretarial College, not the finishing school he'd imagined.

If it is apparent that Worrell was more impressed by the English way of life than its miniature version in Barbados (where he never lived after 1947), it does not explain the astonishing response to this question on race relations.

'Now, do you have any recollection of problems connected with your colour and with meeting white people?' asked Alston.

'Not in Barbados,' said Worrell. 'I think we're more or less culturally homogenous. You find the races went to the same churches, drank from the same communion cup, went to the same schools and we've played in the same teams and there's little or no suggestion of separation between the boys at school. On leaving school you found the chaps of European descent gravitating towards the banks, whereas the only openings for the coloured boys were in the civil service or teaching; and then five or six years after that you find the chaps getting further and further apart. But basically, I don't think there's any suggestion of hatred of the races. It just meant you found yourself in a different clique on leaving school, and there it stayed.'

This description of the social structure of Barbados must have raised quizzical eyebrows. The schools, churches and cricket clubs, practically all aspects of life, were divided along racial and class lines. It is a remarkable statement from a man who would not accept those divisions, who consistently acted in opposition to those mores, and who left his homeland largely because of those inequities.

It is difficult to fathom why Worrell would say it, unless he saw himself as being an ambassador for Barbados with a responsibility to sell it as attractively as he could, especially to promote the Test series. Perhaps Alston found it equally difficult to assimilate this curious tourism spiel, but he did not pursue it, switching immediately to another subject.

This interview was done at the beginning of the series. At the end, after the final match at The Oval, speaking to the British journalist, Ian Wooldridge, of the *Daily Mail*, he seemed more inclined to be candid.

His earlier remark about being a fatalist can be more readily understood if one takes it as a position he had arrived at, perhaps out of a sense of weariness.

Wooldridge wrote about that tour in *Cricket, Lovely Cricket*, and in a published excerpt called 'The Gentle Revolutionary,' he observed that it was typical of Worrell that he did not go out to bat when the match was almost won to give the crowds a chance to say a final farewell. Players, camera crew, the public, he said, 'tried desperately to persuade him to walk out, as Bradman had in 1948, through an avenue of England players to the traditional three-cheers salute.'

Wooldridge said that Worrell refused and instead spent his last dressing-room moments dozing – a habit he had earlier attributed to nervousness when Alston had questioned him.

'He had said a dozen times that these days he would just as soon not bat as bat, that he was even scarcely interested in the outcome of matches any longer so long as the public had their money's worth of entertainment.'

Wooldridge did not think he was as indifferent as he let on, and so, a few days later, he asked him why he had 'dodged the moment that so many entertainers love so much that they even make comebacks for the chance to go through it all again.'

Worrell's answer revealed that he was never that kind of entertainer, said Wooldridge, quoting his response.

'I really didn't feel like facing all that business of a lump in the throat and maybe a few tears in the eyes as well. If I'd been needed to bat I would have batted. But I didn't see much point in just going out there for the sake of saying good-bye.'

Then came the fatalist's remarks.

'That's my way of life now. Nothing really bothers me anymore.'

From the MCC library, where the May 1963 photo ('West Indies "retiring captain"') is lodged, there is another, dated August 26, captioned, 'Frankie Take a Bow.' It shows him standing on the balcony of the pavilion at The Oval after that final Test, waving to the 'vast crowd' beneath cheering for him. 'Looking calm and unperturbed,' by the scenes, the caption said. 'Frank Worrell has been acknowledged as the man who has put cricket right back on the map.'

He stands on the narrow balcony, the team blazer hanging rather loosely over his whites, his right arm upraised, the index finger pointed upward in a regal wave. The eyes look a little misty ... or perhaps it is simply the remnants of sleep.

Wooldridge wrote that he had driven to Canterbury (where the West Indies were playing Kent two days after the fifth Test) to ask Worrell what victory meant to him and what his future plans were.

'…without oratory or bitterness, he took the words mission and victory in a very different context and talked of his other battle, his struggle to achieve social acceptance and end the economic exploitation of the coloured cricketer in the West Indies. I did not raise the colour question with Worrell. He raised it with me and as he spoke the gay calypso image propagated in a hundred headlines to the comfort of a million consciences, crumbled apart. Life, of course, just isn't like that if you were born black in a white man's world. Even if your name is Worrell.'

Worrell told him, 'As a young man, between about twenty-one and twenty-eight, I had a hell of a chip on my shoulder … I was fighting all sorts of issues, both actual and imaginary. This probably sounds unbearably egotistical, but I went on fighting alone for ten years. I lost friends who did not want to become involved. I was described as difficult to get along with. Perhaps I was. But there were principles involved.'

He talked about his battles with white establishment figures in West Indies cricket. 'Even before we left for our last trip to Australia [in 1960] we were offered terms that were completely unacceptable. I protested. I said that if the English players were worth £X in Australia then we were worth £X too. Those of us who protested got £X. Those who didn't got less.'

While he had been consciously waging a battle for civil rights, he was inclined towards expressing himself privately, and much of it was done behind the scenes. However, he was open about negotiating for increased payments and better playing conditions, and he consistently lobbied for his teammates.

He was more frank with Wooldridge than he had been with Alston three months earlier. Then, he was participating in the promotion of the Test series, but at the end of August, with the series behind them, in a corner of a Canterbury dressing room, he was ready for candour.

'It won't happen like that again. You may be surprised to know that there were plenty of people back home who were praying that we would fail. Even now there are some just waiting for me to bow out. Well, I'm going. But things will never go back to where they were.'

He pointed to the maroon blazers hanging on pegs on the dressing-room walls and told Wooldridge, 'These fellows have been well and truly briefed.'

He defined what he felt was the real victory behind the series wins over the past three years. 'It is simply that these chaps can go home as socially acceptable, first-class citizens. For me, there is nothing left to fight against. When I go home I shall go into the background and stay there.'

He made it clear too that he was not interested in political games.

'You remind me that I'm a senator. Well when that happened I didn't really realise that I was being used by a political party. I'm not interested in politics. I am interested in the sociological problems of the Caribbean but I shan't "go to the people," as it were, when I go home. I have already decided the level at which I shall work and that is simply as Warden over the students at The University of the West Indies in Jamaica. I shall be there to help them with their personal problems. But as for fighting, I've done with it.'

Wooldridge ends by saying that in the afternoon when he went to say goodbye, Worrell was still waiting to bat, but 'was stretched out across the dressing-room floor. His head was on a folded sweater, his feet on a cricket bag, and he was ten thousand miles away.'

Within those two interviews resides a narrative that tells of a complex human being who had chosen to live on his terms. Worrell's story cannot be told without exploring the environment that shaped him; the remarkable confidence he had from childhood; the way he negotiated an often hostile world; and how he influenced the lives of many within his circle, and many more who had never even met him.

One of his defining interventions in the cricket world was the joint project between him and Richie Benaud during that historic Australian tour of 1960-61 when the two captains sportingly hauled Test cricket from its doldrums, shook it off and put it back on its competitive feet again. Although the series is famous for the first tied Test in the game's history, it has always been acknowledged as a turning point for international cricket.

It had also been identified as the series that finally transformed West Indian players into a cohesive unit. On his retirement, he said that it had been his greatest desire. 'I have had a great run, and as I have satisfied my greatest ambition in the last two years, I have no complaints. My aim was always to see the West Indies moulded from a rabble of brilliant island individualists into a real team – and I've done it.'

He was a natural mentor, a nurturing spirit who generously shared his wisdom and experience with everyone who came into his sphere, West Indian or otherwise. If contemporary cricketers and administrators could have access to the kind of unconventional coaching he provided, it would make a world of difference to the approach to development, especially within the West Indies.

All around the Caribbean, monuments have been erected to celebrate him, yet given the amnesiac quality of West Indian memory, it is likely that they stand in name only, without context, for a generation whose history has practically disappeared without a trace of its legacy.

PART ONE

CHAPTER 1

DUSTY DAYS IN BANK HALL

In the 1920s and 1930s, West Indian village life revolved around making ends meet. People did what they could to earn a dollar; they went to church regularly; tended the land; did some fishing, and on weekends, the men would have drinks at the rum shops and turn out for the cricket that was always a stone's throw away.

For children in Barbados, the weakened global economy made scarcely any impression. The worldwide depression from 1929 hardly affected their humdrum routines. Rules were still strict and punishments just as severe. Between chores, school and church, the time for outdoor activities was precious and packed. There was football and cricket, swimming and fishing, kites, marbles, spinning tops, and of course, foraging for forbidden fruit hanging enticingly from nearby trees. If they could afford it, they might slip away to matinées at cinemas like the Olympic and Empire, which showed mostly war films, westerns and comedies. The freedoms enjoyed by young boys particularly, made the pervasive poverty bearable.

'You were supposed to be in bed, seven, eight o'clock in the evening. We didn't have radio and television and that sort of thing. In the village, of course, one person might have a radio and when Joe Louis, the boxer, was fighting you'd queue up to go and listen to this thing, and you had to get there early because all the little boys who lived in the area would go by this lady who had the radio,' said Everton Weekes. 'Sometimes the broadcast was not so clear and you had to put yourself in all sorts of postures to try and listen.'

Weekes was a big fan of Joe Louis, the world heavyweight champion from 1937 to 1949. He said those who missed the broadcast because they had chores to do, or were being punished for some misdemeanour, would hear a recap the next day at school. Impoverished conditions were so common that they were accepted as the ordained way. Many children did not think the hardships of home life merited complaint or discussion.

'When you start talking about those days you got the feeling that only you were treated that way, but you realise then the majority of the boys were. They would give you the stories, some of them were ashamed to give you the stories. I don't know why, but later on in life they would come forth and say what transpired in those early days. Some of the stories were really ridiculous. Hearing how tough it was for some children and that sort of thing, especially those people who had four and five children. In my case, it was just the two of us. My sister was seven years older and she was like a mother to me. Seven years' difference is quite a bit when the girl is 14 and you are seven, she puts the whip on you like if she is a cleric, you know,' he said, chuckling.

The boys would not talk about the inequities of the social structure in Barbados, though they were directly affected by it. Yet they could not help but be aware of the sharp demarcations within society, because from as early as the First World War disaffection with the status quo was increasingly apparent. In the villages it was most visible through cricket.

The governing body, the Barbados Cricket Committee, had four teams. Wanderers, founded in 1877, and Pickwick, in 1882, were exclusively white. In response to that exclusion, Spartan was formed in 1893 for the mainly non-white professional classes; the fourth team was Harrison College, the elite secondary school founded in 1733.

The emergence of Empire Cricket Club provided not only a physical space for the black youngsters in the neighbourhood, but its ethos helped shape their outlook on life.

Herman Griffith, a fast bowler who played in the first West Indian Test match in 1928, had the misfortune to be young, gifted and black in a country whose prejudices were aggressively manifested in every space. His talent had been recognised, and a prominent black Spartan member, Lionel Gittens, put forward his name for membership. It was rejected, causing an indignant exodus of Spartan members who went on to form Empire on 24 May 1914, two months before the start of the First World War. The date was chosen to coincide with the celebration of Empire Day, the birthday of Queen Victoria, and as a declaration of loyalty to the British.

After more than a century, the Empire Ground on Pavilion Road in the parish of St. Michael had not expanded its small size – it still counted boundary hits as either threes (on the shorter side) or fours – but its stature had grown immensely, especially because of the quality of its players. By 2023, 13 West Indian Test players and eight Barbados captains had emerged from the club. Among them was a legendary knight of the realm.

Frank Mortimer Maglinne Worrell was born on 1 August 1924, ten weeks after Empire celebrated its tenth anniversary. The house where he grew up, at the back of Pavilion Road, overlooked the club. For him, as it was for almost all the boys in the sleepy village, the ground was an irresistible magnet.

He was the second of three children to his seamstress mother, Grace, and her sea-faring husband, Athelston Theophilus Worrell. Although there was plenty of work for seamstresses and tailors, it was not lucrative; indeed, it barely reached subsistence levels. Women often took in sewing jobs to make ends meet. Though times were hard, there was always a demand for clothing, and stylish garments at that. Dresses were trimmed with frills, and there were collars on bodices with modestly long sleeves. Billowing skirts and petticoats, despite the sweltering heat, were worn by women of every station. The differences would be in the quality of the fabric. Tailors were equally in demand for suits, shirts and trousers.

Grace was an only child, pampered by her doting mother, Florence Eglan Burrowes. All that was known of her father was that he came visiting in a horse and buggy. According to Marilyn Worrell, Grace's granddaughter, the family later surmised he was a white man of some means, and that his surname was Saunders.

Grace was born in 1898, and learnt to sew from her mother. She was a lively, commanding woman, full of flair, and a passion for surrounding herself with beautiful things. She frequently referred to herself as a queen and a lion. Uncommonly beautiful, she was always fashionably dressed and paid great mind to appearances – not uncommon in the middle and upper middle-class families in Barbados. It would be one of her legacies to the Worrell family.

Little is known of Athelston's antecedents, but it seems that he was something of a carouser, a man about town, a 'bad boy,' and that attracted Grace, the lion.

They got married and, in 1920, their first son, Livingstone, was born. Frank came four years later. In 1930, pregnant again, Grace set off with Athelston for the United States. In Boston, a daughter she named Grace, was born, and soon afterwards, she returned with her to Barbados. The trip was meant to provide her daughter with US citizenship.

It is not clear why Boston was the choice of city. Travellers from the Caribbean usually arrived either at Ellis Island or the Boston Port. Perhaps Athelston had connections – many years later, the family would learn that he had fathered a son there, Leroy Worrell, a dentist. Frank had a half-brother he did not know.

Eventually, Grace moved to Brooklyn, where she made her final home. Athelston came, went, and then settled back in Barbados when the marriage finally crumbled.

Livingstone and baby Grace joined their mother in Brooklyn in the early Thirties, but Frank did not want to go to the US. He stayed in Barbados with his grandmother, Florence, who showered her attention on the precocious youngster left in her charge. He was carefree, not carrying the prevailing burden of poverty, and so, occupied a privileged position among his peers. In a remarkable contrast to his later years, he was careless about his appearance. While village boys dressed in hand-me-downs, recycled and patched for as long as possible, Frank's clothes were new; sent by his stylish mother from the US, but typically he went about with his shirt halfway tucked in, as if he couldn't be bothered.

It was widely recognised that Frank was better off than the boys with whom he gallivanted. He was generous and easy-going, yet despite his relaxed manner, his sharp mind and self-confidence made him a natural leader. Perhaps adopting an air of insouciance helped him to feel that he fitted in, which would explain his free-handedness with money. He was often the sponsor of roadside treats, like Mauby, a refreshing drink brewed from the bark of a tree, and biscuits – this childhood generosity was a trait that never left him.

Despite his casual veneer, he had absorbed from his grandmother and his mother a highly developed sartorial sense of elegance that was to become his hallmark. It is likely that because of his childhood carelessness about his appearance, he had it drummed into him that his image was an important marker of his family's social standing. His beautiful grandmother, with her long straight hair and features unlike those of the predominantly black community, had been further elevated socially because of her 'visiting' white consort.

Under her care, he would have been conscious that he came from lofty stock, especially with a white grandfather, and his comportment had to reflect it. Like his mother, he was given to stylishness, and from her he had learnt the attention to detail that distinguished him. She put great stock in presenting herself regally in public, and may very well have given herself a few airs. As an only child, Grace had been pampered, growing up believing in her superior qualities, particularly potent in the status-conscious environment of Barbados.

Once his family had emigrated, Frank worked hard to fit into the community he had to live within. Conscious of his privileged ancestry, he tried to deny its reality around his working-class friends, adopting an air of indifference to mask the enormous adjustments he had to make to cope with a house that had grown quiet all at once.

Even if it was his choice to stay behind, he was still a child, hardly aware what this kind of separation would mean to his daily existence. No mother, no father, no big brother, no little sister. He was no longer the middle child, he was now an only child. There would be many new hours to fill with different activities.

He dutifully attended classes at the Roebuck Boys' Moravian Elementary School, spending a great deal of time with Eric and Leroy Critchlow, George and Victor Hinkson, and the Symmonds brothers, Algy and Noel, with whom he blithely got into typical schoolboy scrapes. They hunted birds with sling shots, went swimming, played football, and flew kites, but cricket was at the heart of everything.

Patricia Symmonds, sister of Algy and Noel, wrote that the death of Tai, as Frank was known, caused great anguish. 'He was my brother Noel's best friend and like a brother to Algy, my older sibling, and me as well.' Noel had come away with his own nickname from their friendship: 'Algy-gi-Tai,' a reference to the number of times he asked his brother to pass the ball to Tai.

For all his life, Frank signed letters to friends as Tai, a nickname derived from his favourite brand of tea, Typhoo, which he could not pronounce because of his stammer. From very young, he stumbled over sentences, stuttering most when he was excited, and often producing words with a lisp. Frank's stammer would have been very noticeable in those days, as he participated in a wide range of sports and games.

Almost all village cricket has its roots in makeshift gear and improbable pitches. Beaches provided a natural playing field, but the Bank Hall group was fortunate to have access to the Empire pasture. With bats made either from coconut tree branches or roughly carved from wood, they took up positions in front of pieces of galvanised steel sheeting propped against old buckets and cans. Making balls involved a little more stealth and ingenuity. They sometimes used young breadfruits, which were plentiful, or marbles or stones would be tightly bound in cloth and stitched together into a solid round. The scrap baskets of women were regularly raided for the bits of cloth, and Frank's grandmother was a regular victim of these cricket crimes.

Roebuck's headmaster, Richard Taylor (Pa T, they called him), had made a case for the Anglican-raised Frank to come to the popular school, despite his religious difference. There, Frank discovered what would become a lifelong love of music and singing, especially hymns. He joined the school choir, performing in a competition that marked the silver jubilee of King George V in 1935, just before he turned eleven. He'd risked his grandmother's wrath to join the cathedral choir. Forgetting to tell her about the evening of the audition until it was too late, he stayed on until nightfall, persuading his friend Victor to wait with him. He got into the choir, but both boys got sound whippings afterwards.

A truly painful incident with profound consequences was to come. One day, as they made their customary scramble over the Empire wall, Frank fell and broke his right arm. The groundsman, John Morgan, took him across the road to the home office of Dr. Charles Duncan O'Neal (later a Barbados national hero). Frank and his friends were terrified to tell his grandmother, but Morgan explained the situation. Hampered by the cast and sling, Frank still could not resist his cricket, but fielding bored him. He started trying to bowl left-arm. Eventually, he became strong enough to do it well and it became another of his hallmarks – that he batted as a right-hander, but bowled with his left arm.

It was not surprising that Frank's friends were afraid to tell his grandmother of his injury. Stories abound of whippings at home and canings at school, mainly over tardiness because boys had slipped away to play cricket and had lost track of time. Torn clothes, sweaty bodies, and forgotten errands – standard signs of a healthy childhood – could easily provoke the wrath of parents, grandparents and school teachers, all struggling to make ends meet in the harsh economic climate widespread across the islands of the Caribbean.

Images of the streets and lanes of Barbados of the period show horse and mule carts, some outfitted for transport, mostly to carry market produce and sugar cane. The men are depicted in suits with hats and berets; more often than not, they walk barefooted. The heat radiates out of those black and white photographs; it shimmers through the layers of clothing and parches the skin just by looking.

A photo of one street in 1906 features various women going about their business, all fully clad in either dresses, or bodices with long sleeves and full-length skirts. Everyone has some sort of head covering: a hat, a bonnet, a head-wrap. Some are carrying baskets with vegetables, ground provisions or fruit on their heads. Women carrying everything on their heads is a striking detail in photographs of the early half of the 1900s, women of a certain station, that is. Another photo, taken three years later, is similar, except they are carrying live birds in the baskets on their heads.

In one photograph, a Mauby woman's bucket sits imperturbably on the wadding on her head. She reaches up with her right hand and turns the faucet at the lower end. The Mauby streams into the glass she holds in her left hand, a good two feet below. Her male customer waits for the glass, or the tot, full of the bark, brewed with cinnamon, bay leaves and cloves, for just a couple of pennies. Mauby women were a large part of the Barbadian landscape from Frank's childhood up to the middle of the century.

Many men had gone off to fight in the First World War and not returned. Work on the Panama Canal had encouraged emigration. The West Indian Census of 1946 noted that for every 100 men who lived in Barbados in 1921, there were 148 women.

Women had to pick up the slack. A cook could earn 12 shillings 6 pence (roughly equivalent to £20 at today's values), a maid would get 10 shillings monthly. Frank's grandmother, Florence, had taught her daughter Grace to sew, but it did not bring enough income to raise three children, especially as her husband was at sea for most of the time. In any case, Grace had grander ideas for herself.

While for many of the working class, emigration to the US and the UK seemed the most viable option, the elite groups within the British territories enjoyed positions of privilege, bestowed by race, social class and the power that emanated from this standing. They were generally of English heritage, inheritors of lands and titles, who had come to the Caribbean to make money. French, Spanish, Dutch and Portuguese colonisers also occupied the upper echelons of the societies over which they had presided.

West Indian cricket had emerged from the belly of this colonial beast and bore its features. English soldiers, garrisoned across the Caribbean islands to expand and defend the holdings of the British Empire from the late 1700s, entertained themselves with cricket matches. As the game spread, slaves and sons of slaves were instructed to bowl to their white owners seeking batting practice. This seeped into the villages and after slavery was abolished, cricket became a popular form of sport and entertainment.

It was the preserve of wealthy whites. Economies based on sugar plantations and their culture essentially constituted the West Indies by the turn of the century. Societies were divided along the lines of class, colour, ethnicity, religion, language, and economic power.

Planters and merchants ranked higher than professionals such as doctors and lawyers, even if they were all white. Coloured people were not yet visible, but in their own enclaves, further distinctions existed based on race and shades; based on religion; based on geography, whether one was from country or town – it was life all over again.

The three dominant islands for the first half of the 20th century were Barbados (despite its small size), Jamaica and Trinidad and Tobago. Considering itself 'little England,' citizens of Barbados believed themselves to be superior to their neighbours and the society was more rigidly stratified. Members of the plantocracy were generally English-born and had direct relationships with their relatives and contemporaries back in the motherland. Control over the island's sugar-based economy entrenched these planters at the high end of the social ladder. The merchant class developed rapidly, but even with their financial success, they could only come close to the prevailing planters. Professionals, mainly doctors and lawyers, who had been educated at British public schools and universities, would find themselves respectably ensconced nearby, but not on par with the elite. While the social stratum was similarly delineated among the other islands, it was particularly pronounced in Barbados. It created peculiar tissues of rivalry, fed mostly by the nature of the personalities occupying positions of influence, leading to territorial sways as power shifted hands. Eventually, British Guiana joined the trio, together forming what became known as the 'Big Four' in the region.

In the early years of the West Indies Cricket Board of Control, leadership remained within their hands. The first two presidents of the WICBC (formed in 1927) were Harold Austin and Laurie Yearwood from Barbados, followed by Fred Grant of Trinidad, then Karl Nunes of Jamaica and the indomitable Errol dos Santos of Trinidad, who was eventually replaced by John Dare of British Guiana. The WICBC was formed by a group of wealthy white individuals, primarily to arrange the first Test tour to England in 1928. Known then as the West Indies Cricket Conference, its mission was solely to plan and execute this venture, and its first official meeting was held in Bridgetown, Barbados, in January 1927.

With the big four at the helm, decisions were made based on their respective perspectives. Constraints wrought by travel, meant that meetings were primarily held in Trinidad and Barbados, as Jamaica to the north and British Guiana to the south meant longer journeys, and thus representation was often dominated by the Barbadian and Trinidadian members.

On the periphery were members of the smaller islands, grouped as the Leewards and Windwards. This was another cause of friction as they felt not only excluded, but denied opportunities to become members of the West Indies teams. Social historian and activist, Tim Hector of Antigua, was a tireless crusader for inclusion. He had written that in the small islands, black captains had emerged long before 1941. 'I contend that the very emergence of blacks in leadership and in near total representation on cricket teams in the Leewards and Windwards had everything to do with these islands being excluded from inter-colonial white-administered cricket, and, therefore from Test-match cricket.'

This was the state of West Indian cricket administration in the first half of the 20th century.

Frank Worrell was himself an indefatigable campaigner for the Leeward and Windward island groupings to be allowed access to training and development programmes. While employed at The University of the West Indies in the last years of his life, he travelled extensively to these outposts, holding coaching and training sessions at the behest of local authorities. He was determined to bring an end to the insular nature of selection processes and, by then, his stature ensured that his words carried weight.

It is one of his legacies to the development of West Indies cricket, but in the early days, cricket was simply a childhood pastime.

CHAPTER 2

AGE OF EMPIRE

The nature of adult struggle is largely invisible in the heat of childhood, where the infinite range of activities can melt away all but the most severe of circumstances. Schoolchildren are gloriously oblivious to the unrelenting Caribbean heat. Frank and his mates cared not one whit as long as they could scramble over the Empire wall on a Saturday morning to earn a free pass to afternoon matches by helping the groundsman prepare the day's wicket.

Empire had been formed as a protest over the overt discrimination of the Barbados cricket structure. With the strongest concentration of English colonisers in the region, the Barbadian sensibility is still distinctly different from the rest of the West Indies. Although relatively small, it has had powerful connections with its colonial ancestry, and social and racial stratifications were very dominant.

Spartan's rejection of Herman Griffith, a junior civil service clerk, symbolised how deeply entrenched those mores were. Although Spartan had emerged as a club where non-white professionals could play their cricket, they still turned away a non-white but talented player because he was not of their class. Even Empire did not allow labourers into its membership in its first few years.

Before Frank was ten, he had already been exposed to bowlers like Griffith, E.A. Martindale (who made his Test debut when Frank was nine, in 1933), and Ernest 'Foffie' Williams, who was born just four days before Empire's formation, right there in Bank Hall on the Main Road. During net sessions, they would often let Frank bowl at them. Chester Cumberbatch (11 years his senior), who captained Harrison College and later played for Spartan and Barbados, lived on Pavilion Road and was one of the neighbourhood group with whom he played in the far corner of the Empire ground on a wicket they prepared themselves.

It was the natural progression after Roebuck Primary to attend Combermere School in Waterford, St. Michael, and in 1937, when Frank started at the school, he had already played a considerable amount of cricket, including in the company of adults. His self-confidence was high.

In Ernest Eytle's 1963 biography, *Frank Worrell: The Career of a Great Cricketer*, Worrell followed each chapter with comments. These summaries were observations and reminiscences about those early years from the more mature perspective of his late thirties. From about six, he was 'observing and emulating chaps like Barney Miller, slow left-arm spinner,' and often watched 'Manny Martindale, Foffy Williams, and Herman Griffith' playing against Barbadian cricketers. 'I seemed to have been playing cricket for a long time when I arrived at Combermere School at the age of 12.'

He was friendly with Harold Gittens Brewster, captain of the Combermere cricket team, and 'one of the most famous of all Barbadian school-boy athletes,' declared one scholar.

Frank entered the school in the September term and by the second week, he was in the Second XI on the recommendation of Harold. A fortnight later, based on his performances, he was promoted by the games master to the First Division XI. Although he preferred batting, it was as a spin bowler he was recognised on the team.

'We had an eleven there called The Starvation Eleven and we started playing at half-past nine in the morning and we played through until about half-past three and then the members of the Empire Club came out for practice,' wrote Frank. As these games went on until there was a result, it helped develop his batting. He recalled that it was around 1941, when he was around 17, that his batting began to flourish. Before then, he thought he was too small to get any power into his shots. '… it was a matter of getting runs by deflections like cutting, gliding or glancing. But very seldom did I get many runs in front of the wicket because of lack of power, and the bounce of the ball (I was fairly short) seemed to cramp me.' (Although there is no record of his actual height, he had grown to a six-footer, and was often described as a tall man.)

He was playing cricket six hours a day, practising in the mornings before school 'in the far corner of our Fourth Eleven field,' and on evenings they would move to the churchyard at St. Michael's Cathedral. There, with the sexton's grandsons, Roy and Eric Critchlow, he played for hours, especially during school vacations when they could be found either there or at the beach.

While Frank roved freely with the boys from his community, his family life was not the same as theirs. With his mother living in the

USA and sending back money, foreign clothes and other household things, he stood out. He had a bicycle, the only one among his friends, and they often borrowed it to go joyriding. He had enough pocket money to treat the other boys to street delicacies.

It made him remarkably popular, said Weekes, who grew up close by in Pickwick Gap in a place called New Orleans. He too was one of the denizens of the Empire ground and remembered Frank riding around with his shirt billowing in the wind, buying snacks for the boys. Although Weekes lived just a short distance away, he was from the poorer side of Bank Hall.

'I met Frank when he must have been about ten or eleven, and although we were only a mile or two apart, the distance was great. Because Frank had a bicycle; I didn't have one,' he said. 'We played a lot of cricket on Saturday mornings at a little place called the Burn House, near the Empire cricket ground. A lot of good players came out from that grouping with the boys from the Lower Westbury Road and the boys from Bank Hall ... and to win a scholarship to go to high school in those days would have been pretty difficult for youngsters like me, for instance. I don't know if it is wise to say this, but it is true that the chief education officer in those days used to be an Englishman and he rode around on Westbury Road and Pickwick Gap and Baxter's Road. And as nearly all Englishmen do, he liked a cup of tea and I was not, my parents were not, in a position to entertain him. So obviously, Weekes would not win a scholarship.'

Weekes had to make sure that when he got home from school, his uniform was carefully aired out, and he did not want to be seen in the clothing he wore at home outside of the house. Frank was always carelessly dapper, but though they saw each other just on Saturdays when they played from nine in the morning, Weekes could see something of merit, 'even at that stage and age one noticed that Frank had a lot of very good qualities.

'He was only six months older than I am. He always carried himself in a way that was admired by most of the boys. And of course, I believe clothes would come for him from the United States of America and there was more admiration for him then ... because he was not the sort of person who thought he was greater than anybody else, which was a good quality I thought.'

41

Although he was more privileged than his playmates, Frank had no airs, they were simply a group sharing the common bond of community and sporting interests. 'He always seemed to have more money than everybody else. I didn't know where it was coming from but I suppose it came from his father, who was on ships,' Weekes recalled. 'And when you had a shilling or two shillings in those days … you didn't have a dollar as such. He always seemed to have a couple dollars with him and he was not selfish with it. He would buy stuff for the boys, Mauby and sweets and things like that. He was a very generous sort of person, and up to when he died he was the same sort of person I knew as a boy. Sharing, and happy to share.'

He was impressed by the way Frank expressed himself, his choice of words, but he had observed the sensitivity of his nature.

'Easily hurt if the wrong things were said; if he was on the different side of general opinion. He was easily hurt by that sort of thing. Not to the point where we would stop speaking, but he would say things like, "I was outvoted," and that was the language he spoke at 11 years. He expressed himself in such a beautiful way it had to be admired. Some very good qualities.'

Moving from puberty to adolescence, Frank focused on cricket, football and other outdoor activities. While cricket devoured a substantial amount of the time and attention of young boys, there was something extra in Frank's obsession, and perhaps this single-mindedness alongside his precocious self-confidence – and his hyper-sensitivity to what others thought – unleashed a profound range of conflicting experiences during this formative time at Combermere.

CHAPTER 3

TRIALS AT COMBERMERE

At the time Frank was admitted, the school was enjoying an outstanding reputation for its sports and athletics. It had traditionally been closely associated with cricket. The headmaster from 1896, George Bishop Richardson Burton, had done much to create and develop cricket facilities, including a playing field. His successor in 1926 was G.B.Y. 'Gussie' Cox, who had spent 31 years at Harrison College and had represented Barbados as an all-rounder. The chairman of the governing body for Combermere and Harrison College was Harold G.B. Austin, the Test cricketer regarded as the father of West Indian cricket, and the two men were friendly enough that Cox was able to get much support in developing cricket facilities at the school.

Cox retired in 1934. By the time Frank entered Combermere, the headmaster was the Rev. Arthur Evelyn Armstrong, an Anglican, nicknamed 'Buff.' He had also been a cricketer, turning out for the Pickwick and St. Ann's clubs and serving as an umpire for inter-colonial matches. During his tenure, the student population grew far past what the already worn physical structure could accommodate. A school designed for 110 students saw its enrolment go to 330 in 1940 and then 418 in 1942: expansion at a far more rapid state than other schools. Perhaps it was a result of its superior reputation for sport.

A sign of the congestion in 1937 was the construction of a wooden structure with a galvanised roof that amplified the midday heat, to house 100 students. It was fittingly called the Cow Shed, one of a series of temporary buildings added on until Combermere was finally relocated to larger premises on Roebuck Street in 1943, the year Frank left with a Cambridge School Certificate.

Despite the inadequate facilities, the school was bursting with sporting and academic energy, and Frank had quickly impressed. He caught the attention of James Edward Derrick Sealy, commonly referred to as Derek, a member of staff in the Thirties (when he represented the West Indies in 11 Test matches). Sealy gave Frank's talent the visibility it needed to bring him to the attention of national selectors later. The games master, Vincent Williams, had also taken a liking to him. The former Spartan cricketer, Owen Alexander 'Graffie' Pilgrim, taught mathematics at the school and from early on, prophesied a great batting career for Frank, even while he was still seen as a left-arm spin bowler.

At Combermere he met Clyde Walcott, nearly two years his junior, but with whom he played cricket until Walcott transferred to Harrison College. Everton Weekes went to St. Leonard's Boys' Secondary School in Richmond Gap – his social circumstances dictated a different path.

Despite the school's passion for cricket, Frank encountered hostility that may have stemmed from the ease with which he had ascended through the teams, his indifference to authority, his penchant for ignoring rules, his absolute devotion to his cricket, and envy.

On one occasion Frank asked his captain, Harold Brewster, for permission to slip away from the match to go to watch a movie, as he was slated to come in low down in the order. He was seen leaving the ground by his house master, Ralph Perkins, whom he believed disliked him, and he was suspended from cricket and received six lashes. It is as surprising that Brewster allowed him to go as it is that Frank asked, and then saw the reprimand he later received as a hostile attack.

Eytle related an anecdote, supposedly to illustrate that dislike. 'The house matches, which started at 4pm and finished at 6, were played to a finish, and went on for several days. In one of these Frank scored a double century. His house master was livid. "Why don't you get out and give someone else a chance to bat, Worrell?" he snapped.'

In *Cricket Punch*, in the chapter 'The Barbados Big-head,' Frank said that master seemed to have targeted him for special wrath. 'Whatever happened he blamed me for it, and he was forever entering me into the black book, which meant a report to the headmaster … and a caning.' He felt he was often unfairly punished, 'and before long I felt resentful and unhappy. I even tried to get out of the school team.'

He was in the headmaster's study at least once a week and it led to 'the worst moment of my life,' when he was reprimanded by Rev. Armstrong in front of his schoolmates. The gist of the admonition was that since he had entered the first XI, he felt he could do what he wanted and had caused nothing but trouble.

'Not only was the accusation unjust, in my own mind, but to stand up in front of the whole school and be called a big-head by the headmaster was more than flesh and blood could stand. Worse than that, after being branded a big-head by the headmaster, I was a big-head to everyone. The senior boys, who had never really liked my being chosen for the first eleven, loathed me more than ever, and my fellow juniors just laughed at me. I was Frank Worrell, the Barbados big-head. And I didn't like it.'

He talked about finding that 'the big-head legend' had followed him from Combermere when he left in 1943. He moved to Trinidad to get away from it, but after a month, returned to Barbados and then went to Jamaica hoping it would leave him alone. Eventually, he figured the best escape was out of the West Indies altogether, and his option was to join his family in the US, but then he received an offer from Radcliffe in the Central Lancashire League and everything changed.

Perhaps it was written this way to suit the tone of the book – targeting an English audience by a man who had already spent a decade on English soil – but this account of that period in Worrell's life is sparse and glossy, sanitised almost. One paragraph, printed in italics, feels like a carefully scripted pair of lines to tie everything together neatly. He lays down the burden of the big-head.

'And, strangely enough, once I left the West Indies I discovered that the legend of my being a big-head had died when I left school. Only in my own mind had it been kept alive.'

Whether or not he was ever able to relinquish that pain, being branded as arrogant and cocky left a profound impact on his life. Weekes, his lifelong friend, had observed that he was 'easily hurt if the wrong things were said; if he was on the different side of general opinion.'

It is not difficult to see why it became such a heavy load for him. That heaviness emerges in the undertone of the first chapter of *Cricket Punch*, 'Don't Shoot the Winners.' Its focus is ostensibly on the 1957 West Indies tour of England: five Tests that resulted in three wins for England and two draws.

It is an unusually indignant tone for the diplomat he had become. He chastised the English, saying 'they don't like winners,' after the press described the West Indies as a weak team, rather than acknowledging that the English had played good cricket. For Frank, the idea that winning was not cause for acknowledging superior performance, but for invoking negative assessments, was not sporting.

It was not a passing comment; he rolled out a lawn tennis story for support. It is the tale of the two young Australian players, Lew Hoad and Ken Rosewall, underdogs in the American world, who rose to Wimbledon stardom amid the support of English crowds – until Hoad won the championship in 1956.

'And what happened? The crowds that had cheered him began to jeer him. They called him temperamental and "big-headed." The Hoad on the way to the top they loved. The Hoad at the top they loathed. And they only loathed him because he won.' He made a similar case for Althea Gibson's 1957 Wimbledon win.

That first chapter lets off steam bottled up since those formative days at Combermere. He had been carrying it for a long time, and in his afterword to the second chapter in Eytle's book he refers to the impact.

'I was unfortunate enough to have been under an endemic psychological and mental strain throughout my schooldays; so much so that by the time I had reached the fourth form I was suffering from a persecution complex. These were the days when child psychology was not a subject demanded of applicants for the pupil-teacher posts that were held in schools; nor indeed did the majority of the masters have the experience of raising families of their own. It was a matter of learning mainly by repetition and retention. There was no allowance made for the original point of view. This is still fairly true of the attitude of so large a section of the population that it can be regarded as a characteristic.'

More than 20 years later, it loomed large enough for the story to have been told again, and for him to add these lines.

'Having had my knocks at a tender age, I tried to insulate myself against subsequent ones. It was, therefore, with a greater sense of pity than annoyance that I ignored the conjectural remarks made every time I revisited.'

His relationship with Barbados was always going to be complicated, and the days at Combermere were to shape his outlook for the rest of his days.

CHAPTER 4

THE WORRELL CLAN

The few people alive who knew the Worrell family in those early years consistently referred only to Athelston's long absences; their vagueness suggesting more a reluctance to discuss the true nature of his relationship with his family than genuine ignorance.

There is an inherent Barbadian reserve about disclosing any information which may seem to be negative about families, particularly if they are prominent members of society. In the case of Frank, it was impossible to penetrate the cloak of discreet silence surrounding the character of Athelston, and the way he related to his wife, Grace, and their three children. It seems he was something of a free spirit. Weekes said you could always tell when he was in Barbados, because there would be loud music coming from his home until late into the night, and he would appear to have had a few drinks as he sang at the top of his voice.

It was not an uncommon lifestyle among working-class men; times were difficult, work was hard to come by: a sea-faring life led to long absences and complicated the capacity to manage interludes back home on solid ground. (Shamont Sobers, father of Garfield, was killed on board the Lady Hawkins, a steam passenger ship where he worked as a 'general servant,' when it was hit by a torpedo from a U-boat in 1942. He was only 34, Garfield was six.)

Weekes eventually revealed that when Frank's mother went to the US, her marriage was crumbling. 'I think there was some sort of separation, because the old man ended up living there, right in Bank Hall, alone in the house. The house is still there. He was a very popular old man himself, he walked around in a tee-shirt showing off his body and things like that.' Athelston died in 1958.

Frank did not talk much about his mother, and barely about his father. Weekes did not think he was close to his father at all, but said that Frank's grandmother was a darling. 'She was very strict, like all grandmothers were in those days, and she was an old grandmother, not a young grandmother the way a girl at 33 is a grandmother these days.'

In *Cricket Punch*, Frank vaguely described his family in only two paragraphs of the entire book. The first simply mentions that he had two siblings, their age difference and that his brother went to live in Brooklyn and played for a West Indian cricket team. No names are given, just as in the second paragraph.

'My mother and father had gone to the United States earlier, so my upbringing was in the hands of my grandmother, who saw to it that I led a normal youngster's life. I got into the usual scrapes, played the usual games of football and cricket and generally enjoyed life.'

He never mentions the estrangement of his parents. This silence, and the deliberate abstinence from discussion of his family life (which extended to his wife and daughter) in a book published in 1959 when he was 35, suggests that he had difficulty with disclosing what he thought cricket fans might not want to hear. The book was published the same year he graduated from the University of Manchester, after a hectic period of juggling his studies and cricket commitments. It was most likely ghostwritten (probably by Ernest Eytle of British Guiana, who had moved with his family to England in 1951 and had become a BBC commentator), and that might account for the singular focus on cricket. Worrell had met Eytle in September 1951, on the *SS Strathmore*, en route to Australia.

That reticence to discuss family matters openly may also have been at the heart of my initial encounters with Grace Hinds (Frank's sister), when she had just passed her 86th birthday. Initially, she had agreed to be interviewed, and we arranged to talk further, but then her manner abruptly changed, becoming almost hostile, and she bluntly refused. Continued efforts failed and she died on August 3, 2018, without changing her mind. Grace had married a Grenadian, Walzid Hinds, a lab technician, and they had five sons. While the children were still young, the family moved back to Grenada for some years. The boys were schooled there, but then Walzid returned to the US, and it was only much later that Grace and their sons joined him.

Grace had been the last living source of childhood memory. The handful of contemporaries, or people who had known Frank in his early years, were willing, but many were ailing and could barely speak, and most have since died. In some cases, memories had become so faulty that the narratives were a mish-mash of stories about different people and places all stirred together in the giant cauldron of a faltering brain.

Livingstone's daughter, Marilyn, a performing artist, educator, and social activist with a background in theatre and film, lives in Brooklyn. She was born on Christmas Day in 1947, and remembered her grandparents and 'Uncle Frank,' although he was an occasional visitor.

He had visited New York in 1945, 1946 and again in the middle of 1947 for exhibition matches, so he would have missed Marilyn's birth, but he had spent time with his mother and siblings, in between visits to nightclubs and sightseeing.

Marilyn dredged up memories of Grampa Worrell (Athelston), whom she said shared a warm relationship with her father. She affectionately described her Grandma Worrell as being spoiled and pampered with an indomitable will. Marilyn had stayed with her in Brooklyn in the mid-Sixties; when she first met her great-grandmother, Florence. Grace had won a lottery, the very popular Irish sweepstake, around 1948. She bought for cash, a 'beautiful, grand, four-storey, limestone house' said Marilyn, 'on Deane Street, 1270 between Kingston and New York Avenue.' The house came with its original furnishings and fixtures, 'beautiful ceilings with crown moulding, mirrored walls, parquet floors, a fireplace, French provincial furniture,' all that was fashionable at the time. 'She was very, very, very grand.'

While Grace, the queen, was acquiring her personal palace as she turned 50, her 24-year-old son was making his new home across the Atlantic in England. In 1948, he had emigrated to take up an offer to play for Radcliffe Cricket Club, and had married his own queen.

Marilyn said Frank often turned to his older brother, Livingstone, for advice. Livingstone, who had not been able to enter Harrison College, although he was very bright and academically inclined, had gone with his mother to the USA. Marilyn described her father as a 'super-intellectual scholar, philosopher, an artist and a humanitarian'. He eventually joined the US Army Corps as an electrical engineer and inspector. But he 'experienced a great deal of racism in his job,' in the 1950s. Her brother, William, has two daughters. Marilyn does not have any children herself, and had been reflecting on the impending closure of the Worrell line. Apart from Frank's half-brother, Leroy, she is the last one carrying the Worrell name.

She had been gathering family mementoes: photographs, letters, clippings; the paraphernalia of decades, footprints for posterity; only to have them lost to floodwaters entering her home.

CHAPTER 5

THE BREWSTER CLAN

In the early Forties, Worrell became a regular visitor to the large Brewster household, a gregarious middle-class home, open to family and friends.

Nine children were born to Esmé Viola Wiltshire and her husband, Mervyn Gittens Brewster, a studio photographer. While Esmé remained in charge of the bustling homestead, Mervyn, and later his son Erard, worked at a photo studio on Broad Street. Harold, who became the Barbados High Commissioner to London, was the eldest of their children, and Velda was the second.

Born in 1922, Velda Elaine was two years older than Frank. They met around 1944, when the family moved to Hindsbury Road from Martindale's Road; close enough for Frank to visit, along with friends of the Brewster children.

At her home in Barbados, Olwen Cumberbatch, the second-to-last child, listed the siblings in order of appearance. Harold, Velda, Erard, Frank, Victor, Hal, Avis, Olwen and De Lisle. Only the last two were alive then. Olwen, born in 1935, was remarkably sprightly and engaging. A gracious hostess, she chatted cheerfully about her family and the relationship with Worrell, but never once dropped her guard. No family secrets would get past her lips. Her father looked after his children well and they enjoyed a middle-class life. Her mother was a perpetual hostess, keeping her house ready and open for the constant stream of visitors.

'I would say what was outstanding about my mother, which is the opposite to me, anybody could come in at any time and get something to eat. She was always there, ready. I don't know how she managed, but she did that. Our friends would come and we could invite somebody and say come and have lunch and there was always something. That is the thing I remember most about her. People who know us would tell you if you go by Mama Brewster man, you sure to get something (laughs), because she was that type of person, but she also had enough to give. Everybody could bring in their friends because she preferred for us to bring our friends home than for us to go to them. So everybody came home.'

Olwen claimed to be the only introverted one in the Brewster clan. 'The others were party people and outgoing, each and every one of the others, very outgoing.' She believed Worrell liked her the most of the siblings, and speculated that maybe it was on account of her quiet disposition.

She couldn't say where Velda had gone to primary school (Velda was 13 years older), but she knew she did not attend a high school. Six of the siblings went to high school, but Velda, Erard and Victor, three of the elders, did not, and Olwen surmised that it might have been a question of money.

She could not recall precisely when Velda and Frank met. He was among the regular visitors alongside the Critchlow brothers, Eric and Leroy, and they would have attended the same church.

As was the norm in many large families, the eldest looked after their younger siblings. Olwen was 'duty-bound' to obey her big sister (Weekes had described the tyranny of a sibling seven years older), and Velda was more of a maternal presence in her life.

'You hear to the person that was older than you. There was no question of it; that was the law,' she paused reflectively. It was the only time that there is a glimpse of the 'quiet one' she had described. 'I looked up to Velda, really looked up to her. We were very close, despite the difference in ages.'

The questions turned to a delicate subject, and as expected, she promptly put up a wall, as sturdy and impenetrable as a giant spider's web.

On 29 June 1944, Velda had given birth to a daughter named Heather. She had already met Frank. He would have known about her status as an unmarried mother. In Barbados, for someone of the middle-class background that Olwen described, that would have been problematic. She was chary about discussing Heather.

'Heather is like my daughter. What you want to know about her?'

I wanted to know the circumstances of when she was born.

'Let her talk to you about it,' said Olwen, deflecting the story of her birth, to a copious summary of her life.

'But she is like my daughter. My son will tell you that she is like my own child. Lana was close too but everybody in my family will tell you that Heather is like my own child. She was born here and grew up here and she went to school here. She went to private school first and then she went to Queen's College. Then she went to Canada after her first marriage. Her first son was born here and he was not yet a year when they left, but that marriage failed. She got married again and her second husband – who everybody adored, I liked her first husband too, not as much as the second one, because I still talk to her first husband, and whenever I go up there, we go out to lunch and so on – but the second husband was really, really nice. He died. Again from a heart attack, but let her talk to you about that because she is living and I don't want to tell her story.'

After a short pause for breath, 'She sends me a ticket to Canada every year.'

It turned out that Heather also visited Barbados regularly, and although she engaged in many short telephone conversations, she put off every proposal for a meeting. I was in Barbados while she was there. I tried to see her while she visited friends in Trinidad for one Carnival and I even went to Canada for an interview which she had agreed to do. As on every other occasion, she agreed to meet then cancelled at the last moment.

But on this hot November day in 2016, Olwen had already closed up shop on that subject as she showed me numerous framed photos, studio-portraits, of the various children of the clan, including a beautiful Heather, smiling and sunny-faced, as they posed expertly for the photographer.

Heather Rollock, née Brewster, exuded Olwen. It must have been a Brewster trait, this engaging personality so light, airy and charming, but superbly adroit at deflection. In our first conversation, which I thought would be a precursor to our physical meeting, she told me that she was raised by her grandmother and Aunty Olwen, and that it was her grandmother's choice for her to stay in Barbados while her mother, Velda, 'was settling herself in England.

'I loved my childhood days growing up,' she said. 'I was spoilt growing up, and I was not selfish,' she added, oddly. When the boys got together to play whist, she would be excited to join in, but one look from grandmother Esmé would tell her that that was not on and she would go to her room. 'We visited friends, we climbed trees; we played soccer and cricket; turn down, pick up, a card game matching cards; jacks,' she said, 'and anybody's mother could scold you.'

Michael Walcott (Clyde's son) described Heather as being more like Velda than Lana was. Although the three of them were very gregarious and loved 'to dress up and look a certain way,' Velda loved cooking (Lana hated it) and was more of a homemaker. She was a 'very social being,' he said, like Heather, and could hold her own in any environment. Lana could be warm and charming, but if she did not take to you, she would simply ignore you.

Heather had the Brewster capacity to speak no ill, especially of the dead. She described Frank as a humble man who always looked out for the poor. 'He was not a braggart or a social climber, even though he lived in that world.' She spoke about his calm demeanour, like a mediator, 'he had to be that middle person,' who would 'always defuse discussions.' She may have witnessed this on the domestic front, because she was never in public with the Worrells. 'On the inside, he was dealing with a lot of egos and passions,' she said. 'Remember the racial tensions of the time.'

Heather never joined her mother in England; instead she got married and moved to Canada in 1969, when she was 25. Her first marriage ended, and she eventually remarried and retired after years as an executive assistant at a bank. She became a widow, with two adult sons. The second boy has cerebral palsy, and this led her to explore alternative medicines and therapy. She said she was eleven when she and Lana bonded – Lana would have been around five – but she would not give any details about the nature of their relationship. She was Lana's sponsor when she emigrated to Canada in 1989.

She also would not speak directly about her relationships with her mother, Lana, and Frank. 'Frank was a wonderful man; decent, kind, hard-working and a good father,' she said, in what was clearly an impersonal description.

It was a curious relationship, and no one was willing to shed any light on its details. Worrell's niece, Marilyn, said that Heather had been very hurt by the way she was excluded from the Worrell home and the Worrell story.

Worrell lived a public life that did not seem to back away from challenging the norms of his time. The rigid conventions of Barbados had shaken him loose from its moorings early, so that even if the Brewster family had decided that the proper thing to do would be to send Velda forth without the stigma of having been an unmarried mother, it is incongruous with his character that Heather would never live with the Worrells, or even be publicly acknowledged, not even after they had settled into their new life at Radcliffe.

CHAPTER 6

WEEKES AND WALCOTT

The cricket career of Everton Weekes had taken a socially circumscribed path. Worrell had come through Combermere and Empire. Walcott went from Combermere to Harrison College. Through the Barbados Cricket Association (BCA) competitions they were granted early recognition along the beaten track.

Weekes came from the poorer side of town, and his early years were shaped by the rough circumstances of his environment. His father had gone to Trinidad seeking work and Weekes did not meet him until he was 19. He had joined the army, and had played in Barbados Cricket League (BCL) competitions. He had often been roped in as a substitute fielder for Pickwick, the club he admired, and while this was influential in exposing him to selectors' eyes, his national debut came three years after Walcott and Worrell had made theirs.

Weekes had been playing in the BCL while at school, but when he left at 14, there were few options. 'I had a couple of friends who had access to a yacht. These two friends of mine were really my seniors and they had this friend who could hook up with the yacht and we used to go fishing, the three of us. I did that to get money for matinées, to go to pictures and that sort of thing. In those days I think it was only a penny to go and see a movie. So I spent a lot of time doing that and reading,' he said. 'Going fishing and reading.'

At 17, he joined the army and spent four 'beautiful' years in the service, representing the army at cricket. As a member of the Barbados Regiment, he played for the Garrison Sports Club, which won the First Division Cup in 1947, but which was disbanded not long after the war. He said that although he was in touch with Worrell, 'I played for the Barbados team, under-19s, but Frank was 19-plus, so he was a couple years before me; he and Clyde. We struck up this very good relationship as young men playing for Barbados and the West Indies.'

He had known Walcott since they were children, as 'Clyde lived only five minutes from me. He lived on Westbury Road, near Baxter's Road where a lot of tourists used to go up and get fish and so on.

We lived in the front road there. So I knew Clyde when Clyde was maybe six or seven years old.'

By the end of the Second World War, the three had been playing alongside each other for a couple of years, competing in BCA and BCL competitions. From 1945, when Weekes was called up, all three were representing Barbados.

Garry Sobers was mesmerised by them as a boy of around eleven. 'I used to score at the Wanderers ground which was just above me on the Pass, the Bay Pass as we used to call it. We used to get big crowds in those days: Wanderers and Empire, Wanderers and Spartan; big crowds. I could stand up and look over their heads and I could see all the great players: Weekes, Worrell, Walcott, George Carew, all of them. I learnt from watching because I used to look at how they played. I didn't watch the sixes or fours they hit. I wasn't interested in that. I used to watch their movements and watch the pitch of the ball and length to see what they do to that kind of ball, how they move. When I went to play, I used to practise with the boys and practise what I saw, because we didn't have any coaches in those days. That is how I learnt.'

There were differences among the three, a result of their distinct personalities and upbringings. Worrell would never be as close with Walcott as he was with Weekes, who revered him. Even while they were students at Combermere, Worrell and Walcott were said to have not got along. Cricket was their bond, and if, at the end of their careers their statistics were remarkably close, it is a measure of how each, with his individual style, pushed the other forward in the spirit of competition.

Weekes was reluctant to admit to any conflicts between them, 'Always tight, as far as I know, we were always very, very, very tight.' Later, he would concede that there were differences between Worrell and Walcott, and between him and Walcott, especially after the Fifties.

If anything other than camaraderie lurked under the public image; the world was not going to find it. Not until death. In Walcott's autobiography, *Sixty Years on the Back Foot*, there are two very short, very dry sentences that say volumes as he describes Worrell's funeral.

'Everton Weekes was one of the pallbearers. I wasn't asked.'

CHAPTER 7

EVERYWHERE IS WAR

The decade of the 1940s was Worrell's coming of age, when the forces that shaped his life coalesced. In 1939, a month after his 15th birthday, the world was plunged into a war, precipitated by Nazi Germany's invasion of Poland. It would be the beginning of a global conflict that went on until 1945, involving the majority of nations and causing millions of deaths and the devastation of economies. Barbados, proudly considering itself an outpost of Britain, devoted itself to supporting the war effort. Despite this preoccupation, West Indians still concentrated on developing their cricket with inter-colonial matches. Through these games, Worrell became renowned throughout the Caribbean during the Second World War. Afterwards, when international cricket resumed, his fame spread globally, opening the highway to stardom in the Fifties.

But the road ahead was not straightforward, and he had to learn to navigate it prudently. After brief stints at trying to earn a livelihood in Trinidad and then Jamaica, he eventually headed to the United Kingdom, which became his home for just over a decade. He would also meet and marry Velda Brewster, the younger sister of Harold, his Combermere captain, and his daughter, Lana was born. By 1949, he was a West Indian Test cricketer living in England, playing for Radcliffe as their overseas professional, with a wife and a baby girl. He was just 25.

But in 1940, he was 16: a student who barely applied himself to his schoolwork, yet excelled at cricket to the extent that he had come to the attention of school masters, often with disapproval. He casually flouted rules, yet did not seem to ever reconcile himself to acknowledging his role in his reputation for arrogance. Accustomed to being singled out for his stylish cricket – at primary school he was already bowling to Test cricketers – it would be surprising if he did not think he was entitled to special treatment.

Even as Worrell's prowess gained acclaim, his love-hate relationship with Barbados escalated. He remained a student at Combermere until 1943, when he was 19. He taught general subjects there for a brief time, then explored the possibility of working in Trinidad. It barely lasted a month (he said he did not like Trinidad's beaches) and he returned to Barbados where he got a job as an agent of Demerara Life Insurance. That too, did not last. If he thought that his sporting success would be easily transferred to the realm of business, he was mistaken. Weekes was convinced that his inability to attract clients affected him profoundly. It demoralised him, made him more driven, anxious to succeed at whatever he did. Suggesting that Worrell was not able to sell life insurance policies because of the colour of his skin, Weekes believed that it jolted him into realising that things would not come easily. 'It hit him pretty hard,' he said.

But his cricket was flourishing. After Combermere, Worrell joined Empire, the most obvious choice given that it had been his childhood stomping ground, and socially, it was the place he could most easily fit in. He played cricket and football for the club, excelling at both, and in 1946, Empire won the championship in both sports. In one game against the Police Club, he scored 201 and took 11 for 78, winning the match almost singlehandedly.

The Second World War had practically wiped out international cricket. Within the West Indies, the inter-regional games continued. The Goodwill tournaments, mainly between Trinidad and Tobago and Barbados (although British Guiana also participated) became not just a big fixture, but were occasions where new talent could be spotted. The first two matches were played at the Queen's Park Oval in Port of Spain in February 1941.

From then to 1946, the two territories played against each other 14 times. In the second year of Goodwill games, Worrell made his debut for Barbados at 18, still a Combermere student – and, it was said, never having seen a first-class match. Clyde Walcott turned 16 on the first day of the third match of the tournament in January 1942, where he made his national debut as well. Together they became regulars of the tournament, building their reputations with outstanding performances.

They did not have auspicious starts: Walcott found it difficult to negotiate the bouncy pitch at the Queen's Park Oval and was dropped for the following match, while Worrell scored 29 and six, but took six wickets for 128 runs. He had made his debut as a batter at No.11, but after two more games at No.10, he was pushed up the order to No.6; his batting had impressed.

Six months later, when Trinidad visited Barbados, Walcott showed his potential, scoring 70, 67 and 50. This was the first time he and Worrell batted together. In the opening match, with the score on 229 for seven, Worrell scored 48 and the partnership added 100 in 90 minutes. He then took five wickets for 47 runs in the first innings.

In that July 1942 visit, Trinidad also scored one of the lowest first-class totals in history in their first innings: 16 in just under 13 eight-ball overs. Derek Sealy took eight wickets for eight runs and 'Foffie' Williams took the other two. Andy Ganteaume top-scored with nine, Victor Stollmeyer made four, and Gerry Gomez was not out on three. If one were to assess the quality of Trinidad's cricket on the basis of that game, one could be forgiven for assuming the worst.

This was hardly the case. The Trinidad team during these Goodwill games of the Forties included players like the Stollmeyer brothers: Victor and Jeffrey, Andy Ganteaume, Gerry Gomez, Lance Pierre, Prior Jones, Kenny Trestrail, and Rupert Tang Choon. The Barbados team included John Goddard, George Carew, Derek Sealy, Clarence Skeete, Frank Worrell, Clyde Walcott and his brother Keith, and later, Everton Weekes. From British Guiana came Robert Christiani, and from Jamaica, the legendary George Headley, and Kenneth Weekes. The games were much more than an occasion to keep cricket going during the war days, they were arenas of fierce contests.

CHAPTER 8

HIM LOVE TO BAT

Worrell's panache was a drawing card at the Barbados Cricket Association (BCA) competitions. He had established himself as an elegant all-rounder, and crowds gathered on Saturday afternoons to watch his graceful moves, especially the late cut, his trademark. He loved to dance, and was always keen to learn the latest moves. With his flair and athletic reflexes, he caught the eye even before he started amassing large scores.

In his autobiography, Trinidad-born Pelham Warner had recommended a large measure of light-footedness and a dollop of light-heartedness. 'I have always loved dancing, and "the polished floor" is good for one's cricket, for it teaches rhythm, balance and footwork, and keeps one young.' That could easily define Worrell's stylishness.

In his sixth Goodwill game, he scored 188, his first century in first-class cricket. In the first innings, Barbados made 452 and Trinidad responded with 428. Worrell hit 68 in the second innings, with Barbados declaring at 273 for five in the drawn match.

In February 1944, Worrell scored an unbeaten 308 against Trinidad at Bridgetown, partnering with John Goddard (218) in a partnership of 502, then the third-highest partnership for any wicket in all first-class cricket. It is still the fourth highest for the fourth wicket. Worrell's triple century also became the highest individual score for Barbados, passing the 304 made by Tim Tarilton in 1920, and he consistently rated it as one of his best performances. From all accounts, the first innings of that match was a thing of beauty. A double century from Jeffrey Stollmeyer and 94 by captain Gerry Gomez saw Trinidad declare on 490 for eight. With Carew, Oscar Robinson and Walcott back in the pavilion, Worrell and Goddard took the score to 650 before captain Tom Peirce declared.

Historian Keith Sandiford put it into statistical perspective. 'The stand of 502 was a new West Indian record for any wicket, eclipsing the 487 that Jamaica's George Headley and Clarence Passailaigue had established for the sixth wicket against Lord Tennyson's XI at Kingston in 1932. Apart from a difficult caught-and-bowled chance to Jeffrey Stollmeyer at 104, Worrell's innings, which lasted more than eight hours, was flawless. While he had taken 211 minutes over his first 100, he spent only 158 minutes over the second, and 135 over the third. At 19 years, 199 days, he became the youngest cricketer to achieve a triple century.'

The December 1945 issue of *Sport and Music Cavalcade*, a Trinidadian magazine published by Brunell Jones and Philip Vieira, carried a review of the Goodwill matches that year. Jones noted that, 'When the big games began Frankie Worrell hit up a sparkling 74 out of Barbados' total of 203 runs in the first innings…' He went on, 'When Barbados batted for the second time in this game Clyde Walcott scored the most attractive century of the series in an innings in which he scored 103 runs all round the wicket, and the newcomer, Everton Weekes, made an unimpressive debut in this match, scoring a duck in the first innings and 8 in the second.'

Appearing under 'World Sports Shorts,' is a photograph of a lean, youthful Worrell with the first shadow of his trademark moustache. Given that he loved the cinema enough to risk getting caught attending during a cricket match at Combermere, it is easy to imagine him sitting in a darkened movie hall gazing at Clark Gable, one of the leading actors of the time, and deciding that he would fashion himself a Gable moustache. Under the photograph, readers were informed that, 'Frank Worrell, back in Barbados from a holiday in New York, where he played in a few cricket games with George Headley's Team, revealed that he discovered he was related to Headley.'

Worrell had already become newsworthy in the region and his record-breaking score was the first of many lengthy innings that became a feature of his cricket.

In February 1946, this time batting with Walcott, a new first-class record partnership for any wicket of 574 was set in a game against Trinidad at Port of Spain. Worrell was unbeaten on 255 while Walcott surpassed Worrell's individual Barbados record with 314 not out. Their record was broken the following year by Indian batters Vijay Hazare and Gul Mohammad, who put on 577 for the fourth wicket for Baroda against Holkar. But for a long time Frank held the title of being the only batter to be involved in two 500-run partnerships. It is still the highest partnership in all West Indian cricket.

By the time he left Barbados in 1947, Worrell had played in 15 matches for his country and scored 1547 runs at an average of almost 74. He had also taken 15 catches and claimed 43 wickets.

CHAPTER 9

JAMMING IN JAMAICA

While still at Combermere, Worrell had gained a fair measure of recognition for his athleticism. His hand-to-eye coordination was superb, he excelled at any sport he tried – football, tennis, swimming – and he had grown into a handsome young man. Always a lover of music and dancing, parties and pretty girls became a fixture in his schedule.

During the war years, the reputations of Worrell, Weekes and Walcott had grown so immensely that they were star attractions wherever they played cricket. In Barbados, their social lives changed. Music, alcohol and women had entered those frolicking days.

Writing of their burgeoning friendship and cricket bond, Walcott described the 'wonderful spirit' among the young players. 'We were so dedicated to our cricket that we vowed we would not drink alcohol and instead spent our spare hours playing cards. But Frank did not observe the ban on alcohol. He liked a drink and he liked relaxing.'

Alcohol has always been a staple of Caribbean life. Sugar cane, mainstay of the economies from slavery and plantation days, led to the development of the world's finest rums. Barbados, Jamaica, Guyana, and Trinidad and Tobago are all premier producers. But the culture of alcohol preceded the production of high-quality liquor. More than once Worrell had spoken about a shared social culture revolving around alcohol. Even if everyone partook of spirits, in the stratified societies they did not drink together.

Having drinks was a way to pass the time, to forget the burdens of life and to unwind and relax after long, hot days. It was true for both the English, who had come from a culture where pubs were second homes for men and women alike, and for workers over whom whips were mercilessly cracked.

Bars, rum shops, recreation clubs, pubs, taverns – the appellations varied – but these establishments were as powerful as the churches as social institutions throughout the region. They were gathering places where news was shared; opinions distributed, and philosophical positions presented. One writer calculated that in the early 21st century, there were a thousand rum shops on the tiny island of

Barbados. Throughout the region, young boys were introduced to alcohol as a way of marking their entry into the state of manhood. It was a rite of passage that encouraged a notion of machismo. A man who could hold his drink was a force to be reckoned with and someone to emulate. It was the same in Jamaica, although older men went to village bars, while the younger would go to places with music and sassy girls.

But even within this regional culture, even within the widely acknowledged tradition of excessive boozing among cricket teams – Australia, England, West Indies – even within these accepted norms, Worrell was often singled out as being the leader of the pack, with Weekes right behind him. Was he a celebratory drinker? Did he drink to escape the realities of the day? His father, who did not appear to be the role model he chose, was a heavy drinker and his mother enjoyed a drink. With all his complexity, Worrell was a man of extremes. He had a large appetite for pleasure and success and he was driven to pursue them, while carefully managing a veneer of urbane sophistication.

All through his adulthood, Frank was known as a dandy, persuasively defined by Charles Baudelaire, the French poet and art critic in his essay, 'The Painter of Modern Life.' His dandy does not aspire to money for the sake of acquisition, that would be too vulgar a pursuit; neither is there 'an immoderate taste for the toilet and material elegance,' these are only 'symbols of his aristocratic superiority of the mind'. What matters most is achieving distinction, a personal originality.

'It is the joy of astonishing others, and the proud satisfaction of never oneself being astonished. A dandy may be blasé, he may even suffer; but in this case, he will smile like the Spartan boy under the fox's tooth.' It can border upon the spiritual and stoical, he wrote, reminding readers that there is 'an energy in all excess'.

It is akin to a religion, and its followers 'all partake of the same characteristic quality of opposition and revolt; they are all representatives of what is finest in human pride, of that compelling need, alas only too rare today, of combating and destroying triviality.'

Worrell's reputation as a dandy may have been confined to a superficial interpretation of the word, but nothing as simple as foppishness could define him, even as a child. His disregard for authority; his pursuit of pleasure; his obsession with cricket; his dalliances, all of it can be found inside Baudelaire's head. His attachment to alcohol is suggestive of that energy in all excess – a man given to extremes.

Yet with all the heavy drinking ascribed to him, how did he manage to keep up the façade?

Several cricketers said that he insisted that they keep their drinking private. On tour, he would keep a stocked bar in his room and they would be encouraged to partake freely, rather than be seen imbibing in public establishments. Weekes said he was the kind of person who encouraged others to have drinks, even mischievously pouring them heavy-handed concoctions without their knowledge. But he also said that Worrell would get drunk quickly, so after just a couple of drinks he would appear to have had more; an explanation that was so hollow that even he laughed at it.

When Worrell had first moved to Radcliffe, the neighbours had reported him as a quiet man, whose only evidence of social activity was the number of beer bottles outside his door on mornings. He had described Barbados as a place where people did not go out in public to drink, but rather, did their entertaining at home. All through his life, he preferred inviting people to his premises to have drinks rather than going out.

Yet there were occasions, especially when he was in high demand for public appearances in the Fifties, when he let his guard down in public. Weekes related what he repeatedly insisted was a 'true story' about a 1950 cocktail party, where Worrell was called upon to say a few words of thanks.

'He started by saying, "At the beginsment of all of this," beginsment he said. Nobody paid much attention to it. When we were coming back home Prior Jones asked him what's this beginsment thing. He said, you know when you stutter and you're thinking faster than the average person, you get begin and commence. He could make a joke of that sort of thing. Prior said, "I only want to know if it will be in the dictionary next".'

Weekes was telling this story to illustrate how his stutter would emerge, and that it would sometimes be very pronounced, but it was generally unnoticeable, unless he had been drinking heavily.

Walcott, it seemed, was less fond of the bottle than Weekes and Worrell. But during the Forties, they were in their twenties and those were years of uninhibited carousing, at every imaginable level.

A few days after leaving Harrison College, Walcott got a job as a clerk in a wholesale provision store. Within a couple of weeks, he switched his clerkship to become a geologist conducting a survey of the water supply in Barbados. He stayed there for two years, mainly because it did not interfere with his cricket. By the time he and Worrell and Weekes hooked up in 1945 in Trinidad to play cricket for Barbados, they had already been creating a stir.

None of them could be said to have been very well-off, although Walcott was clearly in a more comfortable position, so their activities were limited by their financial constraints. Weekes was a lance corporal in the army, playing for Garrison Sports Club (GSC). When he was called to play for Barbados, he was expected to provide his own gear, but could not afford it. The GSC covered the cost, and alongside his small army pay, he tried to live on the stipend – $30 a match – to get by. (The currency was the British West Indian dollar.) Weekes believed that Worrell got help for his kit from his mother. They were very close friends by then, spending a lot of time together at the beach and training at the Garrison Savannah … 'just the two of us together. He liked the Garrison, we would go to the Savannah when they had horse racing and he always had access to the American currency. The old lady was minding him from the States. She would send money to her mother and the grandson would have it.'

In any event, they were young, full of promise, revelling in their youth and popularity. The world was opening up and they were going to explore it.

In 1946, the trio were invited to be part of a team going to New York for a series of exhibition matches. It would be for three months, and their expenses would be paid. Weekes could not get leave from the army and went instead to play in the regional matches, first in British Guiana, then Jamaica. Walcott decided to quit his job rather than miss the chance. Worrell had nothing to lose, and it was an opportunity to visit his family in Brooklyn.

Walcott was amazed at the fast pace of life in New York. They were to play their matches with the Barbados Club and the Trinidad Club, 'busy and flourishing institutions,' at the Randall's Island Stadium from July to September. He was even more astounded by how 'money-conscious' the matches were with the betting that accompanied the games. Special feats were rewarded by the passing around of a hat for contributions. 'I remember hitting a ball out of the ground and the next thing I knew was that a spectator had dashed out and thrust a ten-dollar bill into my pocket.'

The trip turned out to be a financial success for them, but significantly, it opened their eyes to a different social experience.

The three then went to Jamaica in March 1947 for one of the inter-colonial matches. Walcott said that socially, that trip was the best yet. 'Everton, incidentally, revealed himself as a master of the "jitterbug".' Weekes had truly enjoyed Jamaica and the friendship and mentorship he found in George Headley. Among the eyes noticing him was the influential Ruel Vaz, a well-known businessman and entrepreneur who invited him to Jamaica, to play for the country.

'I was in the army, and could not accept the invitation,' Weekes had written. 'But I did tell him that Frank would be interested in setting up in Jamaica, and that is how it started.'

He would not have gone in any case, although Worrell encouraged him to see it as a career move. 'I was not unhappy here. I couldn't see that far, because I'd gone to school here, a boy without a degree. I was not looking that far ahead. I was just looking to get comfortable.'

Vaz needed little persuasion to extend his offer to Worrell, who had already decided to stay on in Jamaica and was working, first at the Government statistics office in King Street, Kingston, and then as a public relations officer for the Reynolds' aluminium firm in Ocho Rios. Later on, when he returned to Jamaica, he was linked to Reynolds Jamaica Mines Ltd, a bauxite company in Claremont. He was soon turning out for the country and for the Kensington Cricket Club, alongside George Headley. He mixed freely in society, moving comfortably between the working class and the wealthier citizens who were part of the Vaz milieu.

On the website of Jamaica's Cricket Hall of Fame, the citation for Worrell's induction, written by director Michael Chambers, remarked on his popularity. 'Worrell made hosts of friends in Jamaica even among people who cared little for cricket. While staying at the Vaz's he would often visit an ice cream parlor called The Commissary near the Rialto Theatre sipping sodas and talking with everyone discursively inclined far into the night.' Chambers, a former writer for the *Jamaica Times*, described his impact on Jamaican cricket spectators. 'Worrell, an ambidextrous youth, quickly endeared himself to our big-hearted galleries with the delicacy of his strokes, his swift fielding, and calculated medium pace left arm bowling. He did not display the savage power of Everton Weekes, nor the catapulting force of Walcott; but he had the qualities to arouse the soul of the poet and artist.'

He identified features that made Worrell stand apart from other players, traits that became the subject of gushing tributes by sportswriters over his career. 'There was the perfect upright stance, the left toe slightly raised like a ballet dancer, poised for the cover drive, the masterly drive between the bowler and mid-off such as against Lindwall at Sabina Park in 1955, the flick off his pads past mid-on, the one step backward dance to pull to mid-wicket; the prayerful hook on his knees to square leg or fine leg, the rapier square cut or the divinely delayed late cut – these were part of the Worrellian repertoire that charmed cricket watchers in many lands.'

Life at the Vaz household was a world removed from the stodgy environment in Barbados. Vaz was a genuine supporter of cricket and was earning a substantial income from his various businesses. Worrell was made to feel so welcome in the house at Windward Road that right to the end he referred to Vaz as his godfather.

The new world he inhabited was far less inhibiting than the judgmental place he had found Barbados to be. He could come and go as he pleased without feeling eyes watching his every move.

Easton McMorris, who made his Test debut in 1958, recalled that he and a couple of friends sneaked into the grounds of Ruel Vaz's home where one of his lavish parties was going on. It was in the early Fifties, and they could not resist the urge to see the famous trio, and the beautiful girls 'the best looking in Jamaica' who were guests. They settled themselves on the periphery of the festive occasion covertly checking out the men and women as they partied the night away.

This was the kind of life that lured Worrell to Jamaica. In this milieu, he could abandon himself to the pleasures of the flesh without the sanctimonious scrutiny of Barbados.

Women were seeking him out, and he enjoyed the attention. For the rest of his life, this would be the pattern. Numerous dalliances were credited to him; wherever in the world he travelled, he formed attachments. The Indian cricketer, Bishan Bedi, euphemistically described him as being the 'most romantic' of the West Indian cricketers. Yet, he was by nature a reserved man, and he kept his sexual activities as private as he could. He did not discuss his exploits, and it is remarkable that none of the people interviewed would reveal any of the secrets of his liaisons. Many would concede that he was very active; one story was told of him having to scramble through a window to evade an unexpectedly returning husband.

While privately, Worrell may have been something of the libertine, he was very conscious of presenting a respectable veneer to the public. It was one of his personal codes: a dignified manner at all times; which was partly why he did not indulge in boisterous celebrations on the cricket field. His naturally reserved disposition, especially in public, would have been a direct contradiction to the braggadocio that was generally on display around male sexuality.

In the sporting world, or any sphere for that matter, where men come together, there is an atmosphere of competition. Alpha males strut their stuff; bragging about female conquests is the thing to do. In cricket, it is no different. For many young cricketers, especially those from modest, working-class backgrounds and limited exposure, to be suddenly thrust into an adoring spotlight was beyond their wildest dreams. Sexual prowess, sexual conquest, having beautiful women flock to their arms was a powerful status symbol, especially in an environment where they were often treated as second-class citizens on account of their origins and their race. They were not successful financially in the West Indies, but they were fit and famous. There was nothing to deliver them from temptation.

In 1947, Worrell was just 23, Weekes and Walcott were around the same ages. They were already stars and they had not yet played in the 1947-48 MCC tour of the West Indies, which would confirm their status to the rest of the cricket world. This was the time to explore and enjoy the extraordinary perks of their cricketing excellence. In the middle of the year, another tour to New York for exhibition matches was organised. This time Weekes made the trip, his first outside the West Indies.

He remembered it as the time he discovered live jazz music and how enraptured he was. The sound of big-band bebop coming from Dizzy Gillespie simply blew him away. It was the beginning of his lifelong love for jazz. Up until then, his exposure to live music was mostly singing hymns in the church choir and the folk music of Barbados.

'I went to New York in '47 with some of the West Indies team, Frank, Clyde, myself and George Headley, Andy Ganteaume, Prior Jones, and I heard this trumpet player and he was different (he made a sound with his mouth, a warbling trill of notes), not the ta-ta-ta, and I saw it was coming from his trumpet. And I thought, what is this? And I couldn't imagine this great trumpet player, this great man, Dizzy Gillespie. My aunt lived on 115th Street, and I was staying with her in New York, ten blocks away from 125th, where everything happened, the Apollo, so every time I had a chance I would go and listen to this thing, and it was so different and I got hooked on it.

'Frank and Clyde enjoyed it too, but they were not a fanatic like me. They were not so crazy about it that they would want to rush and get into a group to line up to go and get it. We had a lot of fun. Clyde liked the glass too and of course so did Frank,' said Weekes.

They were visiting clubs, listening to live music from the big bands with their swing jazz and blues, and honing their dance steps as they tried out new numbers. It was the beginning of a higher level of sophistication. Weekes had been so transformed by that experience that he named his home in Barbados 'Balcony Rock' after a mellow Dave Brubeck composition.

The year in Jamaica transformed Worrell; while his social life had expanded considerably, he was also developing the personal philosophy of mentorship that would come to be his hallmark. His reputation had grown, and it seemed all was well in his corner of the world. The arrival of the English for the series of 1947-48 would result in far more than the impressive scores he tallied for his debut Test series, it led to another physical move; this time to England, and marriage to the girl he had seemingly left behind in Barbados.

CHAPTER 10

AFTER THE WAR

From 19 May to 22 August 1945, just two weeks after the end of the Second World War, the English population flocked to a series of matches between a combined Australian Services XI and an England side. The five three-day matches were crowded, as spectators thronged to see the first international encounters after five barren summers of war. Although they were called the Victory Tests, they were never officially recognised as such, but were recorded as first-class matches. The first proper Test after the war took place nearly a year later, in March 1946, when New Zealand played Australia at Wellington, losing by an innings and 103 runs.

The last encounter between the English and the West Indies had been cut short, (although they managed to play all three Tests) when the war had broken out in 1939. Many things had changed in those intervening years and there was a sense that English cricket, preoccupied with the war effort, had not taken into account that there had been steady competition in the West Indies through the Goodwill games. By 1946, Jamaica was one of the four countries taking part in these regular matches. West Indians had not abandoned their cricket.

The MCC sent out a team to the Caribbean for a series of four Tests from January to April 1948. The team, under the leadership of Gubby Allen, was not regarded as the best available. They did not win a single first-class match on the tour, losing the Test series 2-0.

Worrell had been selected for the first Test, but came down with a bout of food poisoning and had to sit it out. It must have been a tremendous disappointment to have his Test debut thwarted by flawed food. He'd lost his chance to play under the captaincy of George Headley, who was injured and missed the remainder of the series. Headley had been named captain for the first Test in Barbados, but after his injury, John Goddard took over and was named captain for the fourth Test in Jamaica. Headley's promotion was the first time a black man had been officially appointed to captain West Indies. (Learie Constantine had only led the team briefly years before when captain Jackie

71

Grant had been injured on the field.) Gerry Gomez ended up as captain in Trinidad, standing in for the injured Jeffrey Stollmeyer, who had pulled a hamstring during one of the first-class matches; at 26, he missed that early chance at captaincy. Goddard led for the final two Tests.

Stollmeyer attributed this naming of captains according to where the match was to be played, to 'the distance between the islands and the difficulty of communication'. West Indies cricket 'was still in its formative years, and often compromises, of a nature inexplicable in present times, had to be made by the administrators'.

At its formation in 1926, the West Indies Cricket Board of Control (WICBC), a collection of white men mostly from the planter and merchant classes, oversaw the affairs of the region's cricket. Initially, the organisation was created to manage the logistics of planning the visit to England in 1928, where the first West Indian Test would be played. There was no question of which colour would lead. Sir Pelham Warner, known as the 'Grand Old Man' of English cricket, had to make a case for black players to be even included in teams.

The practice of naming white men to the captaincy continued for decades. The social stratification in the colonies made it unthinkable for leadership to come from any other than white hands. It was actually revolutionary for the times, and a testament to the respect for Headley as a cricketer, that he was chosen to lead in the 1948 Test against England. Although the captaincy was the provenance of the white players, it was not a simple affair, and the appointment of different captains based on where the matches were being played would have been an attempt to smooth egos. The wrangling that ensued was based mainly on whichever territory felt it had the best candidate. By the 1950s the grumblings grew to include the issues of race and meritocracy. That decade was full of strife, both internally at WICBC level, and externally, as an increasingly vocal public made its feelings known.

On the ground, the stage was set by the performances of the three Ws in the latter half of the 1940s.

Walcott and Weekes had made their Test debuts at their home ground in Bridgetown; Walcott scoring eight and 16, and Weekes 35 and 25.

Three weeks later, Worrell made his Test debut at Queen's Park Oval in Trinidad on 11 February 1948. It was the first time the three Ws played in a Test match together. Worrell was joined by the compact, elegant Andy Ganteaume, whose legendary score of 112 was his first and last Test century, leaving him with a Test average that always needed to be explained (it was his only Test). Worrell made 97, an attractive knock, containing nine fours, a six, and was full of strokes during the three-and-a-quarter hours he was at the crease, *Wisden* commented that despite Ganteaume's defiance, 'everyone was admiring the cultured batting of Worrell'. Just short of his hundred, he was caught behind by wicketkeeper, Godfrey Evans off the bowling of seamer Ken Cranston, a disappointing end to his first Test innings. West Indies had put on a first-innings total of 497 in response to England's 362. The match ended in a draw after England posted 275 and time ran out when the West Indians were at 72 for three. Worrell had a go at bowling too, taking the wicket of fellow debutant Billy Griffith, who scored 140 before being out lbw.

In the third Test at Bourda in British Guiana, Worrell confirmed his class with his first Test century, described as a glorious one. His 131 not out in the first innings was the top score with 15 boundaries on what was deemed a difficult pitch. The West Indies declared on 297 for eight and won the match easily after England managed only 111 and were sent in again, this time posting 263 and leaving West Indies with just 78 for victory. Worrell's bowling was again called into service.

On 27 March, the fourth Test began in Kingston, Jamaica. This time West Indies won by ten wickets; with 490 and 76 to England's 227 and 336. Weekes led the way in the first innings, scoring 141, while Worrell hit 38 and Walcott 45. West Indies had won the series 2-0 and the three young men had presented their credentials to the world of cricket, which was slowly recovering from the deprivations of war.

For Worrell, that season was successful because, apart from his attractive performances in the Tests, he scored a century for Jamaica in the second colony game, enhancing 'his reputation as the leading batsman in the region', said one commentator, with an average of 147 and a total of 294 runs in his four Test innings.

Changes were coming rapidly for Worrell; Radcliffe Cricket Club wanted him as their overseas player. The club's president, Arthur Hampson, had been on a Caribbean cruise during the England series, and had been so impressed by Worrell that he sent a telegram to Jack Lowe, a textiles trader who had been scouting for a professional for the club. Lowe contacted Lancashire's Jack Ikin, a member of the touring party, who confirmed Worrell's ability, and on that recommendation Lowe made Worrell the offer of a salary of £500 for the 1948 season with a second year in the offing. By the second season, the figure had gone up to £700.

There were perks: air fares and accommodation were covered. If you took five wickets for 30 or under, or scored 50 runs or more, the collection bucket would go around and you could end up with £50 to £60 on a good day.

It was the perfect opportunity for a young man with talent and ambition and a desire to make it big. Coupled with his unhappiness in Barbados, there was every reason for him to move with alacrity.

'I wanted to get right away from the West Indies, to a place where they didn't know me, where there would be no bitter memories of canings for imaginary offences, no sneers about my conceit,' he had written. The offer from Lowe felt like salvation. 'This was my escape route. This was the way I could get right away from the West Indies.'

When the series against England ended in early April, he quickly relocated to Lancashire. Surprisingly, in light of the carefree carousing of Jamaica, he had decided to marry Velda Brewster, and he 'sent for her' said her sister, Olwen. They were married soon after at a quiet ceremony on 28 May 1948. Worrell was determined to make a break from the West Indies, and he felt he needed the kind of companionship and partnership that Velda could provide.

He hardly had time to plan the details. He had been based in Jamaica for almost a year when the Radcliffe offer came, while Velda had been in Barbados. They had a simple wedding at St. Andrew's Church in Radcliffe. None of Velda's family attended. Olwen said the family would not have been able to afford the journey by ship. The fact that Velda went to England on her own before the wedding and none of her family accompanied her, or attended the wedding, suggests that there might not have been complete approval of the marriage. Frank's niece, Marilyn, said that the Worrell clan believed that the Brewster family had not thought Frank was good enough for Velda. None of Worrell's family attended either. His mother was busy setting up her newly acquired fancy home in Brooklyn, and perhaps the speed with which events had unfolded made travel too difficult to arrange.

It was a complicated environment for the young couple. He was setting out to make a living thousands of miles away from home in a profession that did not have a tradition of providing a comfortable lifestyle. Not only did he and Velda have to adjust to the different climate – he spoke about spending more of the first six months huddled under blankets than being outdoors – but they faced new social and domestic arrangements. Velda was no longer part of the swirling, gregarious Brewster household with its constant domestic hubbub. Worrell was away from his friends and whatever support systems he had in Jamaica and Barbados. They were on their own in a foreign country, starting off practically from scratch.

Their first home was provided by Radcliffe, a house with an outside lavatory on Ulundi Street. Later, they would buy a house at No. 8 Bury and Bolton Road, but in the beginning, things were simple and sparse, and building community and friendships was their major focus.

The small town, with a population of around 27,000, was itself emerging from the war. With abundant coal seams, mines were a significant feature of its landscape. When the Worrells got there, that was coming to an end. Its major industries were based on cotton and paper – by the end of the war, the Radcliffe paper mill had more than 600 employees. At one point there were 60 textile mills and 15 spinning mills, but although things were changing, the town still had the feel of a simple, uncomplicated community.

English writer Tanya Aldred visited Radcliffe CC for an article on Sir Garfield Sobers, who became the club's professional ten years after Worrell. She spoke to John Heaton, who had once been the club chairman, and he described what the town was like in the 1950s.

'Life then was much simpler,' said Heaton, 'you went to work, you did your job, you enjoyed yourself at night. If you wanted to watch sport you had your local football teams like Bury or [Bolton] Wanderers, or you watched the cricket. There wasn't a right lot else to do. Two or three cinemas, a dance hall, lots of pubs. For the youth a lot of activity came from the churches. It was difficult to get around – I'm not sure Garry had a car till the third or fourth year. You had to use buses, you had to live your life in the area you lived. To play for the club, you had to live within a certain distance of the ground, so the players really were all local.'

More than 60 years had passed since Worrell had recommended Sobers to succeed him. The ground had fallen away from neglect with weeds poking out of the concrete steps, and a forlorn bench here and there. A corner of the bar was dedicated to Worrell: black and white photographs around a sculpture of him. 'Running above the windows the whole length of the bar is a pictorial hall of fame: faded gilt-framed photographs of Radcliffe's professionals – Worrell, Sobers, Sonny Ramadhin, Cec Pepper, Cec Abrahams…' Aldred wrote.

Back in the day when the six disappeared turnstiles were busy at weekends, Worrell had found his place and he would soon have companionship. A year later in 1949, Weekes accepted an offer from Bacup 16 miles away, and then in 1951, Walcott turned up to play for Enfield in Accrington.

Weekes described Friday-night gatherings at the home of the Worrells, where Frank would cook, music would fill the air, and drinks would flow. With great amusement, Weekes recalled an evening when Frank had decided to cook a Barbadian one-pot specialty: split peas and rice, with pork chops on the side. There were six of them at the house.

'He's got the record for being able to cook split peas and rice and it came out in three different forms. It was burnt at the bottom, fairly well cooked in the middle and hard at the top. Three different layers, and he boasted about how well he could cook. It was a lot of fun.'

Weekes himself became known for his cooking skills, and many raved about having had the pleasure of eating at his home in Barbados.

'We used to meet at his place on Fridays,' Weekes recalled 'His place was always more central. He was that type of person that any youngster who came to the league, any West Indian from any part of the West Indies he would try to entertain them and give them some ideas of what to expect. He was that type of person.'

Ivo Tennant wrote that Worrell's colleagues at Radcliffe found him to be quiet; it might simply have been that he was adjusting to the new environment.

'Their recollections are of a shy young man dressed in a brown suit and possessing little else other than his cricket boots. He would let his hair down only with Walcott and Weekes, then league cricketers elsewhere. "There would be a number of beer bottles outside the door when we put our milk bottles out," recalled his teammate, John Schofield.'

Worrell had been slowly arriving at the conclusion that he had to be careful with his reputation. He seemed to be most at ease in the company of West Indians. On Sundays, they would meet in Manchester at a Trinidadian's home to cook and share drinks. Worrell enjoyed cooking, favouring dishes of Indian and Chinese origin, though he also liked the 'Lancastrian dishes such as hot pot and black pudding as much as the more spicy Bajan fare.' (Black pudding is actually a very popular part of Bajan cuisine, as are the pigs' trotters Tennant cites.) It is likely that the three-layered rice and split peas that Weekes remembers was one of his occasional lapses.

Weekes also wrote of the 'fairly heavy drinking' of the Radcliffe days. It was whisky, brandy or beer then, but the heavy drinking had begun much earlier in the West Indies, and continued through his life. Being conscious of his public image, especially if he was seen drinking the night before a game and then did not perform well, he confined his consumption to nights at home; not in public, nor with his Radcliffe team. That need for discretion was something he constantly preached to players long before he became captain.

In the meantime, the West Indies tour of India was approaching, and it turned out to be a significant marker in Worrell's relationship with the WICBC. Many accounts place money, or rather compensation, at the heart of his absence from the tour. This may not have been the reason, but it became part of the lore surrounding him, and earned him the reputation of a cricketing Bolshevik.

For Worrell, money was an enabler, not desirable for itself, but as a means to live luxuriously. It was not about acquiring the social status it afforded; he preferred a more urbane reputation. Simply, he wanted it to spend it. He had been known for generosity, even when things were tight personally. He was steadfast in his belief that he should be adequately compensated for his professional services, and he saw himself as a premium package, so he was one to negotiate for better terms, for himself and teammates.

His free-handedness and his insistence on being paid well came from childhood exposure to the hardships of his contemporaries. From early on he was close to older cricketers, playing with them in the nets even before he went to Combermere, and he could see their struggles. He felt he was better placed on account of the remittances that were sent back to Barbados by his family. After all, he was the son of a queen. It was a way for him to assuage some measure of guilt for his fortunate circumstances; a way for him to fit in and gain approval despite the allegations that he was a 'big-head' who was cocky and careless. But it might also have been that he genuinely wanted to help others – mentorship was always a part of his life.

Worrell had big dreams, seeing the world as a place to conquer, but he knew his companions' ambitions were limited. He had tried unsuccessfully to persuade Weekes to leave Barbados and get out into the world. Weekes thought it was enough to stay at home and do well in the locale that gave him familiarity and comfort. He admitted that he shared none of the bold visions of Worrell. Someone from his background, he thought, could never aspire to grandeur.

The tour of India had been set for October, just six months after Frank and Velda's marriage. They were still settling into the unfamiliar climes of Radcliffe. They could hardly have been said to have found their feet while shivering under blankets. While he had tried to negotiate fees with the WICBC, this was not the only factor in his omission from the squad.

Eytle glossed over it saying that 'Worrell had been forced to miss the India tour of 1948-49, because of his league commitments and his desire to study in England.' Tennant disputed this, saying that it was for disciplinary reasons. 'Against MCC he had turned up late for matches, had upset Gomez, his captain, with his request to go to the airport and he was generally considered to be self-willed and erratic. He asked, as a professional cricketer, to be paid £250 to tour [some say it was £300]. The West Indies Cricket Board of Control refused. It was the start of his wrangles with the Board over pay. "Frank told me later that the shock of being excluded from the touring party was the best thing that could have happened to him," Gomez said. "He did all sorts of silly things in those days but he came to value discipline."'

Describing the fourth Test in Jamaica, Jeffrey Stollmeyer corroborated the Gomez account. 'An incident took place in the dressing room shortly before the start of the match which may have had a significant bearing on the future of West Indies cricket. Frank Worrell arrived at the ground in a lounge suit a few minutes before the start of play, after we had lost the toss and were going out on the field. We already were one player short (Weekes) and there was a frantic search on for a second substitute. Three West Indies Board members, who were also selectors, happened to cross his path at the time. They followed him into the dressing room and Frank was quite rightly at the receiving end of a severe "lecture". Previously on the tour he had asked permission to leave the ground while fielding in the Test match in Trinidad in order to meet his sister at the airport. This request had been quite naturally turned down. It appears that the Board decided that our most promising player was in need of some discipline and he was not selected for the tour of India.'

Worrell makes no mention of that missed tour in his autobiography, nor does he comment in Eytle's account. Neither does he dispute the claim that he had written to the WICBC asking to be paid £300 as a tour fee for the trip, which was refused. Even Weekes had cited this payment issue as the reason he declined to go to India. It is more likely that he did not decline, but was omitted from the team.

The incidents carry a strong echo of his behaviour back at Combermere that had brought down the ire of the masters there, followed by disciplinary measures to punish his 'self-willed' conduct. In the request to meet his sister, Grace, at the airport, there is a shade of the lad who felt he could ask for permission to leave a match to go to the cinema. He had left Combermere in 1943, it had not even been a decade since his secondary school days. He was now a famous cricketer, with a wife and new independence in a foreign country. It is quite plausible that Worrell, at 24, had not yet divested his teenaged outlook even as he was coming to terms with his professional life.

PART TWO

CHAPTER 11

1949-50

INDIA AT LAST

As the MCC had decided against touring India in the 1949-50 season, a Commonwealth team was appointed in its stead. The team had been put together by George Duckworth, once an England wicketkeeper. The 48-year-old Duckworth gathered players from the Lancashire and Central Lancashire Leagues, where he had spent many cricketing years. There were nine Australians, including the captain, Jock Livingston, five Englishmen, and two West Indians.

The first touring party would visit India, Pakistan and Ceylon (now Sri Lanka) starting in October 1949. The schedule was 21 first-class matches, including five against an All-India XI, which were dubbed unofficial Tests. This meant travel, mostly by long train journeys, to 18 different cities across the three nations over a period of six months.

The West Indies had toured India just a few months before, without Worrell. It was a trip full of highs and lows for the players, especially in terms of living arrangements. In his diary, Stollmeyer spoke often of dingy, insanitary accommodation; food that was inedible (in Indore, he said, 'the flavour of the "good old roach" was ever present'), the long, unpleasant rides on crowded, dusty, smelly trains, and the poor umpiring. He placed the blame on both sides. 'If ever a cricket tour was mismanaged, this one was. I am afraid that in addition to the lack of consideration shown for our team by the Board of Control for Cricket in India, we, in our turn, have been only a little less guilty. Our manager has shown very little enterprise and initiative,' he wrote, adding that he had no 'guts.' Walcott also complained about the same issues. 'It would be idle to pretend the Indian tour was a particularly successful, or happy one.' When asked which country he'd felt most comfortable in, Weekes immediately said England, but then added, dryly, 'Of course, India was easily the worst.'

Despite those reports, the chance to make that journey seemed attractive to Worrell, and when he was invited to join the Commonwealth team, there was no hesitation.

J.K. (John Kenneth) Holt from Jamaica, who had also not gone on the Test tour, was the only other West Indian. It was a team comprising mostly professionals from the leagues and the counties, 'players who were either on the periphery of Test cricket or had played in the odd Test match,' wrote Worrell. They were men hoping that this tour would propel them towards international recognition. 'As a result there was much less cohesion than we might have had.'

In November the team headed to Pakistan for a few matches. A brochure commemorating the visit was circulated, and Duckworth described his team as 'one of the most interesting band(s) of players ever gathered together.' He boasted of the number of all-rounders and spin bowlers, adding, 'There will never be a makeshift side put into a match because there is solid all-round ability right through the tourists.'

He made a prediction about multi-national teams that was one of the most significant effects of that tour – which, up until then, might have been seen simply as a group of Lancashire professionals setting off on an adventure.

'If things go well for the side, they may easily prove to be one of the most successful sides ever to undertake a tour, and they may set a pattern for similar cricket events in the future. They even challenge the whole set-up of first-class cricket organisation, for no team has ever left England on such an ambitious trip except when composed exclusively of county men.'

The brochure also featured a piece by the Premier of Sind, Yusuf Haroon, who noted that, 'This game which is credited with the power to inculcate the spirit of discipline and teamwork deserves the wholehearted support not only of sportsmen but also of all patriotic Pakistanis...' as he welcomed the team. From the Governor's House in Karachi, came brief welcoming greetings from Governor Din Mohammed, 'Both Sind and Karachi can legitimately take pride in their Cricketers, and I hope they will not disappoint their distinguished guests and play a good game.'

The brochure carries photographs of the Commonwealth players and the Pakistanis. Worrell is the youngest, and from the youthfulness of his features it is difficult to imagine that he is not a gangly teenager but a celebrated cricketer and a husband and father.

His daughter, Lana, had been born on July 16: barely three months before he would be padding up for the first match of the tour at the Brabourne Stadium in Bombay on 9 October. Lana would be nine months old before he would see her again. But he had finally got a long, intimate look at India, a place he seemed to enjoy tremendously as his 'inquiring mind' absorbed the country he described as one of 'strange fascination'.

He had many reasons to like India. Perhaps he wanted to reassert himself after having missed the previous tour; perhaps he was inspired by the exploits of Walcott and Weekes, who had been explosive earlier in 1949; perhaps he found the conditions favourable to his style; or perhaps he found himself free to abandon any inhibitions brought on by the need to maintain appearances; perhaps he found that the alcohol he drank to pass the otherwise monotonous routine of play-travel, play-travel, made him more daring on the field. There may be no single 'perhaps' – perhaps it was all, some or none, but Worrell cut loose in India.

His batting dominated. In the five unofficial 'Tests,' he scored 647 runs, nearly 200 more than his nearest rival. This included 223 not out in the fourth at Kanpur, an innings he consistently described as his best. 'It was just one of those innings in which nothing will go wrong for a batsman,' he wrote. 'I shall always consider that my greatest innings, far better than my two more famous ones at Trent Bridge, both of which were made too easy by that feather-bed wicket on which they played cricket at Nottingham.'

Duckworth reported afterwards that the unfamiliar matting was a challenge for the batters. '...it was left to Frankie Worrell to play the innings of the series in Commonwealth's first knock. His 223 not out, out of 448, will rank as one of the best efforts of his career, and like most other great performances there was the element of luck attached to it. Had [Madhav] Mantri held a snick from Worrell off Gaikwad [Hiralal Gaekwad] the scoreboard would have read 29 for 3 wickets with Worrell 8. Fortunately for all except the bowler and wicketkeeper this chance was missed and stroke play worthy of all the great masters of all time was shown by the West Indian. The batsman was the first to admit that this was the hardest struggle he had ever had against the spinners of Ghulam Ahmed and Gaikwad. The bowling analysis utterly fails to show the great skill of these two men.' For Worrell, the struggle for the runs was what had made it so special.

His average in those five games was 97.71, way ahead of everyone else. He took scored two centuries and also took seven wickets. In that first tour overall, in 17 matches he scored 1640 runs and averaged 74.54, with five centuries.

Weekes and Walcott had been equally impressive when they had visited India earlier. Weekes had scored centuries in four consecutive Tests, adding to the one he had scored against England in the final Test earlier in 1948, thus etting a record for centuries in successive Tests. On the tour, he ended up with six centuries, and an average of 90 in 15 innings, with a total of 1350 runs. Walcott had scored five centuries as well, but his total was 1366 at an average of 75.88. In India, he scored the first of his magnificent Test centuries, powering his way to 152 in the first Test in Delhi before he was run out.

The Indians had received a scintillating introduction to Walcott and Weekes, and, not to be outdone, Worrell was determined that he too would give them something to remember.

Yet Tennant said there were those who thought he was capable of even better had he not consumed so much alcohol.

'When asked once if he ever drank before an innings, Worrell cited his double hundred in India: "There was nothing else to do but drink. I saw so many balls I couldn't miss!" He said to Ramadhin on the voyage out for the third tour: "You had better prepare yourself now for the drinking you're going to do in India". There are those who felt Worrell would have been a better batsman, perhaps a more consistent batsman, had he not drunk spirits. Yet his technique was so correct that he still outstayed others.' Ramadhin was a teetotaler at that point, although later, after cricket and Worrell, he developed an intimate relationship with alcohol, becoming a pub landlord in England.

There might be a closer connection with the tales of Worrell's enormous appetite for 'spirits' and the accounts that he could always be found, padded up, asleep, in the dressing room during a match. Reverent stories are repeatedly told that he was always so relaxed during a game that he would not watch from the pavilion, but enjoy a snooze while awaiting his turn at the crease. The legend of his extraordinary calm is invariably illustrated by the example of his capacity to nap during a game (he had told Alston it was due to nervousness). Quite likely, he was simply sleeping off the heady nights before.

CHAPTER 12

1950

THE THREE Ws BEGIN

After his visit to India with the Commonwealth team, Worrell took part in the historic encounters of the summer of 1950. West Indies won their first Test against England on English turf in a celebrated match at the MCC's home at Lord's. Coming after seven visits (three before their Test status); winning three of the four Tests made the victory all the more precious.

From 1928, when West Indies first fielded a Test team, the two sides had played each other 21 times, with England winning eight and West Indies five, while eight were drawn. Winning the series in 1950 carried a special significance.

Arising from that tour was the christening by the media of Walcott, Weekes and Worrell as the Three Ws, an appellation that would bind them together in life and in death. Would they have been grouped together as a unit if their surnames had not begun with the same letter, or if they had not all been born in Barbados? Fate has a way of creating arbitrary alliances.

Other important unions were formed: Alf Valentine and Sonny Ramadhin, both Test debutants, were twinned; and an opening partnership was firmly established between Jeffrey Stollmeyer and Allan Rae. After this tour, Weekes, Worrell, Valentine, Ramadhin and the England wicketkeeper Godfrey Evans were named the five *Wisden* Cricketers of the Year in 1951.

In the build-up to the series, a one-minute British Pathé promotional newsreel shows the West Indian players having a net session as the narrator outlines their strengths.

'When the flannels come out at Lord's, summer can't be far away, only the weatherman refuses to play and, it's most un-cricket-like weather that welcomes the West Indies touring team to the Mecca of the bat and ball brigade. Led by popular John Goddard, they represent a powerful challenge to English cricket. Everton Weekes, a Lancashire League player, is their batting star, while googly man Cecil Williams may well be their key bowler. Clyde Walcott, a good hitter, is the man behind the stumps. Most feared of their fast attack is the West Indies' Lindwall shock-bowler, Lance Pierre, here sending them down to Everton Weekes. Speed merchant number two is Prior Jones, here in action against all-rounder Gerry Gomez. Completing the spin attack is that slow left-hander Alf Valentine, here bowling to stylish Robert Christiani. With fast bowler Hines Johnson to open the attack, the West Indies look good enough to give England a run for their money.'

While the English believed the West Indies would be a strong enough team to make for interesting matches, the general feeling was that it would be good practice for England's upcoming Ashes visit to Australia. Walcott wrote that at one of the numerous official functions they had to attend, the speaker said it was 'a good chance to try out some of the young English players for the tour of Australia in the winter.'

The squad was led by John Goddard and contained Barbadian players Roy Marshall, Walcott, Weekes, Worrell and Cecil Williams; with Robert Christiani from British Guiana; Gerry Gomez, Prior Jones, Lance Pierre, Sonny Ramadhin, Jeffrey Stollmeyer, and Kenneth Trestrail from Trinidad and Tobago, and Hines Johnson, Allan Rae and Alf Valentine from Jamaica. Of the 16, nine were white, six were black, and Ramadhin was the only one of Indian descent.

Worrell felt it was a well-balanced team with experienced players. That would have been an important element of its strength as previous and future squads demonstrated. He said that 'the players got on well together, both on and off the field'.

Weekes thought the camaraderie was more of a public charade.

'The team spirit was, um, certainly on the field it always looked good, but sometimes off the field it was not very good because the white and black thing would put its ugly face somewhere out there, somewhere along the lines. I am not comfortable discussing that because I think there was a lot of ignorance … for you not to be liked because your skin is not the complexion of somebody else's. As far as I know there is only one way.' He was unwilling to get into details. 'That is not the sort of thing I would want to do because it calls for names, naming people and their behaviour and that sort of thing and I would prefer not to go into that. I think that people could see from the distance when some players are acting and they should be in the acting field rather than playing sport.'

Competitions would be arranged to fit these categories, and included the labels of Amateurs (the Gentlemen who played without a fee) and Professionals (Players). The distinction between Amateurs and Professionals was eventually abolished at the end of 1962, coming into effect during the English season of 1963.

Weekes recalled that most of these conditions still applied during his playing days in the Forties and Fifties. 'It was very prevalent then. In fact, in 1950, it was not finished yet. We saw professional cricketers coming through one gate and amateurs through another. That was so up to 1950. A lot of amateurs became professionals and that didn't go down too well with some of the amateurs. It hasn't changed. There's been a lot of covering up and so on.'

The racism was explicit, especially in the selection process, and in the way players were treated. Black cricketers were expected to carry the bags of their white teammates, and had inferior quarters when they were on tour.

Weekes was not impressed by Goddard's captaincy in England in 1950.

'John Goddard, the captain, might not have been knowledgeable enough, in the view of some, to be captain and then there was the question knocking around the place about colour. That still prevails, not in the West Indies because white people don't play cricket anymore in the West Indies. I don't see them,' he said.

In *Cricket Punch*, Worrell did not address any of this. It was a strong West Indian team and their opponents were not at their best. 'England had to scratch and scrape to find a team worthy of a Test match, and probably never before had England been so low in cricketing talent.' The English called on 24 players during that series; West Indies used half as many.

Weekes and Worrell had already spent time in the leagues, and Stollmeyer and Gomez had toured England in 1939, but the rest of the squad were unfamiliar with English conditions, and this was expected to be a major disadvantage.

Worrell was committed to mentoring inexperienced players in the league, even if they represented the opposition. He helped to prepare teammates for conditions they would find on English soil. Sonny Ramadhin recalled that he taught him how to manage social expectations at various functions, such as how to use a knife and fork.

They played 31 first-class matches; starting off under such cold and wet June conditions that even Weekes was praying for balls not to come to him in the field because his fingers felt like ice. The weather was as variable as an English summer can be, and the players had to adjust to its effect on the pitches and the movement of the ball.

With the exception of Valentine and Ramadhin, whose inclusion was a calculated risk by the selectors given their inexperience, the rest of the squad had already established their credentials. Previously, West Indies would depend on one or two individuals to carry the team; there were many on this squad who could easily fill that role. During the tour, eight players scored more than a thousand runs.

In addition to the power of the Three Ws, there was the elegant batting of Stollmeyer, and the sturdy defence of Rae, who often anchored an innings firmly enough for the others to play freely. Christiani was one of the eight who passed a thousand runs. Marshall played in none of the Tests – only 12 of the 16 were called up – and Gomez was used often as a bowler, reducing his batting opportunities, as was the case for captain Goddard, who batted down the order.

The bowling attack was to be led by the seamers: Jones, Johnson and Pierre, with Valentine, Ramadhin and Williams as secondary support. Nothing could have prepared anyone for the astonishing success of the two newcomers. The combined tally for all the matches from the spearhead bowlers was 91 wickets, while Ramadhin and Valentine took 258, nearly three times as many. It was spin, not pace, that made the difference. Ramadhin said people didn't understand that the mystery of his bowling was that he was a finger spinner.

Five days were allocated for each of the Tests instead of three, so matches had time to be completed. The change was made after the previous summer's encounters with New Zealand, when all the Tests were drawn.

Norman Preston, the English sports journalist who succeeded his father, Hubert, as editor of *Wisden Cricketers' Almanack* in 1952, reviewed the tour, and admired the contributions of the Three Ws, who had collectively scored 20 centuries.

'For beauty of stroke no one in the history of the game can have excelled Worrell. A fairly tall, lean figure, there was something like a dreamy casualness about the way he flicked the ball with nonchalant ease: but how it sped to the boundary!' He felt that his 261 in the third Test at Trent Bridge was his masterpiece. With Weekes he had added 283 for the fourth wicket, then a West Indies record for any wicket.

Worrell had described his innings of 223 not out at Kanpur in India as his greatest, 'far better than my two more famous ones at Trent Bridge.' Yet, the 261 at Trent Bridge (the other was 191 not out in 1957) invoked superlatives from every writer who witnessed the match, and anyone who had ever written about it, whether they saw it or not, had been driven to the extremes of adulation.

Horace Harragin, a Trinidadian journalist, spoke about the 'hidden strength' in Worrell's batting. 'It was often an effortless destruction such as an extraordinary six he struck off the back foot when facing leg-spinner Roly Jenkins during his 261 at Trent Bridge in 1950. It caused the bowler to remark: "I don't believe it!" Whereupon umpire Frank Chester replied: "Neither do I, Mr Jenkins, but I'll still signal six".'

If C.L.R. James had not been living in the US at the time, it is likely he would have constructed an edifice to Worrell based on that performance. As it was, the adjectives surrounding descriptions of his batting could all be synonyms for stylishness – it is this similarity that makes the gushing plausible. The innings was flawless, stylish, elegant, fluid, graceful, exquisite, chanceless, a dance, refined, poised – words of writers who have wandered into the domain of the artist.

Two days after Worrell's death, Neville Cardus wrote in an obituary that, 'Worrell's strokes were literally strokes, smooth and polished, sending the ball here and there at his sweet will and leisure, with the minimum of matter to be moved.' His cricket was an expression of the man himself, 'engaging, companionable, lithe, effortless,' and of his wristwork, he said, 'they were not wrists of iron but of finely tempered steel.' He had watched the Trent Bridge 261 with the former Nottinghamshire and England batter George Gunn, who told him, 'he is late-cutting the ball almost out of the wicketkeeper's gloves.' Cardus agreed, 'Worrell leaned over his late cuts with time enough to spare to enjoy, without offence to the bowler, his own delicacy of touch.'

But even his effervescence could not suppress a flash of the stereotype of the West Indian cricketer, although it is meant as part of the praise song he titled, 'Like Hobbs – never a crude or an ungrammatical stroke.'

'There was nothing in his play as batsman, bowler or fieldsman of that hint of primitive impulse which has usually marked even the most civilised of West Indian batsmen; never a rush of blood to his head. During the past few decades, West Indies cricket has gained in a sophistication which has merged it with English and Australian cricket, so much so that it can now fairly be called non-racial and international. Worrell was the first fine fruit of this harvesting of refinement and poise.' The first fine fruit!

On that tour, Worrell scored 1775 runs, with six centuries. In the Tests, he tallied 539 at 89.83. He took six wickets at Trent Bridge; his tour total was 39, establishing him as a medium-fast bowler who could get swing both ways. With Weekes he had shared two triple-century stands against the counties.

In one of those matches, against Leicestershire, a curious story emerged, depending on how you look at it. 'This was the match in which we had two huge stands in double-quick time. First, Roy Marshall and I put on 247 for the second wicket in just over two hours, and then I helped Everton Weekes to an unbroken third-wicket partnership of 340 and we declared at the fantastic total of 682 for two. Weekes was not out for 200, and he scored his century in a mere sixty-five minutes, the fastest of the season. My contribution was 241 not out and Marshall scored 188,' wrote Worrell.

It seems straightforward enough, but in *Mastering the Craft*, Weekes related a version that suggests there might have been an undercurrent of competitive jousting in the details. Weekes recalled the fast hundred as an exciting moment. He said Worrell had told him he would give him the strike and encouraged him to go for it. He said that when he went in to bat, Worrell was already past 150 (and perhaps tired?) and after Worrell spoke to him, he really did allow him to face the majority of the balls. (Elsewhere, Weekes said that Walcott would not have done something as generous as that.) By the end of the day's play, Worrell was on 225 and Weekes was on 190, and Goddard opted to let him get to his double century.

'The next day I went out with Frank and it took me 40 minutes to get the ten required runs. Frank deliberately took the strike for himself. It was his way of protesting the captain's decision which he thought would kill the game,' wrote Weekes. 'Frank felt I was accustomed to scoring double hundreds and that another one at the moment was no big deal. He was convinced that Goddard should have declared the innings, and press for a team victory. So it took me 65 minutes to get a hundred and 40 minutes to get ten runs. I believe he was of the opinion that the game had fallen into vanity, and he wanted no part in it. I read it as a vote of confidence in me. When he urged and facilitated the first hundred it was his leadership ability coming to the fore.'

The way this story is related by Weekes speaks to the unwavering loyalty he carried for Worrell, but it makes one wonder whether he genuinely believed the motive he attributes to Worrell.

This was a three-day match against Leicestershire, the seventeenth game they had played, and already batting scores were high and flashy. That first innings was declared at 682 for two in 132.1 overs. Marshall had already scored 188, Worrell was on 241; if Weekes was allowed to continue, then Worrell would not be the only one scoring a double. Is it possible that this was a greater motive for his obstruction? Leicestershire took 152.3 overs to get to 352, 20 more than the West Indians had taken. It would likely have been even fewer overs if Worrell had not kept the strike for himself. If he believed that delaying the declaration was wrong, it seemed odd that he would choose to protest in a manner that would affect the statistics of Weekes. Weekes went on to say that perhaps Worrell thought double hundreds were not a big deal for him since he would have had reports of one he had scored earlier that year against British Guiana at Kensington Oval. Perhaps that was his subtle way of suggesting that there was some competition between them. As the Three Ws, comparisons were inevitably being made about which one was best.

By the end of the tour, Weekes had scored more runs than the other two. His tour tally was 2310, with seven centuries, five of them

91

doubles, and he had scored an unbeaten 304 at Fenner's. Walcott also scored seven centuries, and totalled 1674 runs. He scored his lone Test century at Lord's, an unbeaten 168. As wicketkeeper, he took 30 catches and made 18 stumpings.

Preston had ended his *Wisden* report by saying that, 'Goddard's men were popular wherever they went and deservedly they took home a handsome profit of £30,000 which will stand West Indies cricket in good stead for some time to come.'

Yet Walcott complained that the players did not benefit substantially from the profits. 'We were classed as amateurs and received just five pounds a week and that had to pay for meals taken outside the hotel. So if we entertained anyone to dinner, half our allowance would disappear in one evening,' he wrote, conceding however, 'the Board did pay us a bonus of £150.'

Gate receipts at the Tests were £94,000, with 372,000 spectators attending the four matches. Overall, West Indies played 38 matches, of which they won 19, exactly half, and they only lost three.

The entire team had glittered and it was truly a surprise for the English, who had felt that the success of 1948 was the result of a weak team going out to the Caribbean – not that the West Indians had a strong squad.

Although they had been successful in most of their early tour matches, the defeat in the first Test had reinforced the idea that the 1948 victory in the West Indies was a fluke, and that the loss was due to poor captaincy by Goddard. England needed just four days to win by 202 runs. Worrell made just 15 and 28 as West Indies were bowled out for 215 and 183. Goddard was criticised for persisting too long with Ramadhin and Valentine but they took 15 of England's 20 wickets in a match dominated by spin. Slow left-armer Bob Berry, making his Test debut on his home ground, took nine wickets while leg-spinner Eric Hollies finished with eight. England had been 88 for five when Godfrey Evans, batting at eight, made a counter-attacking century, putting on 161 with Trevor Bailey. The pitch was found to be so cracked that West Indies lodged a complaint at the next meeting of the Imperial Cricket Conference (ICC) during the Lord's Test.

'I have never seen a Test match started with cracks on the wicket of the dimensions of those at Old Trafford,' said Walcott. In *The*

Daily Telegraph, E.W. Swanton agreed. 'No Test match in modern times has begun in fair weather on anything resembling this Old Trafford wicket,' he wrote.

Michael Manley thought the match exposed the weakness of Goddard as a tactician. 'There are many who feel that [Godfrey] Evans could and should have been contained on that first day during which the fate of the match was sealed.' 'I felt there were times when the honest length of Gomez might have been Goddard's answer,' said Swanton.

The second Test at Lord's, when victory by 326 runs was declared on 29 June 1950, saw another display of breathtaking batting. The match began on Saturday 24 June. Goddard won the toss and sent in his openers, Stollmeyer and Rae. Stollmeyer's innings was short, but delighted the crowd, wrote Manley. A 'wristy, forcing shot off his pads past mid-wicket's right hand' was followed 'by a classic off-drive with a full flow of the bat which rocketed the ball just beyond the reach of extra-cover's left hand'. At the other end, Rae, who eventually made a century, was laying the foundation for what was to come.

'Stollmeyer's departure opened the door for an experience which none there would ever forget. Frank Worrell arrived at the wicket. Within minutes he had played the most delicate of late cuts. It was so impudently played, with a nonchalance that all but disguised its skill, that it had three results. His score advanced by four runs; the crowd came to its feet, and the England fielders accorded the stroke the final accolade: to a man they clapped. In the next hour and a half Worrell played every stroke in the book, driving, cutting, and pulling as well. When he went, astonishment wrestled with disappointment.'

Worrell made just 52, but Neville Cardus was beside himself, dramatically proclaiming that 'A Worrell innings knows no dawn. It begins at high noon.' Although he was far from being the top scorer in either innings (he made 45 in the second) – Walcott compiled a powerfully struck 168 with 24 fours in the second innings; Weekes was run out on 63 after a mix-up with Walcott; Rae hit a solid 106 in four hours, 40 minutes, and Gomez had made a stylish 70 in the second innings – his batting invoked a torrent of praise.

The victory unleashed a wave of celebrations throughout the Caribbean. Barbados and Jamaica declared public holidays. At

Lord's, spectators completed a spontaneous victory lap. There is a celebrated photograph of a band of them, joyfully sauntering along to the strumming of a guitar by the calypsonian known as Lord Kitchener. That photograph, that guitar, and that song, 'Victory Test Match,' have all been inextricably woven into the lore of that triumphant moment of celebration.

Their origins are worthy of some scrutiny, as they became as much a part of the history of West Indian cricket as the music and dance that surround it. The story often repeated is that a large band of spectators trooped onto the field, dodged the security and started an outfield party, the likes of which had never been seen at Lord's. The group was led by Lord Kitchener (Aldwyn Roberts), the man at the extreme right of the photograph is Lord Beginner (Egbert Moore).

Rex Alston was commentating as the match ended and the players left the field.

'There are one or two West Indian characters coming out on the field waving their hats as the West Indies players walk quietly off the field [he had earlier said they were running off]. Yes, there are several West Indian supporters running from the far end and they are going to escort their team off the field. The score is 274. Goddard running in with his stump being chased harem-scarum by lots of West Indian supporters. Such a sight never been seen before at Lord's.'

As the spontaneous ensemble formed, he went on to say, 'They are determined, I think, to give us a little song … a band of about a dozen of them. One in a bright red cap, one in a bright blue shirt and they are dancing out into the middle and there is a press photographer chasing after them but I think they will be herded tactfully off the middle. In fact, there is a policeman now telling them to go away and they are singing and dancing off the pitch and the English section of the spectators is giving them a round of applause.'

Stories about hundreds of spectators storming the ground are also refuted by the writer Martin Williamson. On the final day, a Thursday, fewer than a hundred spectators, mostly West Indian were present.

'At lunch, England were nine down, and the end came shortly afterwards at 2.18pm when Johnny Wardle was trapped lbw by Frank Worrell. Sadly, both BBC radio and TV missed the event as there were the distractions of Wimbledon tennis and *Woman's Hour* to contend with. There was a scramble among the West Indies team for stumps as spectators rushed to the middle. John Goddard, the West Indies captain, led the sprint for the pavilion as well-wishers mobbed his team. "Frustrated in their efforts to get near the players, [the crowd] then joined up in a follow-my-leader fashion and victory jog around the field," reported *The Gleaner*. "Bottles of rum were produced as if by magic and toasts were drunk to Goddard." About 30 policemen barred the fans from getting too close to the pavilion itself.'

While the looming loss might have kept English fans away, one would imagine that the portent of that first victory would have drawn even larger groups of West Indian supporters. The bulk of emigration to England had not yet happened, and thus the number of West Indians in the country was not substantial in that period. Were 30 policemen necessary to keep the celebrants at bay? It is a reflection of the attitude towards West Indians, especially those who had the gall to sing, dance and play musical instruments at Lord's.

Despite the restrictions, celebrations persisted. The calypso linked with this event is more commonly known after its first line, 'Cricket, Lovely Cricket,' than the title under which it was recorded 'Victory Test Match'. There has always been some ambiguity about who really composed it.

The two contenders had both arrived in England aboard the *Empire Windrush*, which set sail from Jamaica carrying Caribbean immigrants and docked at Tilbury in 1948. Both were from Trinidad, where sharing compositions was not unusual for calypsonians and it is likely that the song eventually recorded was a joint effort.

Williamson had two bits of evidence to offer. Along with Kitchener and Beginner on the *Windrush* was Sam King, who went on to become mayor of Southwark. He, too, was at Lord's. In 1998 he was interviewed by *The Guardian*. 'I was about going home, about 20 voices said, "Sam, you can't go home, man. Kitchener going to make a song." I said, "What?" They said, "Just come." We sat down on the grass and Kitchener says, "Cricket, lovely cricket," and someone said, "Put Ramadhin in, man." And he put Ramadhin in, and he went over it, and in 30 minutes he wrote the song, "Cricket, lovely cricket, at Lord's, where I saw it. Yardley won the toss, but Goddard won the Test, with those little pals of mine, Ramadhin and Valentine." I was there. That was history.

'That account was backed by E.L. Cozier in *The Gleaner* who said that Kitchener had "already composed a calypso on today's victory and they will be playing it tonight at the Paramount and the Caribbean, two London night clubs most frequented by West Indians." He added that the song had been a work in progress throughout the final day. "I heard Kitchener with its beginnings before the match this morning, but it's probably undergone considerable changes since then."'

What is clear is that it was not the song that made its way around the outfield at Lord's, as some have said.

In 2009, the airline magazine, *Caribbean Beat,* offered this unreferenced explanation. 'Decades later, Kitchener would share his memories about what happened at Lord's, and, later, in the heart of London, Piccadilly Circus: "After we won the match, I took my guitar and I call a few West Indians, and I went around the cricket field singing. And I had an answering chorus behind me and we went around the field singing and dancing. So, while we're dancing, up come a policeman and arrested me. And while he was taking me out of the field, the English people boo him. They said, "Leave him alone! Let him enjoy himself. They won the match, let him enjoy himself." And he had to let me loose, because he was embarrassed.

'So I took the crowd with me, singing and dancing, from Lord's into Piccadilly in the heart of London. And while we're singing and dancing going into Piccadilly, the people opened their windows wondering what's happening. I think it was the first time they'd ever seen such a thing in England. And we're dancing Trinidad style, like mas, and dance right down Piccadilly and dance round Eros.'

Lord Kitchener was known for surrendering to his muse at arbitrary moments. It is easy to imagine him feasting on each day's play with the percussive thud of bat on ball, the trumpeting of the crowd, and the lulls and crescendos of a day spent at the cricket, and coming up with a melody.

On the other hand, Lord Beginner had long established his proclivity for writing calypsoes on cricketers and matches. From as early as 1929, when he composed one to celebrate Learie

Constantine, he had consistently written chronicles and odes of this nature. There are eight such recordings by him from 1929 to 1953. In that first one on Constantine, the refrain went, 'Learie Constantine / That pal of mine.'

It might have been fortuitous for him that Valentine also rhymed with 'mine.' Since the refrain that made history for 'Victory Test Match,' was 'With those little pals of mine / Ramadhin and Valentine,' this might be a strong clue that Beginner at least, had something to do with the composition.

In any case, shortly after, it was Beginner who recorded 'Victory Test Match,' accompanied by the band, Calypso Rhythm Kings. Lord Kitchener followed soon after with his recording, '1950 Victory'. It was one of six calypsoes Kitchener wrote on cricket.

Composing calypsoes on cricket was not uncommon and there are more than 200 known recordings on the subject. Three focus on Worrell, and 24 mention him.

The celebration that had started at the ground didn't end at Piccadilly; they cavorted all the way back to the squad's base at the Kingsley Hotel, where the front of the building had already been draped in Caribbean flags. The party had begun to swing, but a shy young man, who had made a stunning debut, was not comfortable with the revelry.

'Sonny Ramadhin, who took 11 for 142, recalled that he was not part of the party as he did not drink alcohol at the time. "I used to wait outside in the street until everybody had finished, just biding my time," he smiled. "All I ever drunk was ginger beer. When everybody went out celebrating in London, drinking champagne, I just had a quiet meal with some friends from Trinidad who were in England as students"', he told Williamson.

At his English home in Delph in 2016, Ramadhin said his extreme shyness was the main reason he did not participate in the festive evening. His dinner companion was Ralph Narine, a Trinidadian from the southern part of the island where Ramadhin was born. Narine was studying at Gray's Inn and qualified as a barrister two years' later. He later became a Justice of Appeal in Trinidad and Tobago. He had played cricket with Ramadhin's brother, Ramsamooj, back in Trinidad, and Ramsamooj asked him to meet Ramadhin at Waterloo Station when the West Indians arrived in April. Ramadhin was so taciturn, that it took a week of daily meetings for Narine to realise it was on account of his shyness and how overwhelmed he was by the alien conditions. They became friends for life.

Walcott, who said he was not much of a drinker then either, admitted it was one time he went freely and joyously at it. Perhaps his memory of the event remained a little hazy, as he wrote, 'Thousands of our countrymen came racing on to the outfield, singing and dancing, and I can remember the scene clearly. They were singing the game's most famous calypso, 'Cricket, Lovely Cricket,' [By the thousands! On the field! What fast learners!] with its tribute to "those two friends of mine, Ramadhin and Valentine."' [Pals, they were.]

As the centurions, he and Allan Rae were invited to take the first gulps of champagne that had been provided in the dressing room by MCC. 'After we emptied our glasses, we hurled them to the floor to the cheers of our team-mates.' Goddard had brought a crate of Goddard's Gold Braid Rum to England from his family's distillery, and by the time the outcome of the match was known, he had prudently had it released from its bond, so they had enough spirits to keep them and their friends going all through the night.

They went back to Room 326 (the winning margin was also 326) at the Kingsley Hotel to party, Walcott said, 'having invited some West Indians who had supported us to join in.' His memory may still have been hazy because he inaccurately said, 'Frank Worrell, who was taking an economics degree at Manchester University, had to be in Manchester later that night and decided to lock himself in his room for a couple of hours before going to the station. Unfortunately, he overslept and missed the train. He spent the night partying with us instead.'

Worrell had enrolled for a course of study in Optics at the Manchester Municipal College of Technology and this was what Walcott was referring to. It was later, in 1956, that he was accepted for a BA programme.

Even if Walcott's recollections of details may have been faulty, what remained irrefutable is that the victory at Lord's, and the taking of the series 3-1, was an enormous milestone in the journey of West Indies cricket, and West Indians had every reason to celebrate.

They had beaten the English for the first time on foreign soil, and had done it emphatically. After England won the first match comfortably, the expectations of the series as a warm-up for the forthcoming trip to Australia seemed reasonable. The victory at Lord's was a jolt, but it turned out not to be a fluke. West Indies won the next match at Trent Bridge by ten wickets. They arrived in Nottingham brimming with confidence while England were beset by injuries: Len Hutton joining Denis Compton on the list of absentees. On the opening day, Worrell bowled magnificently in tandem with Hines Johnson. England were 75 for five before Derek Shackleton, 42, and Roly Jenkins, 39, steered them to a more respectable 223 all out an hour before the close.

The next day belonged to Worrell, his innings of 261 in 335 minutes including 35 fours and two sixes sent shockwaves through English cricket. He was on 110 when joined by Weekes for a blistering fourth-wicket partnership that was eventually worth 283. '...virtuosity we may not see repeated in our lifetime,' wrote John Arlott. The assault on the leg-spinners Jenkins and Eric Hollies was especially brutal. Worrell used his feet to Jenkins to such an extent that at one point the bowler called out, 'For goodness sake, let me loose it out of my hand first.' Worrell finished the day on 239 and there was speculation in the press that he would break Len Hutton's Test record score of 364, but he fell to Bedser on the third morning, and although the innings fell away, West Indies still established a lead of 335. England recovered some pride in the second innings, Cyril Washbrook scoring his final Test hundred in a total of 436, but West Indies had no trouble knocking off the 102 they needed to win to take a 2-1 lead in the series. Between them, Alf Valentine and Sonny Ramadhin took 12 wickets, continuing to plague the batters.

By the time the fourth and final Test at the Kennington Oval arrived, the generally dismissive remarks of commentators and spectators had evaporated. The tourists had won all of their county matches, save the one against Warwickshire, on the eve of the final Test. But the loss only proved to make them even more committed to the series victory that was now possible.

The opening pair of Stollmeyer and Rae set the tone against the bowling of Trevor Bailey and Alec Bedser. Rae was his usual stoic self, determined to occupy the crease and allow the stroke players to have their way. He had made 109 before Bedser bowled him;

Stollmeyer had been out lbw to Bailey for 36. Worrell joined Rae, at first shakily, and before lunch he was almost out twice. After what must have been a fortifying meal, both he and Rae went at it; by tea, Rae was on 99 and Worrell 66. Rae completed his century shortly after the tea break, taking four hours, including 75 minutes to score his first seven runs. Weekes came in to join Worrell and scored a quick 30 before making room for Walcott. Early on the second day, Worrell had to leave the field because of a stomach ache which required medical attention; Gerry Gomez took his place. Rae would later recall that Neville Cardus was ready to leave because Worrell had departed. 'I don't want to see any other,' he told Rae, who advised him that it was only a temporary departure. Thus reassured, Cardus returned to his seat. Worrell returned and, riding his luck, made 138. He was dropped by Freddie Brown, the newly installed England captain, off Bedser on 69, and the same bowler was unfortunate when stand-in wicketkeeper Arthur McIntyre was a fraction too late taking the bails off with Worrell on 99. Nevertheless, Worrell still produced some shots full of his trademark brilliance. West Indies finished on 503, effectively extinguishing England's ambitions of levelling the series.

Len Hutton's masterful 202 not out brought a flicker of hope. Like Rae, he took around four hours for his first hundred, but then he freed up. Charles Bray, writing for the *Daily Herald*, remarked that, 'Two cover drives were of such perfection and majesty that the first reaction of the huge crowd was an audible gasp.' But England still trailed by 159, Valentine and Goddard each taking four wickets, and West Indies enforced the follow-on. This time, England subsided miserably to 103 all out, utterly unable to deal with West Indies' spin attack. Valentine took six for 39 and Ramadhin three for 38. Inside four days, they won by an innings and 56 runs. There could hardly have been a more emphatic way to complete their first series victory in England.

CHAPTER 13

THE COMMONWEALTH BAND

When George Duckworth had gathered his team of professionals to head to India, Pakistan and Ceylon in 1949, he envisioned this assembly as the forerunner of a different kind of international participant in cricket: the multi-national team.

Such an assemblage already existed. The West Indies Cricket Board of Control presided over a team with members of different nationalities, who happened to belong to a philosophically constructed nation. The first tour by the Commonwealth XI found enough success in India to be repeated the following year and the year after that. Worrell played in these, and in England as well, from 1951 to 1955 and again in 1958.

In February 2021, Indian batter, C.D. Gopinath, a member of the team that recorded India's first Test victory against England in 1952 at Madras (now Chennai), gave an interview remarkable for the strength of his memory at 91. Asked who he would have a drink with if he could travel back in time, unhesitatingly he named Frank Worrell.

When he was around 19, he was opening the batting against the Commonwealth XI in their unofficial Tests, and he was nervous. As Worrell walked past him, ball in hand, he said, 'Gopi, I'm going to bowl you a long hop to break your Test duck.' He thought he was joking. But Worrell did bowl the long hop and he gratefully hit it for four. At the end of the over, Worrell told him, 'and now I'll get you out.' He laughed with delight at the memory, saying, of course he didn't.

They met again in the Lancashire League, and became friendly. He said Worrell invited him to his benefit match, and Gopinath happily went around with a hat collecting donations for his 'very good cricketing friend'.

Those collections were contributions demonstrating the appreciation of spectators when batters got to 50 runs. They motivated league players because they bolstered their incomes. Sobers laughingly recounted that when he was new to Radcliffe CC, Frank would tell him that when he got to 50, 'don't you get out till you hear the last penny drop!'

Worrell moved to Norton in the Staffordshire League and Sobers replaced him at Radcliffe in 1958. Inexperienced and practically alone in England, Sobers was often invited to visit the Worrells on Bury Road and there he would play games with Lana and enjoy home-cooked meals from Velda. It helped ease the loneliness.

'I used to go round by him on evenings and sit down and kill time because I didn't know anybody in Radcliffe. It was very comfortable. I wasn't one of these runaway people. I was on my own at the age of 22, and it was great to have somebody like Frank around. You could go and sit down and talk to him about the game, and he would tell you about people that he played against and what kind of players they were, that kind of thing, and look out for this and that.'

Worrell's nurturing was not confined to West Indian youth. The legendary India left-arm spinner, Bishan Bedi spoke warmly of the profound impact of meeting Worrell and how it inspired him to model his cricket after-life with the same mentoring spirit.

He made his Test debut in the 1966-67 series against West Indies, and Worrell had been watching the matches. On 4 February 1967, Worrell was conferred with an honorary doctorate by Punjabi University, and addressed the students at Chandigarh, where Bedi was a law student and captain of the university team. He was seated somewhere up front and was mesmerised by the 'brilliant orator' with the 'loud, husky voice' who was telling his peers that their university education came with a responsibility to help develop their societies.

Worrell had observed the lanky Sikh in the audience and sent word that he would like to see him at the Hotel Mountview, where he was staying. Bedi had been selected to tour England with the Indian team in 1967, and the 20-year-old was bemused at the invitation. Lounging in the five-star hotel, just the two of them, he was given advice that was parental and coach-like in its intent and substance – don't sit on the wet grass; remove damp clothes immediately, you could easily catch a chill; look out for those hidden big holes left by bowlers in the sodden field when you're bowling; the English women are treacherous, beware of them – for close to three hours Worrell shared the kind of titbits that many would not have thought important enough to pass on. For Bedi, 'these tiny little things, from a man, giant as he was then, to be telling an absolute beginner, I was very touched'. It seemed inconceivable to him that he would make time for a 'non-entity,' who was not even West Indian.

Just over a month later, Worrell was dead, and everything that had passed between them on that fateful day, assumed greater significance.

'He was willing to impart his knowledge, to share it with an actual beginner, and that is what has stayed with me. I learnt that from him, and I don't mind sharing it with anybody,' said Bedi. 'Knowledge is of no value if it is not shared.'

Tales of generosity and instinctive mentorship are a motif of Worrell's life, the foundation of the reverence with which he is remembered away from the cricket field.

He continued to win hearts, and by the third tour, he had become embedded in the Indian imagination even though he had to leave prematurely to take up Test duties.

The second tour, during the 1950-51 season, was led by the former England wicketkeeper, Leslie Ames, who also played for Kent. He was no longer participating in international Test cricket, but had reached 100 centuries in 1950. During the Second World War, Ames had been a squadron leader in the RAF, and by the time he set off for the Commonwealth tour, he was plagued by back troubles that ended his career soon after. He became friendly with Worrell, and they would share drinks on evenings, although Ames said, 'He was one of the nicest men I ever met, but he did not take life seriously enough.'

On this tour, Pakistan was not included, and the team played 27 first-class matches, six more than previously, including the five unofficial Tests against an All-India XI and one against an All-Ceylon XI. This time, J.K. Holt was replaced by Sonny Ramadhin. They did not lose any matches, winning 13 and drawing 14. The captaincy had fallen often on the shoulders of Worrell as Ames's back injury worsened. He rose to the challenge not only as a captain in three of the four 'Tests,' but also topped the run-scorers with 1900, and in the 'Tests,' was the leading wicket-taker with 18. *Wisden* reported that Worrell had been a 'capable captain,' on the many occasions he had been called to lead the team.

He found this experience convivial and attributed it to a more harmonious group than on the previous visit when players were focused on enhancing their reputations. 'There were no personality conflicts as on the first tour,' he wrote. 'A greater bunch of troupers for an unofficial tour couldn't have been selected. We went through India, smilingly taking the rough with the smooth. As a consequence of this attitude from an international relations point of view, this was one of the best tours to India undertaken by any team.'

The team's success may also have been a result of the kind of leadership Worrell brought. Many accounts had been given of unsatisfactory conditions associated with touring India. Worrell did not add to those complaints in any written form. It was quite possible that he was smoothing many things over behind the scenes, unlike the manager of the West Indies team, Donald Lacy, whom Stollmeyer had scathingly called useless.

Ramadhin, timid and inexperienced, said Worrell was his best friend on his first trip to India, helping him to learn how to socialise and cope with the astonishments of this new world, and introducing him to the pleasures of alcohol. Ramadhin came from a sheltered rural Hindu community in Esperance, Trinidad; India was revered as his ancestral home. It had made him very nervous, and coupled with his shyness and apprehension about fitting in and understanding the culture, he leaned heavily on the reassuring shoulders of Worrell, who represented the height of sophistication in his mind.

Worrell had made friends with the Indian all-rounder, Dattu Phadkar, who batted in the middle order and bowled handy medium pace with good control of swing. In the 1948 fourth Test against Australia at Adelaide, Donald Bradman's team amassed a first-innings total of 674 and the Indian captain, Vijay Hazare, scored 116, while Phadkar made 123. India managed 381, but Phadkar established his class.

In the first of the unofficial Tests during the previous tour by the Commonwealth XI, Phadkar had also scored a century, although his team lost by ten wickets. In the third, at Calcutta, Duckworth had reported, 'The Bengal bowler troubled Worrell as the latter had never been troubled before and he was his side's bowling hero.' It was the beginning of a lifelong friendship, that deepened when Phadkar went to play for Nelson (Learie Constantine's club from 1929 to 1937) in the Central Lancashire League in 1951.

His daughter, Lalita, remembered Worrell's care for her father.

'What is perhaps less well known is how he stood by my father and mother when my father fell ill in 1953 in England. Uncle Frankie was already in the League, playing for Radcliffe. The two men were friends. My father always spoke in later years of Frank Worrell as one of the "nicest people in cricket". He admired his integrity and generosity of spirit and enjoyed the intelligent conversation which was a mark of the man.'

Just half a month into the season, Dattu contracted double pneumonia and had to be hospitalised. 'This was not only scary from the point of view of being strangers in a strange land, it was also a financial catastrophe for my mother and father. Nelson was forced to hire substitute professionals for the League matches. Clearly they could not support my father as well. Uncle Frankie stepped in. He himself substituted for my father in some of the matches. It is my belief that he spoke to the other professionals who were substituting. Sir Frank ensured that the "professional take" from the league matches Nelson played in went almost completely to my parents. Moreover, my mother used to recall that he was always a friendly cheery presence at the bedside, rallying my father and as he recovered, ensuring that he kept his spirits up with the deadpan humor he was known for.'

Lalita, elegant and beautiful in her early seventies, had shared this by email. She had many photo albums with pictures of the Worrells and the Phadkars, but when we met in New Delhi, she did not bring them, though the few she sent digitally were evidence of their closeness.

There are two photos of a New Year's Eve party at the home of the Phadkars in Calcutta in 1966, where Worrell had quietly disclosed his illness to them, bringing tears and sadness to the evening. Another shows him with the Phadkars at Eden Gardens during the December 1966 Test, and on board the ship travelling to the West Indies for the 1952 tour, a group shot with little Lana holding the hands of Velda and Dattu, with Sonny and Frank alongside. The quality of the photographs was not good as they were taken from inside photo albums and the plastic coverings caused blurry light reflections; but it was enough to see that they shared a close relationship.

With Phadkar recovered, Worrell was once again getting ready to head to India; this time the Commonwealth team was going as part of the BCCI's Silver Jubilee celebrations. That tour, during the 1953-54 season, was not quite as successful as the previous trips. Worrell returned for West Indies duty at the end of December 1953 for England's tour of the Caribbean. As a drawing card, it was he who had brought the most excitement and pleasure to spectators. The *Times of India*, in 1949, had reported that the BCCI had 'levied a tax of four annas per seat per day' for matches against the Commonwealth team. Worrell was thrilling to watch with his elegance and weight of runs, let alone his wickets. While Weekes and Walcott had brought differing forms of powerhouse play to the Indian pitches during the Tests, Worrell had practically danced his way into their hearts with the Commonwealth team.

He took part in matches until 29 December, when he and Ramadhin left on the *Comet* for England. The diary of one team member, Paul Gibb, described the evening. 'Later, I went to the farewell party for Frankie Worrell and Sonny Ramadhin at Maxim's nightclub. The whole thing was a bit of a flop. We sat at a long, narrow table down the side of a smallish dance-floor, beyond conversational range of any but our nearest neighbours. Many of us had not eaten and there was no attempt made to serve us dinner until about 11.15.'

More than once in his journal entries, Gibb remarked that Worrell's absence was a big loss. Roy Marshall had joined the team, but did not shine the way Worrell had. In the ten games he played before departing, Worrell scored 833 runs with four centuries. In the two 'Tests', batting three times, he made 102 runs.

The first match, against the Cricket Club of India (CCI), in Bombay from October 10-12 yielded a remarkable story.

The cricket world has often heard the story of the fateful blow to the head suffered by Indian captain Nari Contractor from a ball by Charlie Griffith in a tour match in Barbados in 1962. Frank Worrell's blood donation has perpetually linked the two in cricket's history. Contractor never met Worrell again after that incident, but he recalled that the first time he had met him, he was just about 19 years old, and they both played in this CCI match. At his home in Mumbai, while recovering from hip surgery, the 84-year-old haltingly related the extraordinary episode.

'My first meeting with Frank was in 1953 when he came as a captain of the Silver Jubilee Overseas Cricket team, SJOC, as they were called. He was batting; he had scored a few runs and a leg-spinner was bowling to him. And the first ball of that particular over, he hit for a six onto the first floor of the CCI, the second ball, he hit a six onto the second floor, the third ball went onto the third floor of the CCI and the fourth ball went the fourth floor. Four consecutive balls.'

He paused and chuckled with delight, savouring the memory he had from his position at deep square leg. The unfortunate bowler, he said, was Desai. The records show that Worrell scored 76 in that innings, Contractor 26, and Avinash Harkant Desai, whose bowling style is listed as leg-break/googly. The SJOC team did not bat again and the match was drawn.

'After the match, I spoke to him, in the sense that he presented me with a Frank Worrell cricket bat with which I got a hundred at Bangalore within a month,' said Contractor.

When Worrell left the tour it continued, still under the captaincy of Australian Ben Barnett. While the tourists had voiced many complaints about their treatment in India during the various tours, they were often guilty of obnoxious, racist behaviour themselves.

Gibb, who did not seem to approve of the conduct of his colleagues, noted that it was said that the current group's behaviour was far better than their predecessors.

He related one incident where Roy Marshall flung away an autograph seeker's book, shouting at him to 'muck off,' and another where they poured lemonade onto the heads of spectators trying to get a glimpse of them in their dressing rooms. Stollmeyer's diary had a similar entry for the West Indies tour. 'Allan Rae, Gerry, Jimmy and I walked the three-minute walk from the ground to the hotel and locked ourselves in Allan's room. Eventually, to get rid of the autograph hunters who, at Delhi and at Poona were positive menaces, we threw a jug of water at them. The type that collects autographs in India is usually a miserable little runt, dirty and with no manners or reasoning, whatever. They are uncontrollable and add greatly to our discomforts.'

In one entry, Gibb writes, 'Raman [Subba Row] was a bit upset about the behaviour of the lads at the table. We are waited upon by household servants trained to take a pride in attending people who are immaculate in their behaviour. Our lads perform in such a way as would never occur to them at home. They help themselves to cigars and cigarettes, putting them in their pockets if they don't want to smoke them. They clown around with the cutlery and slobber their food in imitation of certain Indians they have observed. They call their servants names and beckon them in imperious manner. The servants call them "sir" and "master" and wait upon them with their tongue in cheek and, I have a feeling, with the hope that they won't have to tolerate this sort of thing for long.'

Another entry: 'Had dinner with Jack Iverson and Ken Meuleman. I must say I often loathe eating in the company of these Aussies. They are so frightfully rude and aggressive to the waiting staff.'

In yet another incident, the 'lads' charged at a rickshaw carrying two of their mates, and upended it. 'The frightened rickshaw wallah hung grimly on to his shafts with panic all over his face. He was wafted into space and left dangling. Des, Bob and Allan then got between the shafts and dashed off, the bemused rickshaw wallah padding alongside. They charged through the gates of Government House as red-coated sentries sprang up all round them. At the main door was an Indian policeman – with a sense of humour. He held up his hand, brought Reg and George to a halt, and said all cars to be parked here please, indicating a space to the rear.'

These were the 'larks' the tourists felt no qualms about indulging in at the expense of the hapless locals of the working class. It was the kind of behaviour that Worrell publicly denounced. What would he have done if he had still been there?

CHAPTER 14

1951-52

AUSTRALIA AND NEW ZEALAND

After the victorious series in England in 1950, Worrell, along with Weekes, Ramadhin, Valentine and Evans were named 1951 Cricketers of the Year by *Wisden*. It is the most prestigious individual title bestowed in the sport, and it provided formal recognition that confirmed his celebrity status in the global cricket community.

The decade had begun with Worrell in India with the Commonwealth XI, followed by the Test series against England, before he headed back to India with the Commonwealth XI. Then came the tour to Australia and New Zealand in the winter of 1951-52.

During the 1950 tour, Walcott had been approached by Enfield Cricket Club, also from the Lancashire League, to join them for the following season. He discussed it with Weekes and Worrell and decided to take the position. But he felt it would be prudent to provide himself with some support, and so on 31 January 1951, he married his girlfriend, Muriel. Two days later, Weekes followed suit, tying the knot with Joan Manning. The Three Ws, along with their spouses, were now together again in England, and close enough to each other to socialise regularly.

Since the Worrells had moved to England, there had been several overseas trips lasting months, and in between there were the Test matches and the regular league games. The India trips alone lasted at least six months each; the Australia and New Zealand tour, roughly the same. There were two Test series against India and then England in the West Indies, and in the 1954-55 season, another Australia tour. Worrell would have spent at least half of those first five years of marriage abroad. Velda did not accompany him on those trips, although she and Lana joined him when he returned to the Caribbean.

Their circumstances had improved significantly since they had first emigrated – they had moved to their own home at Bury and Bolton Road in Radcliffe; they had made friends, and were much better off financially – although they had also developed fairly expensive tastes. Worrell had quickly realised that he had to maximise his income in order to provide for Velda and Lana. Velda had suffered a miscarriage in those early days, but it did not mean there was no prospect of more children in the future.

Long separations are not easy to manage in any relationship, and this must have been an intensely stressful aspect of their marriage. Worrell's reputation as one of the world's leading batters was at its peak; he had become a celebrity and the cliché about the connections between stardom and wine, women and song was evidently apt during this period. It was the beginning of a stealthy estrangement between them, though they did not betray the myth of a happy marriage in public.

Still, for Worrell, it was a time of growing maturity. The more he toured and interacted with diverse groups of players, the more he travelled, the greater became his inclination to behave as a statesman. His cosmopolitan outlook, with its genesis in his early visits to the US and Jamaica when he was fleeing the insularity of Barbadian society, made it easy for him to adapt to diverse environments. He was very conscious of his public image; evident in the debonair way he dressed and spoke, but also in the care he took to present a sophisticated veneer. The days when Ames could comment that he did not take life seriously enough were disappearing from his public persona, but not entirely from his private self.

Sensitive to the inequities faced by cricketers because of social stratification, he used his personal standing to act upon it. For the tour of Australia and New Zealand, he discovered that his contract offered him more money than some of the other players and he protested to the WICBC. They narrowed the differential, but were displeased about having to negotiate terms, something they were not accustomed to doing.

After the victory in England, the chance to beat Australia on their home territory was seen as an opportunity to be recognised as world champions, as Australia had also beaten the English in the winter of 1950-51. The winners of the series could claim to be the best team in the world.

Worrell, Weekes, Walcott, Ramadhin, Ken Rickards and Marshall sailed on the *SS Strathmore* that September, headed for Perth from where they would fly to Sydney to meet the rest of the squad.

Walcott described the journey as 'a very enjoyable one' with 'all manner of shipboard games which gave good exercise.'

Eytle travelled with the six cricketers. 'The days of sailing were punctuated with games of table tennis, quoits [a game where players toss rings at a stake of some sort], dancing and swimming in the ship's pool,' he wrote. They had agreed that by the time they got to Bombay, the parties would give way to a strict training regime. Worrell decided to arrange a last hurrah as a surprise.

'First we knew about it was when all members of our party were ordered to foregather in Frank's cabin. One by one the players descended below deck expecting perhaps a meeting to discuss policy, training schedule or the like. Instead, we were astonished to see the spread Frank had arranged for us, because, as he said, nobody had thought of a morning party, and it was time someone did.'

Eytle said this was just one of many similar acts on his part during the tour. The grand gesture, the unassuming authority (although Goddard was captain, when the players were summoned to Worrell's cabin, they expected it to be a team meeting), from early, his leadership was established within the West Indian team.

Eytle's first impression of Worrell was that he was 'neat, affable, always dapper and seldom seen without a disarming smile,' and that he was 'reserved, yet friendly, enjoying life to the full.' At the Sunday morning services, Worrell and Weekes would join in the singing of hymns from their position at the back of the congregation.

'He is tremendous fun at a party and is always happy until the talk turns to cricket, then he slides away to a corner, preferring to talk of other things,' he wrote, adding that Worrell was a non-smoker but with more than a passing interest in alcohol. Worrell's complaint was that the trip was ten days too long, and with all the partying – which he said they could not escape – getting back into shape was 'particularly arduous'.

It is a contrast from the aloof way Goddard generally interacted with players. Keith Miller, the extraordinary Australian all-rounder, had reported that at a party at Goddard's home, he had enquired about the absence of the Three Ws. 'We do not mix socially,' was Goddard's reply.

Worrell had related a grand story about Miller's unconventional and aggressive character. Like Worrell, he believed in playing for the love of the game, and not simply for victory. At one of the matches, things had taken a soporific turn and spectators and players alike seemed to be nodding off. Miller decided he was going to wake everyone up, so he alerted Worrell, who was at the crease. 'I am going on to bowl and the third, fourth, and fifth balls of my over will be bumpers.'

He did and, forewarned, Worrell was able to take 'evasive action' as the ball whistled past his head. It did the trick; the crowd sprang to life, booing Miller, who did not bowl for the rest of the afternoon, having achieved his goal.

The tour turned out to be an unpleasant one. The dissent has been attributed to the feeling that Goddard had been unfairly credited with excellent leadership in the 1950 series. Players had tactfully written that his was a 'democratic' style of leadership which encouraged players to share their views on strategy. In fact, they felt they were the real tacticians, and he should have acknowledged their contributions.

Even before the party set off, the schedule was a source of dissatisfaction. They played 22 first-class matches and won nine, losing eight and drawing five; and they won only one of the five Tests. Lamenting how the tour turned out, Worrell wrote, 'The first mistake was made before we left home. Only one first-class game – against Queensland at Brisbane – was arranged before we went into the first Test match. That left us too little time to get accustomed to Australian conditions, and our officials must have realized this when Queensland beat us by ten wickets.'

He claimed that the rift that had developed after the 1950 tour was the major factor in the team's 'poor showing.' Many players had made 'good suggestions' to Goddard, yet all the praise had gone to him, and there was no acknowledgment of the team's input. 'The annoyance was so great that on our tour to Australia the advice was withheld, leaving Goddard a captain without officers – and we drifted on the rocks.' Worrell said Goddard had depended on this advice since he took over the captaincy in 1948. 'Relying on such "sure" support he never really took a decision of his own, which meant there were no trial and error impressions on his mind. Having not assimilated sufficient cricketing knowledge up till 1952, to weather this sort of storm, he floundered and the team with him...' It was the 'withdrawal of the brains,' when they were most needed.

He was prepared to stand by his captain, until an 'unfortunate event' forced him to take a neutral stance 'where I endeavoured to earn my livelihood as a worker following the instructions of the respective captains on the tour.' Worrell would play the role of the subordinate cricketer, obeying the masters. They would not, however, benefit from his knowledge.

The incident that caused him to pull back occurred about five minutes to stumps in the Brisbane Test. Worrell told Weekes to stay at his end and he would play out Doug Ring's over.

'Ring bowled a ball which was a leg-spinner and wide of the off stump – a ball I had no need to play at, but as if I were drawn out of my crease by some supernatural force I just found myself moving down the wicket attempting a defensive stroke to the ball. I was stumped and had no explanation to give in the light of my intentions and discussions with Everton Weekes a minute before. John Goddard, as nightwatchman, walked to the wicket in a huff, immediately received a full toss from Doug Ring and played the most "un-nightwatchman-like" stroke I have ever seen. He drove it back into Ring's hands and was caught.'

The following morning, Worrell was going down to Sunday breakfast and was alone in the elevator at Lennons Hotel when Goddard entered and 'refused to speak to him'. That made him decide 'to be a neutralist member' of the team. He said the team never recovered from the 'splinter groups' of this tour 'until Gerry Alexander began to mould the team in 1958.' Even in 1960 some of the members of the teams of the Fifties 'tried to impress Alexander that there was a division in his side' that played against England in the West Indies.

'These individuals had the "benefit" of active participation in this sort of non-alliance and were well schooled in thinking in this manner. So it was perfectly natural for them to interpret as sabotage certain cricketing situations that cropped up. What is especially annoying,' he ended, 'unsuspecting Alexander very nearly fell for it.'

While Worrell and other players had complained about the short-sightedness of the itinerary, Goddard would find that his captain's privileges did not extend to airing his grievances to the media. The WICBC was having none of that public dissatisfaction. President Karl Nunes issued a statement. 'If we have not the wisdom, temperament or ability to adapt ourselves to the conditions of other countries as we expect them to adapt to ours in the West Indies, and if we cannot take what we give, we do not measure up to the calibre of Test cricket.'

The Board suspended Goddard for three and a half years. Goddard later said, 'In the 1950s cricketers did not consider suing for restraint of trade. But if Worrell or Sobers had been suspended there would have been an outcry.'

The rifts from the 1950 series would persist throughout the decade. Their roots were embedded in the social and racial demarcations entrenched in the West Indies that, naturally, pervaded its cricket. Cricketers had existed under these conditions for so long that they took it for granted that white players would always hold the positions of control. The more Worrell asserted his influence, the greater the disparities appeared.

Those power dynamics did not apply only in the relationships with coloured and white players, but were also major aspects of the dealings between the white players. A case in point was the stiff relationships among Stollmeyer, Gomez, Goddard, Marshall, and even Sir Errol dos Santos. Stollmeyer and Gomez had been friends from childhood, but they clashed with Marshall and Goddard. Stollmeyer and Sir Errol were often at odds, and the latter always got his way.

Colour was always near the surface. On the voyage out to Australia, Walcott said they had been warned about the 'colour prejudice' in Australia. He said the Australians on board seemed to accept them, except for 'one old man.' He said he heard him ask another passenger, 'Why is it that these coloured boys mix so well with you people? I suppose it must be because they are cricketers.'

In effect at the time was the Immigration Restriction Act of 1901, which essentially legitimised what was known as the White Australia policy. This policy was meant to keep out non-white migrants. The National Museum of Australia records that after the Second World War the policy was relaxed as population growth was low. The policy was basically dismantled in 1966, and in the 1970s it was replaced by laws such as the Racial Discrimination Act of 1975. The West Indians could be said to have been granted an 'honorary-white status' to play there.

When the Australians visited the Caribbean in 1955, Alan Davidson noted that as they landed in Jamaica, they were greeted with some hostility. 'We arrived and there were all these placards at the airport, you know, people having a go, White Australia Policy, go home – all this sort of stuff.'

Despite complaints from players about the conditions of the tour, they agreed that the Australian hospitality was its redemption. A general conviviality on both sides meant having drinks together – heavy drinking was the order of the days and nights – and Walcott told of calypso exchanges, making fun of each other from both sides. Stollmeyer, the vice-captain, was fond of calypso and was a ready hand at extemporising, so the sessions would have been lively, entertaining, and high-spirited, to say the least.

Another aspect of their pleasure at the Australian hospitality, apart from the endless booze, was the availability of women, who flocked towards these 'exotic' men.

Personally, Worrell had not fared badly, given the overall outcome of the series. The Australian fast bowlers, Ray Lindwall and Miller, unsettled the West Indies batters, just as Valentine and Ramadhin made the Australians uneasy in a different way. Worrell stood his ground with bat and ball, and in the fourth Test at the Melbourne Cricket Ground scored 108 in the first innings. Victory in that match would have squared the series at 2-2, but Australia squeaked home by one wicket to establish a decisive 3-1 lead. In the third Test at the Adelaide Oval, West Indies' sole victory, Worrell took six first-innings wickets as Australia were bowled out for 82. Worrell also passed 1000 Test runs, joining Jeffrey Stollmeyer and Gerry Gomez in reaching that milestone during the series. Worrell ended up as the highest West Indian run-scorer with 337 overall and 17 wickets.

The next stop was New Zealand for two Tests. West Indies won the first by five wickets but were thwarted by rain in the second. The first match was a high-scoring affair for the tourists. Opening partners, Stollmeyer and Rae hit 152 and 99 respectively. Walcott made 115, Worrell 100, and Weekes 51, for a first-innings total of 546 for six declared. Worrell fared well on this part of the tour as well, He was the top run-scorer with 233 from his three innings at an average of 116.50, further enhancing his growing reputation.

Roy Marshall wrote that the tour was marred by inter-island rivalries and other disputes among players. He reflected that he might have fared better with Stollmeyer and Gomez if he had learnt to keep his mouth shut. He was never at ease on this tour, particularly because of differences with the white Trinidadians, and it is ironic that the victory in the third Test was set up on Christmas Day when he and Stollmeyer opened (Rae had been left out) and put on 72 in a partnership Marshall called 'the best of the series by any side'.

In New Zealand, four matches were scheduled, one of them against Otago in cold and blustery conditions at Dunedin. Marshall scored a hundred for which he said he had Worrell to thank. He was on 82, and they needed only 18 more for victory.

As they went out to bat after lunch, Worrell asked, 'Would you like a century, Roy?'

'Of course, Frank. Nothing would suit me better,' he responded.

'Well, I'd better make sure I don't score any runs,' Worrell told him.

Marshall wrote, 'And he didn't, but he almost forgot himself once. One of the New Zealand bowlers sent him down a waist-high full toss. Instinctively Frank shaped to clobber it for six, was halfway through his stroke before he remembered his promise, checked his bat and almost popped up a catch.

'I got my century thanks solely to Worrell's kindness. That was the kind of man he was.'

Back in England, Worrell continued enjoying regular club cricket. Jamaican academic, John Figueroa (brother-in-law of Gerry Alexander), described a game between the W.I. Wanderers and the Surrey Club Cricket Conference, where Worrell got five wickets in a row. He and Harold Brewster had 'come down from the North to play with us'. Having scored around 65, they were wondering how they could stave off what seemed like an inevitable defeat. Figueroa heard Worrell say he felt like bowling and he promptly relayed that information to his captain, Ernest Eytle.

'The field looked like an Australian rather than Club Cricket effort – three slips, gully, two leg slips, a deep fine leg and a mid-on and mid-off. The first three balls missed both inside and outside edge, then on the fourth ball there was an attempted sweep to leg which went high up in the air and was well held by young Shirley (son of Dr. I.O.B.) at fine leg. The next two balls were wickets too and they brought up the end of the six-ball over. With the first two balls of his next over Frankie took two more wickets and so performed the remarkable feat of five in a row.'

CHAPTER 15

1952-53

A RETURN TO THE CARIBBEAN

When the Indian team travelled to the West Indies for the 1952-53 tour, Frank, Velda and Lana went with them from Southampton. It was a rough journey, and the passengers spent most of the time in their cabins struggling with sea-sickness, Worrell included.

Gulabrai Ramchand, an all-rounder who later captained India for one series, shared his memories of that voyage. 'The team left by flight for London from where we took a boat to Barbados. It was a banana boat, a small cargo vessel that carried bananas from Barbados to the UK. Most of the players were sick because of the high seas and the rough weather.'

Built in 1949, the *SS Golfito* was actually a passenger-carrying boat of the Fyffes Line. These vessels were used to export British manufactured goods, but featured refrigerated cargo holds and thus were able to transport perishable fruit, such as bananas, which could go off in a short time. The term banana boat suggests sparse facilities for travellers, but the Golfito had three decks with cabins for 94 first-class passengers, public rooms and open-air deck spaces. One person who had travelled on the Golfito in that period, remembered that it was 'quite comfy' and had a swimming pool. 'On the Jamaica to UK leg with bananas aboard, the captain would address the passengers and make it clear that the well-being of the bananas was his prime responsibility.' The WICBC received substantial discounts, as much as 50 per cent, when their cricketers used the line.

Eytle said one night they were having drinks at the bar and Worrell abruptly said he was going to check on Velda and Lana. Concerned when Worrell did not return, he went down to their cabin.

'When I entered I saw young Lana chasing a ball around the cabin, Velda sitting on the edge of her berth her hand on Frank's head, and heard unmistakable groans in a deep male voice.' He returned to the bar, leaving them to the roiling waters, which settled as they got to Bridgetown.

It was their first return to the Caribbean in five years and a large crowd gathered at the Careenage. It was Worrell they had come to see. Paying scant attention to the tourists, they chanted, 'We want Frank,' lofting him off to parts unknown on their shoulders. The Indian team was left to make their way to the cars waiting to take them to their welcoming reception.

When it was learnt that Worrell would not be playing in the Barbados team, the disappointment led to a public outcry. A match between Barbados and any visiting team was regarded with just as much, if not more, anticipation than a Test involving West Indies. Once again, Worrell had stepped into a Barbados environment which resurrected his negative memories of that society. 'There are still some who have never forgiven him for his change of allegiance,' wrote Eytle. Worrell was now representing Jamaica. He would never play for his homeland again.

It was to be a series of five Tests, beginning in Trinidad. In all, nine matches were played with seven draws. West Indies won the Test series 1-0. The six-day Tests began in Port of Spain, on Wednesday 21 January 1953, with the Sunday and Monday being rest days.

The Indians made 417 in their first innings, with Polly Umrigar scoring 130. He top-scored again in the second innings with 69 in a total of 294. The West Indians replied with 438 in the first; Everton Weekes leading the way with 207 and Bruce Pairaudeau next with 115. The match was drawn.

Ramchand wrote that the Indians, led by Vijay Hazare, had to adjust to the unfamiliar jute matting in Trinidad for the first and third Tests. 'Fortunately for us, West Indies had only one genuine quick bowler in Frank King. It was imperative for us to post big totals if we had to match the might of the Three Ws – Frank Worrell, Everton Weekes and Clyde Walcott. We ended up with honourable draws in four of the five Tests.'

Ramchand was top scorer in the first innings of the third Test, making 62. Madhav Apte had no difficulty with either the jute or the bowling, scoring 163 not out in the second innings, and Vinoo Mankad didn't seem to be troubled either, scoring 96 before he was run out.

Weekes seemed unstoppable on his way to 161 before he too was run out, and he added an unbeaten 55 in the second innings, while Stollmeyer blazed his way to 104 not out. The match ended in a draw. Worrell's scores so far had been moderate. Walcott had struck 98 and 34 in the second Test in Bridgetown, and at Bourda in Georgetown in the fourth, he had charged to 125, with Weekes making 86.

It was only in the final Test that Worrell matched the consistency of Weekes and Walcott. In Jamaica, the trio sparkled. Worrell came good with 237; Weekes made 109, and Walcott 118 in a first-innings total of 576. India replied with 312 for nine and 444 in the second innings and the match again petered out to a draw. The only match to produce a decisive result was the second at Barbados when West Indies won by 142 runs with Ramadhin and Valentine taking 13 wickets,

Despite the stalemates, it had been an intriguing contest, with both sides employing different strategies.

After the bitterness of the Australia tour, Stollmeyer was determined to reshape the approach to captaincy. In his memoir, he set out his agenda and strategy.

'I was all too aware of the naïve approach to the serious business of Test cricket, not only by our captain John Goddard, but equally by some of the members of our team.' He felt that many of the players were not sufficiently trained in the finer points of the game, 'nor were we paying sufficient attention to tactics and strategy. Surely anyone who aspires to play at Test level must try to learn not only cricket technique but also cricket tactics?'

He described his approach with Trinidad before the selection of the team for Australia. In a match against Barbados, he decided to use 'defensive tactics to carefully set fields,' bowling at the batters' pads, a ploy then described as 'leg theory.'

The objective is to bowl the ball on the leg side, with a cluster of close fielders positioned there, waiting for the cramped batter to defensively edge a ball. It usually slowed down the rate of play and prevented run scoring, and was one of the reasons for dull cricket. (In the 1932-33 Ashes series, the English had employed fast leg theory, using high-speed, short-pitched deliveries, in what was called Bodyline, during the controversial series against Australia.)

Stollmeyer was afraid that the robust Barbados team would demolish his Trinidad side and he went on the defensive. The match was drawn, but his methods offended the Barbadians, and he cited this withering editorial in the *Barbados Advocate* which was full of rebuke.

'It was indeed unfortunate that many schoolboys were at Kensington on Saturday to see how the game of cricket should not be played, and how one of the greatest outdoor sports, devised to test the skill, determination and sportsmanlike qualities of the players, can be made to look ridiculous by grown men. No one who saw the game on Saturday will continue to wonder why, in certain countries, cricket no longer has the support it formerly did. Mr. Stollmeyer let down Trinidad badly.' The writer conceded that while Trinidad were not world beaters they were not such a 'third-rate combination' that they had to resort to 'defeatist tactics.' The paper hoped that such behaviour would not be 'copied by local cricket captains in the belief that because an international player adopted them they are stamped with the hallmark of great captaincy.'

Conrad Hunte, Clyde Walcott, Everton Weekes, the Marshall brothers, Roy and Norman, the Atkinson brothers, Denis and Eric, John Goddard – these were the eight Test players on the Barbados side Stollmeyer was up against. Theirs was dashing, attacking, spirited cricket. Defensive be damned.

This was the kind of cricket that Worrell wanted. This is what he and Richie Benaud promised when they came up against each other nearly ten years later. It was the opposite of the dowdy caution calculated to minimise the risk of defeat, even if it meant simply focusing on playing for a draw. This English way had been oozing the life out of cricket. If Stollmeyer felt it was the way to go, the Barbadians were not tolerating it. When the Indians arrived, he would get a taste of his own medicine.

He had defended his position, saying it was wrong to expect any captain 'not to do his utmost within the laws of the game to win'. He referred to the Bodyline of the Thirties, saying, 'When this form of attack was outlawed some time later, and the rule whereby only two fielders are allowed behind square leg was introduced, I was among the first to approve. The Indians of 1953 in the West Indies used this tactic to great effect against us, and when at the receiving end I could easily see how the game could be spoiled and brought into disrepute by its indiscriminate use.'

But he remained convinced that he was making wise choices, saying that he again used that plan when England visited in 1954, and he contended that strategy and tactics must always be evolving. Implicitly, it was a criticism of Goddard. 'It was not entirely surprising, therefore, that the West Indies Board decided on a change of policy and appointed a new captain for the home series against India.'

The Indians had also come up with their own strategy for the West Indian attack, and Hazare decided that Ramchand should use some leg theory to thwart the batters.

'Bowling to the Three Ws was no joke. They were merciless. You got one out and another W emerged. Our only hope was to keep them relatively quiet. Gupte and Mankad both bowled their hearts out; Gupte bowled 65 overs and Mankad 82 in the first innings of the final Test, in which all the Three Ws got hundreds.'

Weekes and Walcott were on fire. 'Worrell was grace personified, he would bat superbly for 30 or 40 runs and invariably got out to a marvellous catch. We used to tell Frank: "The other two Ws are murdering us, why don't you get some runs?" He would reply: "Don't worry, it will come soon." And it did, in the final Test, where he got 237,' wrote Ramchand.

Off the field, there was a great deal of socialising. In Trinidad, the excitement within the communities of Indian descendants was high. This was the first time a team from India had visited, and there was a scramble to host events for them. For roughly two weeks before the first Test, exhibition matches were arranged, some at the Queen's Park Oval, and at Skinner Park in the southern town of San Fernando. Invitations to tea parties, cocktails, dinners and dances were flooding in for the Indian tourists, as influential citizens vied for opportunities to meet the visitors from the land of their ancestors.

The manager of the team, Cotar Ramaswami, praised the conduct of the tour all round, but admitted that he had misgivings, despite the charming reputation of the hosts. '...the West Indians have the reputation of being a gay people, given to bohemianism and with a taste for the good things of life, as they say. My charges were not only young – the average age of the team being about twenty-five – but they had earned the reputation of being the most handsome team visiting the West Indies even while we were sailing from Southampton to Port of Spain, Trinidad.'

This aspect of the Indian cricketers had not escaped the notice of Worrell, who mischievously cautioned him.

'My misgivings deepened after I was pleasantly warned by the great West Indian cricketer Frank Worrell: "Mr. Manager, you have got very handsome young men and you have to look after the lads carefully as the young ladies in the West Indies are too forward and free." This well-meant warning was later confirmed by a story I heard from Mr. Jaipal, the Secretary to the Commissioner for India. Mr. Jaipal had to answer an enquiry from a young lady, presumably belonging to the Indian community about the number of married men and bachelors in the Indian cricket team. Being a shrewd and diplomatic person, Mr. Jaipal replied: "I have no statistical data regarding this aspect of the players, but I can assure you that whether they are married or not, none of them have brought their wives with them"'.

The article was accompanied by a photograph of Subhash Gupte, saying pointedly that he 'had a wonderful tour in the West Indies'. It was obviously based on Gupte's immense popularity and his subsequent marriage to a Trinidadian. At a welcoming tea party arranged by Andrew Goberdhan in San Fernando, his daughter, Carol, was helping her father at the event, when Gupte saw her.

'Hello, how are you? May I be so bold to say that yours is the kind of face that I would like to see every morning at my breakfast table?'

This was the line their daughter, Carolyn, would record as his opening approach to the woman he would marry four years later at his home, Parna Kuti, in Bombay. They lived for some time in England. When his cricket career ended, he returned to Trinidad in 1963, where he spent the rest of his days. But at that time, he was the exciting, attractive Indian leg-spinner, one of the stars of that tour.

'In contrast to Ramadhin, our leg-spinner Subhash Gupte did very well on that tour. He got 27 of the 62 wickets that we picked up in the series,' wrote Ramchand. 'What made Gupte so effective was that he deceived batsmen with his flight, and had a good wrong 'un. He got fine support at the other end from Vinoo Mankad, and the two of them were backed up by brilliant fielding. It was said that the 1952-53 team was the best Indian fielding side to visit the West Indies, with J.M. Ghorpade, C.V. Gadkari, Polly Umrigar, D.K. Gaekwad, Madhav Apte and myself.'

He had done well on the tour himself, and his only complaint, he said, was that his captain, was not a leader ... and maybe, that he should have allowed him more chances to bowl.

'If there was anything we lacked, it was strong and aggressive captaincy. Vijay Hazare was a great batsman and an unassuming person, but his personality did not infuse confidence in the side. There was no planning, no team meetings or discussions of tactics. He did everything in a mechanical fashion and had confidence in only two bowlers – Gupte and Mankad. There was no fixed batting order. There was no planning, no thought as to which bowler should bowl to which batsmen. Someone like Dattu Phadkar, the all-rounder, could have made a difference had he led the team. He had the courage, the will and the stomach to take chances and his body language reflected that.'

Stollmeyer would have had a fit at the thought of such a lack of structure and planning.

CHAPTER 16

1954

ENGLAND AGAIN, AND HUTTON

When England returned to the Caribbean during the 1953-54 season, the defeats of 1948 and 1950 were still fresh. This time the team was headed by Len Hutton, the first professional to lead an English side. Although he had been tentatively handed the captaincy when India had visited in 1952, he took to the responsibility so well that they won three of the four Tests.

It was not his first visit to the Caribbean, having been summoned during the last stage of the 1948 tour when it was already too late for his bedraggled teammates. He was determined to ensure that conditions were different, and the rigidity with which he enforced his ideas may have been the major factor in creating an aura of sourness that characterised those first four months of 1954.

In all, ten matches were played, with England winning six. The five-Test series ended 2-2, with a draw at Port of Spain.

Perhaps Hutton felt that England's downfall in 1948 was because they did not take the competitive element seriously enough. In the past, relationships between the opposing teams had also been influenced by friendships and shared business interests. A tour to the Caribbean was an opportunity to enjoy the tropical pleasures of the region, while deepening commercial ties.

Stollmeyer had written fondly that in 'those happy days, although Test cricket was a serious matter, an overseas tour to the West Indies was a more leisurely business and there was more time for entertainment and relaxation. There was much fun and camaraderie off the field and the players of both teams mixed rather more freely than obtains in today's "rat race."' The gentlemen who mixed socially on both teams were predominantly drawn from the same class. Hutton's background was somewhat different from these gentlemen, according to his *Wisden* obituary.

'He was born at Fulneck near Pudsey into a family in which there was a healthy respect for the old virtues of discipline and self-denial. It was also a keen cricketing family, and the boy seems to have nursed ambitions deep in his heart to become a great player. He devoured anything he could lay his hands on about the art of batting.'

Hutton's upbringing influenced his approach as captain. In 1938, a year after he was selected to play for England, he scored a record 364 at The Oval. *Wisden* reported that, 'Hammond wanted 1,000 on the board to be certain of victory and Hutton, suiting his game perfectly to the needs of the occasion, obliged by staying at the crease for 13 hours 17 minutes until 770 had been scored.'

He had been commended for his handling of his fellow Yorkshiremen Fred Trueman, the young terror of a fast bowler with a vicious temper, during India's visit to England in 1952. Trueman would not be so easy to handle in the West Indies.

In reviewing the tour that gained notoriety for its ill-will and bigotry, *Wisden* criticised several of its elements. The behaviour of the players and the quality of the umpiring came in for the harshest words. Hutton was congratulated for his outstanding batting performance, but gently chided for his management of the team.

'Earlier and firmer handling of the most recalcitrant member, the fiery Trueman, might have avoided several situations, but, anxious not to dim the spark of Trueman's hostility and aggressiveness, Hutton probably waited too long before calling his lively colt to heel.'

A much deeper sociological background shaped this encounter. The Fifties had seen a burgeoning movement towards independence and self-rule throughout the dominions of the British empire. Intense debates would result in the formation of a West Indian Federation in January 1958. It was a period of alarm for the English natives who had taken up residence in the Caribbean. Their status was under threat and they leaned towards the visitors for some assertion of superiority, at least on the cricket field.

'Every day on the tour we were being invited to social functions, invariably with the white people, and it was difficult to refuse. All the time they would be saying to us, "For God's sake, beat these people, or our lives won't be worth living." It became a big millstone round our neck. We were almost afraid to talk to a white person. We knew what they were going to say. We wanted to win, but not for them. After a while it ate into our souls,' said Charles Palmer, who was both manager and player on the tour. The article was headlined

'The second most controversial tour in cricket history,' taken from a reference by its author, Stephen Chalke, to that description by *The Times*. E.W. Swanton referred to the tour as 'a diplomatic and sporting disaster of the first magnitude'.

The English-born and their descendants were anxious to show off their Englishness and thus their equal standing with the visitors; what the political philosopher, Frantz Fanon, had termed the assimilationist phase of colonisation. If it provoked angst among the tourists; it was causing even greater divisions within the local populations.

It did not help that Hutton had instructed his players to avoid fraternising with their opponents. When that became known it caused further rifts, even within his team.

Chalke wrote that, 'In each island there were complaints about the English team: from slights supposedly inflicted at social functions to the incident in the final Test at Kingston when Hutton, leaving the field for tea with a marathon double-century to his name, did not stop sufficiently to receive the congratulations of a large, flamboyant man in a white tailcoat: Alexander Bustamante, the nationalist leader who had become Jamaica's first Chief Minister. A few moments later Palmer, in the dressing-room, was being grasped by the lapels and lifted off the floor by a 6ft 5ins member of the Minister's retinue. "This is the crowning insult," he said. "Your captain has insulted our prime minister." I said, "Put me down first of all, and we can talk about it." I was then involved in 48 hours of nonstop diplomatic consultations. Morning, noon and night something was happening. It got to the stage where I didn't know where the next arrow was coming from. All I knew was that it was coming.'

On the other hand, Stollmeyer had been looking forward to reconnecting with Hutton, whom he considered his friend, and whose batting technique he admired. 'We were also both involved with the firm of Slazenger's Ltd, he as a signatory of their equipment and I as a shareholder in the local company which represented their merchandise. Communication would be no problem or so I thought.'

In Jamaica, where the first Test was played, he invited Hutton and his vice-captain, Trevor Bailey, to a dinner party which included Gomez and Worrell. 'It turned out to be less than a success. Conversation and pleasantries did not flow as easily as I expected and it set me to wondering if anything was amiss,' he wrote. 'It was only some time later on the tour that the truth leaked out through other members of the England team that Len had asked his players not to mix with their West Indian counterparts. His reasoning was, apparently, that you could not get tough enough with the opposition if you fraternized. Although this was apparently the policy enunciated to our visitors, I can't say that it worked because, as the tour wore on, there was fraternization and very little ill feeling engendered between the two teams.'

Stollmeyer was being generous. Although most of the complaints stemmed from the behaviour of Trueman and Tony Lock, there were several reports of unfriendly and unsportsmanlike conduct.

Walcott was scathing about the attitude of the English players. Right from the start, he wrote, they complained that the sound of dogs barking had kept them awake at their hotel in Jamaica. They had arrived determined to be disagreeable. While he conceded that there were umpiring mistakes, he felt that half the players on the team would have been fined or suspended under the ICC code of conduct that was later instituted.

'Some of the language directed against our players was appalling and would not be tolerated today,' he wrote. '... I am afraid Len Hutton, England's first professional captain, had much to answer for on that tour. ... His players were allowed to get away with far too much and I can confidently say that if a West Indies touring side had behaved in the same way, they would have run the risk of being sent home.'

England's visit so soured relations that a goodwill tour by an E.W. Swanton XI was scheduled for 1956 to act as a soothing unguent to the wounds. Worrell took no part in this tour, and Stollmeyer did not play because of his injured heel, so Allan Rae was captain for this friendly encounter.

Worrell devoted two chapters in *Cricket Punch* to the 53-54 tour, and his criticisms were as sharp as his recollections. In the first chapter, 'The Truth about Trueman,' he declared that the fast bowler was being made a scapegoat for far worse conduct from other members of the team. He did not try to exonerate his behaviour, but he believed that there was nothing personal in his hostility and cited instances to illustrate the point that it was all part of his temperament. '... there is not one West Indian player who loathes

Freddie Trueman. We know Trueman as a hard, tough character who plays to win. We know him as a great cricketer. And we know that he was not the cause of all the trouble during the tour.' The British public had been misled, 'the whole sordid business has been hushed up and rumour allowed to run wild.'

Weekes offered this laconic observation. 'Some of us did not see a real problem because the rough and tumble of league cricket in Lancashire had prepared us to deal with the Yorkshire personalities we found in both Trueman and Hutton.'

In the other chapter, 'Let's Forget 1954,' Worrell said it was 'the unhappiest Test series' he had ever experienced, and the 'bad atmosphere' was there from the beginning. He described going to the hotel when he arrived in Jamaica, expecting that both teams would be there, socialising. He greeted an English player, who responded in monosyllables, but he shrugged it off, thinking it might have been the effect of tiredness, until he encountered the same cold response from another player. Weekes and Walcott later told him that for the entire week all their attempts to engage the English had been rebuffed. Word soon got around the islands about these snubs. 'Never once, however, did the members of the MCC party show that they wanted our hospitality, and their attitude distressed us beyond words.' The team continued its friendly overtures, 'but there were frequent clashes between the touring party and the Press and spectators.' This 'hostile attitude' persisted for the tour's entirety until they realised it was a deliberate policy.

'Our visitors adopted what are often called the Australian tactics of having no fraternization with the opposition, but these tactics went down badly ... and they were not even Australian tactics, for the Australian cricketer, hard though he is to beat, is the friendliest of characters off the field.' By the end of the first Test in Jamaica, which West Indies won by 140 runs, the English began to thaw, and after that, their performances improved.

The *Wisden* report of the tour raised some of the troublesome issues, and seemed inclined to share blame equally.

'To set out the origins and assess the responsibilities for the tension which marred so much is anything but simple. Certainly the early insistence of so many people that the cricket championship of the world was at stake did nothing to ease the situation. Nor did the constant emphasis upon victory which the MCC players found to be stressed by English residents in the West Indies.' Tension before a ball had been bowled, noisy crowds, and 'ceaseless torrid heat,' frayed tempers, said the report, noting that twice the crowds had become 'menacing'.

'Convinced by the happenings on the field that the general standard of umpiring in the West Indies was not adequate for Test cricket, the touring team felt that the crowd atmosphere made the work of the men in the middle even harder than it should have been. The MCC players sympathised with umpires threatened with physical violence, as marred the first and third Tests. When, as the West Indies players admitted, the majority of disputed decisions, usually at moments of match crisis, went against MCC, they wondered how in the circumstances any umpires could remain completely calm and controlled.'

Saying that although the English were provoked beyond forbearance, their 'dramatic gestures of disappointment and untactful remarks' caused resentment among West Indies officials.

The report recommended a different process for the selection of umpires for Tests in the West Indies. There was no mention of a general modification of umpiring selection criteria everywhere; although the game was full of complaint about the quality of umpires and the propensity for biased decisions; though in fairness, the report was specifically about that tour.

'As it was, in every Test England had to accept umpires from the colony in which the game was to be played. Even when Hutton in British Guiana objected to the two colony match officials standing in the Test, the West Indies Board would not agree to umpires being brought over from another island. After hearing their emphasis on the danger of creating inter-island jealousies, Hutton reluctantly agreed to two other Georgetown umpires, one of whom he had never seen in charge of a game.

'A panel of umpires, drawn from all the islands, who could be inspected by the captains before the Tests began and from whom officials could be chosen for the whole series, appeared to be the only solution and one which was to be recommended emphatically.' It seemed a reasonable suggestion. Umpiring had been the cause of fractiousness from spectators.

Worrell did not play in the first Test match in Jamaica; the finger he injured during the Commonwealth tour still had not healed. Headley had been selected, a decision that was greeted with mixed responses.

Jamaicans welcomed it, but at 45, Headley was felt to be past his prime. Stollmeyer wrote, 'The question of Headley's selection was the first of many disagreements which I was to have with the then President of the West Indies Board, Sir Errol dos Santos, disagreements which were to cost me dearly in the future.'

It did not help that Headley scored 16 in the first innings and one in the second, Tony Lock taking his wicket twice. Walcott said that Headley was dismissed in the second innings 'with the most flagrantly obvious throw I have ever seen.' Lock's bowling action was the subject of much controversy; yet his was the last Test ball faced by Headley. Lock also took Walcott's wicket in both innings, for 65 and 25. Lock's bowling, said Walcott, 'was just another drop in the ocean of resentment.' Lock was no-balled for throwing on three occasions on one day in Barbados. He eventually changed his action.

Michael Manley wrote that the match was marred by an unsavoury incident. 'Holt was given out lbw at 94 by an umpire of sound reputation, Jamaica's Perry Burke. There was a very real question whether Statham's delivery was lifting over the height of the stumps.' Holt was a Jamaican favourite whose Test debut had been felt to be overdue, and he had seemed comfortably on course for his maiden century. The crowd erupted angrily. 'The near riot which attended the decision, and necessitated a police guard to see the umpire home, must be seen as a sordid example of mob behaviour, but more significantly it can be understood as a kind of social exclamation mark to the particular sequence of events.'

Stollmeyer himself was booed by the crowd for not enforcing the follow-on, and again when he lost his wicket for eight in the second innings. He was also regarded as a possible target of violence.

'So ended a turbulent Test match,' he wrote. 'I was afterwards told that I had been placed under police protection for the latter period of the match, and had the result been otherwise, I wonder whether I would have been here to tell the tale!'

West Indies won the second match at Kensington Oval, with Walcott and Holt dominating. Weekes did not play, and Worrell, after being bowled for a duck by Brian Statham, made 76 not out in the second innings.

The third Test took place at Bourda in British Guiana, and England won by nine wickets. As Holt had injured his leg, Worrell opened the batting, but was caught by Godfrey Evans off Statham for a duck. The same thing happened after he had scored two in the second innings, though this time he was not opening. The match was also marred by a bottle-throwing incident shortly after Clifford McWatt was run out on 54 in West Indies' first innings. Walcott believed that several factors contributed to the violence, including an incident involving Trueman when an lbw appeal against Christiani was turned down during the earlier colony match.

At Hutton's request, two different umpires were deployed, E.S. Gillette and 'Badge' Menzies, the latter also being the groundsman. This, Walcott said, furthered the discontent already festering, and so, when the local boy McWatt was run out, although he was clearly short of his crease, violence erupted, most likely because of a drunken response that got out of hand. Hutton stoically insisted on staying on the field and the game eventually came to a sporting conclusion.

Up to this point, Worrell had not been among the runs. Walcott said, 'Frank was in the middle of the sort of run of bad form which comes even to so great a cricketer and he was playing in front of a crowd that was somewhat less than friendly.' Worrell felt he was not popular in British Guiana and as a result, he tried too hard, 'he is constantly on edge, and so his natural game tends to be obscured.' But Eytle said that because Worrell had scored his first Test century at Bourda, 'he always cherished a fondness for the Bourda wicket'.

Worrell had himself written that the Bourda wicket had less bounce than other Caribbean pitches which meant that 'the ball comes through stump high at uniform pace and height, and anything short of a length can be driven back past the bowler with ease.' He had no complaints about it, saying that it was the easiest to score on. 'It is a delight to bat on that wicket.'

But he was candid later about what might have accounted for his moderate performances. Every West Indies home series meant he had to leave England in the middle of winter. He could not leave right after the league season because of his studies, and adjusting to the heat and the glare of the Caribbean was almost 'intolerable' for the first two weeks.

'This, the intense heat, coupled with the fact that you daren't admit to your friends that you were feeling the heat, put you at a psychological disadvantage. Comes the first Test match and out in the middle you can hardly keep your eyelids apart. Before you know it the ball is hitting the bat instead of the bat hitting the ball and before long you are back in the pavilion.' It was exacerbated by the fact that usually there were no matches between the Tests to help acclimatise.

'So you move into the next Test with a failure behind you. Next stop is probably Trinidad. You are well and truly looked after by your friends, and for those of us who are partial to the kind of entertainment we give and get in the Caribbean the temptation to accept readily is strong indeed.'

The acclimatisation he referred to applied to his return visits to the Caribbean, although that process would have also been relevant to the English players, and was not singularly applicable.

The fourth Test was in Trinidad, and the entertainment went both ways. The Three Ws each scored centuries in a first-innings total that was declared at 681 for eight. Weekes scored 206 in six hours, while Worrell put on 167, and Walcott 124. It was the second time they had each scored centuries in the same match.

The history of the jute-matting pitch – laid in 1934 – had made a draw seem likely, and it ended with a feast of runs. England scored 537 in their reply with centuries from Denis Compton and Peter May. In the six days of the fixture, 1528 runs went on the board, with only 25 wickets falling. Statham had pulled a rib muscle and could not bowl for the remainder of the tour, and Valentine was out, nursing a sore finger, but the bowlers were utterly undone by the pitch.

The final Test in Jamaica would be the decider, and it was expected to be a keen contest. It was the debut of Garry Sobers, who had come to people's attention when he first represented Barbados in the colony match against MCC. It was for his bowling that he had been included, and he did not disappoint, taking four wickets in his first innings.

Hutton and his team were determined to win, and applied themselves with a purposefulness not seen in earlier matches. Trevor

Bailey took seven for 34 as West Indies were hustled out for 139. At tea on the third day, England's reply stood at 390–six, with Hutton on 205. As he and Wardle headed in, the unpleasant non-encounter with the Chief Minister of Jamaica, Alexander Bustamante, occurred. It is unlikely that Hutton would have recognised him, for it was the custom that before a game teams would be presented to the Governor, not the Chief Minister, although he might have noted the flamboyantly dressed character. The tea interval was mainly spent in trying to defuse the situation and Hutton resumed play in such disturbed spirits, that he was caught behind by Walcott without adding to his score.

Still, West Indies could not recover sufficiently in their second innings and England were left needing to knock off 72 to win and square the series.

The lowest point for England had been the third day of the second Test, 'when, in five hours, they scored 128 runs from 114 overs and lost seven wickets – in perfect conditions. Their methods merited and received much criticism,' reported *Wisden*.

The Almanack paid tribute to the Yorkshireman whose bearing and strategy defined the series. 'From first to last no batsman compared with Hutton. His performance in leading the Test averages on either side, with 96.71, was overshadowed by the mastery he showed of every bowler in every innings of any length. In concentration and certainty, he stood alone and, when inclined, he produced his most majestic attacking strokes, without ever allowing the wine of them to course to his head. In the last three Tests Hutton's average was a shade under 150, and throughout he was the bulwark of England's batting.'

This was Len Hutton's tour at many levels, but it would raise several questions about the spirit of the game. He was undoubtedly focused on establishing the right of a professional to lead the team. The MCC was not happy with the use of leg theory and the slow over rates employed by its team. Off the field, the conduct of the players and the unpleasant atmosphere in general was embarrassing not only to the club, but to the esteem of cricket as a 'gentleman's game'.

For Hutton, there was censure and an almighty tussle over his retention as captain for the tour of Australia later that year. Eventually, he was retained, winning the Ashes, and earning himself a knighthood in 1956.

CHAPTER 17

1954-55

AUSTRALIA, AND LEADERSHIP DRAMA

Shortly after England had carried away the Ashes, the Australian team visited the West Indies for a five-Test series that began in March 1955. The Australians, fresh from defeat at home, asserted themselves vigorously and cheerfully, winning three of Tests and drawing the other two, becoming the first overseas team to win a series in the Caribbean.

There were none of the 'ugly' incidents which had scarred the previous English tour, prompting a letter to the President of the Australian Board, Roy Middleton, from WICBC President, Errol dos Santos, seeking to place on record 'the wonderful exhibition of sportsmanship and good behaviour of each and every member of this team'. He said that wherever they visited, 'they won the admiration, esteem and friendship' of everyone. He praised the captain, Ian Johnson, for his 'friendliness and tact' which he thought ensured 'the greatest harmony' everywhere. He ended by noting 'there is no record of the slightest friction'. Middleton responded with pleasure, declaring that his Board was 'very pleased that it was able to arrange this visit to your Country in return for the two visits made to us by your teams'.

But even with the tour rated a diplomatic success, behind the closed WICBC doors, a considerable amount of bickering was going on regarding the selection of Denis Atkinson over Worrell as vice-captain.

Stollmeyer had led the side for the England series, and Worrell had been his vice-captain. For this series, Worrell was replaced by Atkinson, whose inexperience was widely acknowledged. The WICBC regarded it as an opportunity to prepare a white player for the leadership.

Stollmeyer wrote that the decision to replace Worrell as his deputy was 'preposterous in any circumstances and was the cause of much of the dissension and bad cricket played by our team in the series'.

'What am I going to say to Frank Worrell?' He anxiously repeated this question to his friend, Cecil de Caires. He wrote to both Worrell and Atkinson, one letter offered his sympathies and declared that he had no part in the decision, and asked if he would mind if he consulted him during the series. The other was to congratulate Atkinson and saying he hoped he would not be offended if he consulted Worrell.

The Board's public rationale was that with Stollmeyer unlikely to be available for the forthcoming tour to New Zealand in 1956 (he would later announce that he had decided to devote his time to his business interests and retired from the game after his injuries, although it was clear that his differences with Sir Errol had become irreconcilable), they thought it prudent to give Atkinson a chance. It was a flimsy explanation, and given the environment, the conclusions were that the Board was operating within the traditional class and colour hierarchies to select the captain. Many thought it was also connected to the distinction between amateurs and professionals, especially in the wake of the controversy when Len Hutton had been selected to lead England.

On 30 September 1954, the Board had written to Worrell regarding his availability and his terms. He had asked for a fee of £1250 and they had agreed on that. It appears that Weekes was the only other player who earned this sum.

The vice-captaincy had already been offered to Atkinson, who had no qualms about accepting the appointment, although he was aware that the Three Ws were far more qualified. When the appointment was made, Atkinson did not demur. He penned a note to the WICBC president on notepaper of The Barbados Mutual Life Assurance Society where he worked, on 30 July 1954.

'Just a short note thanking you and the Board for my recent appointment. I am aware of the responsibility, and criticism that is bound to be thrown at me. However I see no reason why I cannot make a success of the job. Strangely enough the public here in Barbados have not been as critical as one expected. Guess thats (sic) because they seem to have little regards (sic) for Worrell, especially within recent years.'

As fate would have it, Stollmeyer injured his finger during practice before the first Test in Jamaica, and Atkinson had to step up immediately. There would be no question of consultations with Worrell.

Australia won that opening Test by nine wickets. Stollmeyer resumed the captaincy for the second Test in Trinidad, which was drawn; and the third in British Guiana, where Australia won by eight wickets. Then he damaged his collarbone while fielding and it became clear that he would not be able to play in any subsequent matches. It unleashed a storm within the WICBC.

The Test in Georgetown ended on Friday 29 April, and immediately Kenny Wishart (BG), cabled selectors Edgar Marsden (Trinidad), and Cecil Marley (Jamaica) telling them that although Atkinson had done good work filling in, Worrell should be named captain for the rest of the tour. Under the present position, he considered it 'absolutely necessary Windies do utmost endeavour salvage something from wreck'. After recommending that Worrell take over, he added, 'Worrell obviously most knowledgeable available players and will surely obtain full support so necessary any captain present.'

Marsden said that since he was at an important government meeting, he agreed with the idea without giving it too much thought. On being advised, Sir Errol asked secretary Cyril Merry to cable Wishart and remind him that this was a Board decision, and not solely for the selectors.

In May, Marley would write to the president, quoting the line in the cable that spoke about obtaining full support, and explaining that he and Donald Lacy interpreted it to mean that 'Atkinson did not receive that support in British Guiana'.

On that Friday evening, however, Sir Errol rang Merry to say that he was 'definitely against the appointment'. The Barbados members had cabled him 'objecting strenuously, to any idea of such an appointment'. They proposed that if Atkinson was 'found wanting' then John Goddard should be approached.

Michael Manley had written that Sir Errol had tried to block the appointment of Wishart to the Board. Wishart 'had been the first non-white to captain the British Guiana team,' and had become an 'able businessman and administrator'. (It would be difficult to classify Wishart as 'non-white' from photographs of him, but he was of mixed heritage.) Sir Errol, said Manley, was so incensed when Wishart was nominated that he declared that he 'would not sit with that man!' Sir Errol was renowned for his dictatorial manner, and would never brook opposition from anyone.

Merry was instructed to solicit the views of Marsden and J.G. Kelshall (also of Trinidad). Marsden felt re-appointing Goddard was a 'step in the wrong direction,' while Kelshall felt that if not Atkinson, he would prefer Goddard.

Sir Errol asked Merry to meet him at his office so they could discuss the responses. He told him that with all the cables passing through so many clerks at so many cable offices, it 'might well let the cat out of the bag' and so they decided they would communicate with members by telephone.

Cecil Marley and Jack Kidney (Barbados) voted for Atkinson as first choice and Goddard second. At the end of his polling, Merry reported that a majority of six were in favour of Atkinson being appointed captain for the remainder of the tour; and that the other three preferred Worrell.

Cecil Marley had told Wishart that he was agreeable to Worrell being captain but only for the fourth Test, and that the captain for the fifth should be decided after that match. Marley said he and Lacy would go along with the majority.

Wishart had been led to believe that the votes were more strongly in Worrell's favour from earlier conversations he had had with Board members, whose positions had since shifted. He cabled saying he understood it to mean Worrell for the fourth and a decision pending for the fifth.

Merry duly cabled Board members to let them know that Atkinson had been chosen for the rest of the tour and asked for nominations for a vice-captain. As an 'act of courtesy,' he sent an extended version to Wishart, letting him know how the voting went.

All of this had begun on a Friday night at the end of April; by the Sunday afternoon, Merry would return home to find Wishart's livid and sarcastic cable awaiting him; no doubt having been gawked at by many clerks at many cable offices.

Your cable incomprehensible as Marley Lacy Marsden previously in favour of Worrell stop What a wonderful Board to disregard recommendation its selection committee no wonder we are where we are suggest Depeiza vice-captain and entire Board meet Carricou [sic] select next team.

The reference to Carriacou, a tiny island that is part of Grenada, suggested that the Board could not be taken seriously.

Merry, having reported this chain of events in a memo to the Board in May, said he was not going to leave himself open to that kind of abuse, even from a friend of 25 years, and he submitted his resignation. As it was circulated, Board members reacted angrily to Wishart's outburst and urged Merry to reconsider.

Kelshall wrote to the president describing the offending cable 'which might easily have had its origin in the brain of an ignorant elementary schoolboy of the lower type, appears to have been an attempt to discredit those members of the Board who did not agree with the sender.' He said Wishart should be made to apologise for his 'vulgar invective' over which he must by now 'be thoroughly ashamed'. Other members concurred and the president issued a call for an apology and described his actions as 'unconstitutional and insupportable'. On 5 May, nine days before the fourth Test in Barbados, Wishart offered an apology that was really intended to give his side of the story. In his capacity as chairman of the local selection committee, he had visited Stollmeyer in hospital to discuss the captaincy. Stollmeyer told him it was a matter for the Board's selectors and he did not wish to get involved. Wishart acknowledged that Merry's memo was a faithful record of what had transpired that weekend, but said Merry did not make it clear in his cable to him 'that certain selectors, who are also members of the Board, had changed or modified their views with the result that my previous impression of a 3-1 majority of selectors in favour of Worrell for the Fourth Test no longer had any foundation, but quite on the contrary, was now 3-1 against this player.' If he had known this, he would have left everything at that. He believed then that Board members, apart from the selector-members, had ignored the recommendations of his committee. 'A pity that Merry did not telephone me also.'

Under those circumstances, he felt his comments were reasonable, even if 'hastily and facetiously' written.

'I cannot agree that it is not within the province of the Board's Selection Committee to make recommendations such as were made in peculiar circumstances as then existed and I would assure the President and members that I was actuated by no other motive save the good of West Indies cricket. Please remember that I was present at the Third Test, saw our players on the field, in the dressing room and at their hotel and therefore know what was going on both on and off the field.'

He went on to ask that Merry, his 'friend of over 25 years,' reconsider his resignation as he never meant to direct his ire towards him personally. Before ending on a conciliatory note, he ominously repeated that the atmosphere had been very hostile in BG. 'I do not propose reducing to writing here various unfortunate incidents that occurred in British Guiana during the Test, but one day members will be told.'

(In a letter dictated on 16 March, 1956, ten months later, he would write to the Board objecting to 'preferential treatment' being given to Weekes regarding a £3,000 mortgage loan, adding bitterly, 'It is also not very long ago during the Australian tour in British Guiana when Weekes was heard to make disparaging remarks concerning the Board and, at the time, openly stated that he had no use for us.')

The team had already been upset by the choice of Atkinson as vice-captain before the series began. Atkinson, a white Barbadian who was an insurance salesman, had hardly made the kind of mark on the game that would have earned him a leadership position. Many players were obviously more qualified to fill the role. It was clearly a decision based on his skin colour. Even though men like Jeffrey Stollmeyer and Gerry Gomez would fall into the category of white players who automatically enjoyed a certain status, their cricket credentials were unquestionable. Walcott wrote that they should have known it would be an unrewarding series when Atkinson was selected, 'even though the Three Ws were in the team'. Worrell had said, 'I had the honour of captaining ten white men in India so that must speak for itself.' Walcott said the press and public pleaded for Worrell to lead. 'They rightly made the point that he was the more experienced player and captain, but they overlooked the fact that the thing had been decided in the selection room some time before and was unlikely to be changed then.'

In 1954, long before the Australia series had even begun, the WICBC had surprisingly announced that Atkinson would lead, with Bruce Pairaudeau – a white British Guiana player who had not even been selected for the Australia visit – as his vice-captain for the tour of New Zealand in 1956.

Whilst the public was still in a state of outrage, the announcement had come that Atkinson would also replace Worrell as Stollmeyer's vice-captain. The implications were obvious.

The *Trinidad Guardian* had reported, 'About 2,000 people protested, at the Kingston Race Course, against the appointment of Atkinson, the Barbados all-rounder, as captain of the West Indies for the fourth and fifth Tests against the Australians. They wanted Frank Worrell, who was named vice-captain.'

Fortunately for Atkinson, he helped to establish a world record for the highest seventh-wicket partnership in that Bridgetown Test. He and Clairmonte Depeiza amassed 348 runs; for both men it was their first Test-match century. Atkinson made 219, and also took five for 56 in Australia's second innings. It was a personal triumph, no doubt spurred on by the protests and the fact that he was playing at home, but it was the only time he ever reached three figures in Test cricket.

The Australians won the final Test at Sabina Park, this time with victory by an innings and 82. Despite Walcott's 155 in the first innings and 110 in the second, the Australians had five centurions in the first innings alone, with Neil Harvey scoring 204.

It is quite probable that Worrell's performance in this series was affected by the dissension in the committee rooms. He was close enough to know the nature of the discussions and decisions behind closed doors. It would be reasonable that in his disgruntled state his cricket suffered. He hit 61 in the first innings of that final match, his highest score of the series. He made nine three times and, due to a pulled hamstring, did not play in the second Test in Trinidad; neither did Atkinson. In the series, only J.K. Holt, Weekes and Walcott played in all five Tests.

Wisden declared that the most dominant batter was Walcott.

'By fearless but discriminating batting, he performed feats achieved by no other player in history when both at Port-of-Spain and Kingston he hit a century in each innings of a match and altogether five in the series. Moreover, his aggregate of 827 runs was the highest recorded in a rubber for West Indies. Too often Walcott bore the chief burden of an innings, for though Weekes improved from a moderate start, Worrell never reached the form expected of him.'

Walcott's fiery batting may have been his response to the slight; Worrell's mediocre returns may have been his expression of dissent.

Worrell, Weekes and Ramadhin were the players who had been brought back to the Caribbean with higher fees than the other members of the team. Despite Worrell mising the second Test, Walcott recalled that he was still up to knocking back quite a few with the Australians at the Queen's Park Hotel, where both teams were staying. They had returned from dinner when they came upon some of the Australians playing cards in a room. They were invited in by Keith Miller, and he and Weekes joined in the games. They were 'entertained lavishly,' and Worrell, who did not play cards, 'was happy with the drinks,' said Weekes. The party lasted for quite some time.

The details of what Wishart had witnessed in BG may not have been public, but it is easy to imagine that within the confines of their hotel and dressing room, in an environment where drinking was traditionally hard and fast, many grievances would have been aired without inhibition. Both Atkinson and Worrell played in that match and would have been present.

Manley thought that the 'insult' to Worrell could not be mitigated, and felt it 'contributed substantially' to Worrell's 'increasing disaffection from the game locally between 1956 and 1960'. This might only be partially true, as Worrell was focusing on his studies at Manchester during this period, as well as his league commitments, which were onerous.

But Stollmeyer was right: the decision to name Atkinson as vice-captain and captain invoked a considerable amount of negativity around the tour, and the impact of the Board's decision would have more negative consequences in the years immediately ahead.

PART THREE

CHAPTER 18

1954-67

EMIGRATION AND FREEMASONRY

Harold Gittens Brewster, the eldest sibling, emigrated to England when he was appointed acting High Commissioner for Barbados. He had been popular in Barbados for his athletic prowess, excelling at several sports and he was Worrell's cricket captain in the Combermere days. They had become friendly and it was through him that Worrell came to be a visitor to the Brewster household, where he met Velda.

When Brewster arrived in London, where he was posted and provided with official housing, it was natural for the Worrells to be regular visitors. He had met and married Mercedes Maria de Bernard, and they had two children, Mercedes Alicia and Celso Harold Derek. His daughter, Mercedes was just two years older than Lana, and the two cousins, a lively pair, became close friends.

I met Mercedes, now Leal, at 143 Canopy, where she had arranged high tea on a Saturday afternoon in January 2017. Despite the rain, it was cozy inside where she was waiting, stunningly beautiful and dramatically fashionable at 71, as suited her vivacious and assertive personality. She served up incredible stories that were dazzling in their colour and temerity – and unprintable without corroboration.

She made it a point to mention that because of the sophistication of the acting High Commissioner's quarters, the Worrells would often host their friends at her father's residence. It was part of their preoccupation with image, she said, recalling that Uncle Frank always wore 'custom-tailored' clothes. Although that emanated from his childhood household of stylish seamstresses, and a culture of tailor-made clothing, the Worrells did have an extra eye for fashion. Mercedes remembered being taken to a seamstress with Lana to be measured, and Uncle Frank ordered two suits and two skirts each for them. She considered it extravagant, given his means. She said Velda was the same with 'fancy' clothes.

It meant that he had to be particularly assiduous in financial negotiations, which he was, but he was also quite free-handed with money, and this exasperated Velda.

Brewster, himself a flashy man, moved easily among several tiers of London society. Having established himself in diplomatic circles, he expanded his influence to other spheres. In Mary Chamberlain's *Narratives of Exile and Return*, she writes, 'In November 1955 the Barbados Immigrants and Welfare Liaison Service was established in London in temporary premises in Little Smith Street, and Harold Brewster, a Master at Combermere School, was appointed as the Assistant Liaison Officer, working assiduously to promote employment for Barbadians and continuing to present them as the "elite" of Caribbean workers.'

Even if he believed them to be the elite, they were not treated with any special consideration when they arrived in Britain. John Holder, a Barbadian fast bowler, was not impressed with the treatment meted out to migrants. Writing with Andrew Murtagh in, *Test of Character: The Story of John Holder, Fast Bowler and Test Match Umpire*, he registered his dissatisfaction.

'The Labour Department back home in Bridgetown, in conjunction with the London Transport Executive, were recruiting one hundred conductors, guards and station-men each month to the UK. The Acting High Commissioner for Barbados in the UK at the time was a gentleman by the name of Harold Brewster, the tireless promoter of this recruitment drive. Amongst the new arrivals, there was general scepticism, not to say outright dissatisfaction, about his role in the recruitment. Despite the fact that he was based in London and knew what the conditions were likely to be for the immigrant, he had made no attempt to prepare them for the realities of life in a completely different world to the one they had just left. "All he did," said John, "was paint a very rosy picture about life in London."'

In that chapter on London Transport, Murtagh related Holder's experience.

'Harrow-on-the-Hill may well have been one of the more affluent areas in north London, but the house they were allocated had no heating. There was no shower, only a bath with cold water. "I didn't wash for a fortnight," John admitted with a laugh. He might find it amusing now but at the time that must have been distressing for anyone as fastidious about personal cleanliness and hygiene as he. There was no-one to help them or to advise. They were left to their own devices. And where was Harold Brewster, who was meant to be responsible for their accommodation, facilities and general well-being? "As time went by," John damningly pointed out, "many of us came to the conclusion that he did not really care about us"'

Several accounts describe shoddy treatment of the immigrants. One published in the *Barbados Nation* newspaper gives an idea of the inducements that were offered ten years later, in 1965, when Brewster was still closely involved. The article by Tony Vanterpool tells the story of Reuben Rollock, who later returned to Barbados.

'When I left in 1965 I was advanced $336 [about £80]. That included two weeks' pay for my accommodation. The scheme was very good. There was a group of us and when we got to London we were picked up by a coach from the Barbados High Commission's office. We were welcomed by two officials, Pickwoad, an Englishman, and Harold Brewster, a Barbadian, and driven to Brixton where we occupied an African house. We were shown by the proprietor how to use the various utilities. Although I got into London on the Sunday morning I did not reach my room until six o'clock the Sunday night. The first thing I did was place my chicken in the garbage after it had succumbed to the heat. I didn't stay there too long. I met a Bajan who directed me to a better place for which I paid two pounds a week.'

From these and other accounts, it appears that Brewster was not as concerned with the plights of his compatriots, as much as he was with keeping up robust numbers for the recruitment scheme. In all of this time, he was closely associated with Frank, and there is a striking difference in the way they interpreted the idea of helping out members of the West Indian community. Frank was known to go out of his way to render assistance and support at all levels, including using his own money. Velda had often complained that if Frank was down to his last pound, he would give ten shillings of it to a friend in need.

But Brewster was connected, and Frank wanted to be connected as well, and it is very likely that he was the one who introduced Worrell to freemasonry, although several cricketers were also members.

The ancient brotherhood was a way of networking and providing opportunities for members. In that period, comings and goings were discreet, and membership was very privately held. Intricate signals were used to identify the brethren, so for instance, a particular formation of the fingers in a handshake would be a subtle indicator that one was communicating with a 'brother'.

Gregory Gomez, son of Gerry, related a peculiar story from the early 1960s when he was around 12. He had been an avid tennis player and was taking part in a tournament at the Altamira Tennis Club in Caracas, Venezuela. Gerry, who was a partner in Sports and Games Ltd, a sporting goods store, was on his way to Colombia, to visit their Pro-Keds factory. He accompanied Gregory, his second son, to Venezuela and watched the tournament.

'I had finished my match, a match I was not supposed to win,' said Gregory, because his opponent was rated second best in South America. Buoyed by his unexpected victory, he thought it was an opportune time to ask his father to buy him a new pair of tennis shoes as he used to borrow his mother's. His father refused, saying he did not have any money. But then, Gregory recalled, a stranger made a curious hand signal to his father and his father crossed the road and reached into his wallet and gave the man some money. Nearly 60 years later, he remained convinced that the signal was one of the secret ones used by Lodge members. He remembered that his father's membership was a bitter bone of contention between his parents. (Gerry had married Yvette Pidduck, an air hostess attached to British West Indian Airways, in October 1949.)

On Friday evenings, Gerry would get home early from work, pull out his Lodge robe and apron from a box he kept in his closet and set off for meetings. It infuriated Yvette.

His mother's antipathy influenced his decision not to become a freemason when Gerry took Gregory to Lodge Rosslyn 596 on Alexandra Street to try to persuade him to join when he was in his early 20s. He was not comfortable and asked his father if they could leave. 'We left and there was no more talk of it. It was eerie,' said Gregory.

Many cricketers, particularly of the business community, were Lodge members. Sir Donald Bradman had been initiated into Lodge Tarbolton in November 1929, but did not get past the first stage and resigned in 1934, making it clear that this society was not to his taste.

In his autobiography, Andy Ganteaume proudly claimed his status as a freemason at the Eastern Star Lodge in Trinidad, noting that he had been a member for 45 years.

'I am among those who believe that freemasonry cannot or is not likely to make a bad man good, but my experience is that it makes good men better. In addition to its moral principles, there are facets of the order such as research of Masonic topics and delivery of papers at Lodge meetings as well as holding seminars that are intended to develop the intellectual faculties of the brethren.'

Worrell became a freemason in the mid-1950s. According to the records of the United Grand Lodge of England (UGLE), the governing body for freemasonry in England and Wales, 'He was initiated on 21st July, passed on 18th August, 1954 in Sussex Lodge No. 354 Kingston, Jamaica and raised on 9th December, 1954 by Lodge of Faith No 344 EC Exalted in Sussex Chapter No. 354 EC, Kingston, Jamaica, (under a dispensation) possible on 9th July, 1962.'

He had been proposed for membership in Jamaica by his close friend, Carl Jackman, who would become campus registrar at Mona in 1966, and then University registrar from 1969 to 1989 at The University of the West Indies.

Shortly after Worrell's death, Jackman, a Past Master, presented the eulogy at the Sussex Lodge. He spoke of how intensely devoted Frank had been and said that his 'sustained interest' had been 'unsurpassed' in this Lodge. He said that even as a 'very young Mason,' he diligently researched everything he could to understand the teachings and the workings of the various lodges, and was a regular visitor to lodges in England.

'On his return to Jamaica in 1960, he was assiduous in attendance, coming in each month from Claremont, 50 miles away, for the purpose of attending his Lodge.' The lodge meetings were held on the third Wednesday of every month, and whenever he was in Jamaica he did not miss them.

He decided to join a lodge in Radcliffe near his English home, and the archivist at UGLE, indicated that he was 'passed and raised in Lodge of Faith, No. 344, Radcliffe, Lancashire at the special request of his Jamaican lodge fellow cricketer, Clyde Walcott.' This was in December 1954. Walcott later joined the Mount Olive Lodge, No. 385, in BG in 1955.

Worrell had eventually asked the Radcliffe Lodge to raise him to the third degree. This had to be arranged through the Grand Lodge in London and a formal request was made by Sussex Lodge in Jamaica.

Freemasons can move upward by a system called degrees. The first is as an Entered Apprentice, the second is called Fellow Craft, and the third is known as a Master Mason. At each degree, members are required to memorise the questions and answers specific to that station. They are found in the relevant Masonic catechisms and to move from one degree to another, a member is tested on his knowledge and responses to questions within the stylized format of the catechism.

Worrell studied the catechisms and the rituals closely and would ask Jackman to clarify anything that he did not grasp. Jackman said that his move to Trinidad, first at the request of that Government for him to help with their community development programmes, and then when he was transferred to the St. Augustine campus of The UWI, 'did not allow him to go to the Chair of the Lodge – an honour which would certainly have been his had circumstances permitted.'

The year before his death he joined the Lodge Eastern Star, No. 368 S.C. in Trinidad. Jackman said he had told him that although every lodge he visited made him feel welcome, he felt he had to belong to a lodge and to take part in its proceedings, 'so that he could feel he was living a full life as a Mason'.

Jackman's eulogy made much of Worrell's impact on the world as a West Indian, especially outside of cricket, and he shared some stories.

'The Brethren of Sussex will remember when we honoured him for his Knighthood, how modest he was about it. "We did well as a team," he said, "but the Queen could not knight all seventeen of us; so I have had the honour of receiving the Knighthood on their behalf."'

Another anecdote demonstrates many of his traits: his taste for the fine and the flashy in his choice of car; his irreverence for the same (just as when he was a schoolboy with his fancy shirts carelessly untucked as he rode about on his bicycle); his complete focus on cricket development; his impatience with the glacial pace of officialdom, and his egalitarian outlook.

'When he came to the University and was re-laying the cricket field and pitch, he discovered just the clay he wanted in Yallahs in St. Thomas, but much difficulty was encountered in getting transport to bring this clay to the University. Whilst officials argued and red tape was being untangled, Bro. Frank quietly made several trips in his new Jaguar and brought the clay to Mona. Later, whilst groundsmen grumbled and tried to avoid the labour of rolling a wicket in the sun, Bro. Frank himself took a hand in rolling the pitch hour after hour. Example rather than precept! When he was told a few weeks before his death of the opening ceremony for the cricket pitch in St. Augustine on which he had laboured last year, he called me and asked me to see to it that the "little men," like the house-boy who had helped him prepare this pitch, were not omitted from the list of those invited to the ceremony.'

The work was truly substantial, said one member of the team at the time, having to deal with a significant slope on the ground. For one season the team were without a home while the work was undertaken and had to play elsewhere. 'The lower part took at least four feet of filling. If you see dirt he had to bring there to get an even surface.'

Not much else is known about Worrell's relationship with freemasonry. Tennant had written that he had been refused membership in the Barbados Lodge because of his 'reputation for arrogance'. He also wrote that shortly before his death, when he was already at the university hospital in Jamaica, he asked Harold Brewster to have a Masonic apron brought to him.

The symbolic apron, traditionally made of lambskin or white leather, is presented when a member attains his first degree as an emblem of innocence and the badge of a Mason. It is worn at ceremonies during life. In death, it is meant to be laid alongside the Mason in their final resting place.

CHAPTER 19

1956-59

UNIVERSITY OF MANCHESTER

Cognitio Sapientia Humanitas. Those Latin words, translated as Knowledge, Wisdom and Humanity, are inscribed on the University of Manchester's coat of arms, granted in 2004, 45 years after Worrell graduated. One of its publications, *Portraits from our Past*, shares its nearly 200 years of history (from 1824) and lists some of its illustrious alumni. Worrell is among the 20 Manchester pioneers featured, and one of 11 commemorated with plaques around the campus. His is on the Dover Street Building where he had attended classes. In one of the student buildings, the Alan Gilbert Learning Commons, the floor tiles are engraved with names of outstanding students; he is there also.

He could not have imagined any of this when he decided it was time to go back to school. Worrell's entry into the academic world was influenced by Arthur Lewis, the St. Lucian economist who was knighted in 1963 and awarded the Nobel Memorial Prize in Economic Sciences in 1979. It is not clear how they met, but it would have been in the late Forties when Worrell had just moved to Radcliffe.

Lewis had become the first black person in the UK to be appointed a professor, and had taken up his position at the University of Manchester in 1948 – the year the *Windrush* arrived with its passengers from Jamaica. He had previously worked with the British Colonial Office, as a member of the Colonial Economic Advisory Committee, and the Colonial Economic and Development Council. As a strong advocate for mass education as a key to development, it is logical to conclude that he would have persuaded Worrell to take up some sort of academic training. Weekes said that it was Lewis who convinced Worrell to study Optics and then later advised him to read for an Economics degree.

Worrell enrolled at the Manchester Municipal College of Technology, which then taught University of Manchester technology students and non-university students, but did not yet offer university-level courses.

It became in effect a university in 1956, retaining close constitutional links with the University of Manchester. But when Worrell enrolled there to study Optics, he was juggling his Radcliffe club duties, his West Indies cricket commitments, the Commonwealth tour to India, his newly born daughter, Lana, and building a life with Velda. There were eight courses for first-year day students: Physiology, Ophthalmic Lenses and Frames, Anatomy, Physics and Physics Labs, Chemistry, Optics and Optics Labs and Tutorials, and Mathematics. After about a year, he found it too onerous and stopped.

Lewis, who held the position of Stanley Jevons Professor of Political Economy from 1948 to 1957, had become actively involved in trying to improve the living conditions of West Indians living in Manchester.

Summarising their 2013 monograph on his work, researchers Paul Mosley and Barbara Ingham noted his institution-building activities 'as founder of Community House and the South Hulme Evening Centre, two further education centres which sought to fight discrimination against the Afro-Caribbean communities of Manchester in the 1950s.'

As they outlined the design for his further education centres and Lewis's incorporation of 'activities which build vertical social capital alongside conventional vocational training,' they concluded that his 'social centres had a significant positive impact on Afro-Caribbean income and poverty levels. Through a merger between Community House and the West Indian Sports and Social Club, Lewis helped to create an innovative institution which has endured through to the present.'

By 1953, 'membership of the West Indies Cricket and Sports Club, as it was initially known, was mainly male and its activities heavily focused on sport and specifically on cricket, in which the West Indies side, and the West Indian members of the Lancashire League, were at that time experiencing remarkable success. It was not yet running evening classes of the kind planned by Lewis; but, as we have seen, it was already operating a pardner association.'

Dr. James Peters, the archivist at the University of Manchester, had looked through the university's records to see if there were any organisations to which Worrell was affiliated. He came up with only this, which at least suggests that Worrell was actively involved with West Indian groups. 'In 1958, a Caribbean Society applied to become a recognised University society – this meant that they could use University property for meetings. The request was declined, mainly because the membership of the Society would have extended well beyond University students. The Society seems to have been set up in 1958, and Worrell was its president according to a list sent when applying for recognition. Non-recognition would not have ended the Society as it could have met outside of the University.'

There is little doubt that Lewis and Worrell were not just acquainted, but had a shared concern for the plight of West Indians struggling against racial oppression, poverty and the lack of opportunity for development.

Mosley and Ingham noted that it was the first time this nature of the work of Lewis had been documented. Even the records at the Ahmed Iqbal Ullah Race Relations Resource Centre at the University could not find anything additional in their extensive oral histories collection.

But Mosley and Ingham were clear that Lewis had been personally driven to take up this cause. 'Lewis, academically over-extended as he might be, was determined to do something practical about this predicament, which he felt as the predicament of his own people. Of the three thousand or so black people in Manchester, most were from the West Indies and a good few from his own island of St. Lucia, seeking to get away from the kind of conditions he had himself experienced and described in "Labour in the West Indies." The late 1940s and early 1950s were the time when Lewis was most outspokenly angry about the disparity between rich and poor, and its strong overlap with the disparity between black and white.'

By the time Worrell was ready to try again, this time for a BA, he and Lewis would have already met on Manchester ground. He had switched from Radcliffe to Norton in the Staffordshire League, earning more money and making it feasible for him to begin the degree programme. (He played on Saturdays for three seasons: 1956, 1958, and 1959, the only interruption was for the 1957 West Indies tour of England.)

He had initially applied to do an economics degree, but after the first year (when he did French as well), he switched to the BA (Administration). Dr. Peters outlined the programme. 'The syllabus was very mixed and included politics, economics, sociology and social anthropology. This degree was more geared to government and administration topics than the BA in Commerce, which had more economics content. Apart from compulsory courses in Government, Economics, Modern English Economic History, Public Administration, History of Political Thought and Statistics or a foreign language, Worrell would have taken special subjects. He appears to have done Social Administration, Social Anthropology, British Social Change and Industrial Sociology.'

Although it is likely that Lewis delivered lectures on Economics to Worrell in the year that they overlapped, the University could not confirm this as they did not hold records of the Lewis lectures for that period, and their lecture attendance records stopped in 1951.

Tennant, who had spoken to Worrell's supervisor, Professor Emrys Peters, quoted his rather condescending assessment. 'He was not the most brilliant of students and was a slow worker. He would think getting through two chapters in a week was great. But his English was not bad and he was a thorough reader and a dutiful worker. I thought he would achieve a comfortable pass. He took an interest in social anthropology and gained a much better cross-cultural understanding of attitudes than he would otherwise have done. I never had to discipline him.'

Worrell submitted his application form in February 1956. To the question: What career are you considering? He responded, 'A career in industry and trade.'

Eight months later, he was overjoyed to be accepted as a full-time student by the University of Manchester. By then he was already a cricket star, and Manchester regarded his matriculation as an occasion for celebration. The *News Bulletin*, published by the Manchester University Unions, led its Sports Section with the headline, 'Test Cricketer Arrives' on Thursday, 11 October 1956.

Photographed in a suit and obviously fresh from a barber's chair – such is the exactitude of the moustache and the hair – he is seated with his right hand pensively supporting his chin, looking precisely the part the university was expecting.

'Yet another celebrity was added to the list of students last week, when Frank Worrall (sic), the West Indian cricketer arrived to do a three-year Economics course,' it began, reminding its weekly readers about the last tour in 1950. 'It meant disaster for England and runs

154

galore for the walloping W's, Worrall and Weekes, the dual despair of English bowlers.'

Then followed a series of questions to Worrell, first about how he felt coming to Manchester.

'I'm very impressed with the place but I'm not quite a stranger here,' he said, the writer adding that he had an 'old school friend who graduated in Medicine a while ago.' It is not clear to whom he was referring. (It could have been a reference to Carlos Bertram Clarke, who had qualified in London as a doctor in 1946, and with whom Worrell was friendly.) In a 2017 interview, Rodney Norville, another Barbadian living in England who had attended Combermere – he died in 2019 – said that while Worrell was at Manchester, 'he was able to see more of his friend Dr. C.B. Clarke who also played for the West Indies some years before Frank.

'Because of Dr. Clarke's connection with the BBC Sports Club, West Indian teams used to play one or two practice matches at Motspur Park and this trend continued, so much so, that when I became Captain of the BBC Cricket Club I was honoured and proud to have Frank playing with my team,' said Norville.

The newspaper interviewer then asked Worrell about the upcoming West Indian tour of England in 1957.

'I hope to be selected. If I am I'll just have to fit the games in around my examination,' he said. Asked about his team's chances, he said, 'That all depends on the run of the ball. The opposition is much stronger these days and we badly need a fast bowler.'

He was selected: England won the series 3-0, with two draws, and the fast bowler was Roy Gilchrist. Wes Hall was also in the squad but did not play in any of the Tests.

He told the interviewer he hoped to play for the university team in his second year, and he did. When the Athletic Union of the university celebrated its centenary in 1985, its publication noted with pride that he played for both the Student and Staff Clubs.

With his cricket commitments and his growing international stature, it was a challenge for Worrell to manage his classes and his studies.

Only a few of his course grades at the University still exist, but they tell the story of his struggle to keep up. In Industrial Sociology, of the eight students marked, his grade is the lowest at 41 per cent (the highest was 69 per cent), in Public Administration I, he got 49 (highest 61), in Statistics II, he got a Class III, but in Social Anthropology II, he led with 54 per cent.

Apart from the England series in 1957, he opted out of Test cricket in the later years of that decade. He was absent when Pakistan visited the West Indies in 1957-58 (when Garfield Sobers established a new record Test score with 365 not out at Sabina Park), and then the 1958-59 tour of India and Pakistan. For both those tours he had been offered the captaincy, but declined because of his studies.

The minutes of the AGM held by the WICBC in October 1956 – just ten days after Worrell's arrival at Manchester was being hailed in the sports section of the *News Bulletin* – recorded the discussion regarding the 'tour of Great Britain 1957.' Under the heading of 'Professionals', Worrell's availability came up.

Worrell had written to say that he was attempting to fit three terms' work into two so that he would be free for the summer term at the University and he would be in a position to reply to the Board early in 1957. 'Discussion ensued as to the possibility of using Worrell wholetime for the part of the tour coincident with the Summer Vacation. This would leave him free for all of the Tests other than the first. He would have had games for the University and such an arrangement would avoid the disadvantages of parttime playing.'

The Board agreed that at the end of the year Worrell should be asked to 'state his position' before they made a decision. Two months later, on 12 December 1956, a memorandum was circulated to Board members indicating that Worrell said that he had received permission to have the whole of the last term off, 'provided he attends two-thirds of the lectures given in the session and presents himself for the exam which takes place between May 23rd and 27th and the final paper on June 7th.' It meant that he would miss only three tour matches.

'I shall be glad if members will indicate whether they agree to engage Worrell on the usual terms of £800 and £75 per Test Match to represent the West Indies in the circumstances mentioned. Members may wish also to consider whether Worrell should be left as free as possible for his pre-examination lectures, in which event the Tour Control Committee could be advised to make use of him for the matches most convenient to him, provided he plays in sufficient suitable matches to afford him the necessary match practice before the First Test on May 30th.'

It would have been extremely challenging for Worrell to balance the cricket with his academic workload and his family life. He had to confront this as soon as he entered the university and it is hardly surprising that he chose not to participate in any other Tests until he had graduated.

As a celebrated student, his opinion was often sought on cricket matters. The *News Bulletin* opened an article headlined, 'Worrell tips M.C.C.,' on 13 November 1958 with this paragraph.

'"A couple of weeks ago, I didn't think Australia stood a chance. After the New South Wales match, I had to have second thoughts, but I still think that, with any amount of luck, the M.C.C. team should just about do it." Frank Worrell, famous West Indian Test cricketer, had this somewhat reassuring yet cryptic comment to make in an interview with *News Bulletin* last week.'

He is also quoted as saying that, 'I expect Cowdrey and Graveney to be a success down under, but May must keep a tight rein on Graveney. After scoring 25 runs he is liable to throw his wicket away by rashness.' Later, he surmised that, 'The Australian leg-spinners will probably have a bigger effect than the M.C.C. spinners, because orthodox spinners do not cut much ice in the tropics. England will miss Johnny Wardle, complete with Chinaman and Googlie.'

England won none of the Tests, losing four and drawing one, and the following year, on 5 March, 1959, the *News Bulletin* carried an 'exclusive' analysis by Worrell.

'Along with most other cricket writers, I have been proved wrong in predicting victory for England in the recent series with Australia. However, unlike most of the other writers, I have looked deeply for reasons for this failure. A lot has been written on the subject and in looking for news-value, I am afraid that the critics have not fully analysed the situation.

'The basic problem facing an England team in Australia is that of re-adjustment. Overseas, the pitches are much faster, the light much brighter, and cricket style must be altered accordingly. Very fast bowlers such as Meckiff and Gilchrist, and spinners who use the wrist are required. Especially in this latter department England failed. "On paper" the M.C.C. were strong, but the bulk of the team were unable to make the re-adjustment necessary, with the result that too much depended on too few. The openers in particular never mastered the phenomenon of left-handed fast bowlers and so often the early break-through led to complete collapse.

'In my opinion, the Press has made many unfair criticisms of the English performance. May's captaincy has come under heavy fire but it should be remembered that May is only 29 and has had as much experience and knowledge of cricket as anyone of his age playing to-day. England are said to be stale and over-played, but here again there are no supporting facts. The five-week voyage to Australia and the small amount of cricket actually there gives sufficient time to anyone to lose his staleness.

'Under strange conditions, England were outplayed but at home I think they will still hold their own against anyone. But for future tours, drastic team rebuild will be needed.'

The demands of his coursework did not prevent him from following the cricket. *Cricket Punch* was published in 1959, the year he graduated. Even if it had been ghostwritten, it would have occupied a considerable amount of his time and energy. More than half of the book is devoted to an analysis of the 1957 series against England. It must have been a venture designed to earn him some income at this point in his career, but it was a lot for him to manage. His years at Manchester were extraordinarily packed; studies notwithstanding, he found time to consider a tour to South Africa.

CHAPTER 20

1958-59

SOUTH AFRICA – INTEGRATION AND SEGREGATION

South Africa had officially adopted the policy of apartheid when its Afrikaans National Party came into government in 1948. Under the premise of Baasskap – white supremacy – the system prevailed for more than 40 years, only coming to an official end in 1994 after relentless savagery and abuse. The international community eventually responded with sanctions and ostracism, but one of the areas to feel its early impact was sport.

The circumstances leading up to the invitation to Worrell to tour South Africa in 1959 provide an insight into the thinking behind that offer, and why he was persuaded to accept.

The name Basil D'Oliveira has become the most closely associated with the sporting boycott of South Africa. Having emigrated to England and becoming established in the Test team, he was selected for the 1968-69 tour of South Africa which led to its cancellation and a chain of events that saw South Africa being excluded from Test cricket for 22 years.

In his autobiography, he described his early years. 'I was born a Cape Coloured, one of South Africa's four major groups (the others are white, African and Indian). In those days the various groups had their own sides, although all except the whites would play each other in representative matches, where the atmosphere and the competition would always be needle-sharp.'

Despite the conditions, he was not 'bitter or resentful,' just 'sad' about being denied opportunities to play freely. 'But I never had a hatred for the white man. I knew about the laws of the land, about the "separate development" policy that became Government policy in 1948, and we would have been foolish at that time if we had tried to buck the system.'

He had played for South African Non-Europeans against the Kenyan Asians in 1956 and his team won all of their matches. The Kenyans then invited them to visit in 1958, and he captained that side for 16 matches (they lost only one). They were the first non-Europeans to tour outside of South Africa, and it ignited interest among non-white communities.

'As there was no point in expecting the apartheid laws to be repealed, I had to prove my point that we were as good as anybody in the only place I felt at ease – the cricket field. We even tried to get Frank Worrell to bring his West Indian Test side over to play us in South Africa; in those days, such an informal trip would not have been frowned on, as long as the West Indians kept away from the whites. Excitedly we talked long into the night about asking Frank to "throw" one of the games, so that the publicity about our victory would reach a wider audience – but our hopes were dashed when the tour was called off for no apparent reasons.'

D'Oliveira would not have known then of the debates and negotiations raging over this tour. The first overture had been made to the WICBC in 1958, but the Board had refused the invitation on the grounds that while the policy of segregation existed, it was not considered to be in the best interests of either the West Indian or the non-white section of the South African community.

The non-white South African Cricket Board of Control (SACBOC) did not give up. So buoyed were they by the success of the Kenyan tour earlier that year, they approached Worrell directly, asking him to put together a team for a visit at the end of 1959. Their objective was to prove to the world that South Africa's black cricketers were good enough to play at the level of Test cricket.

Author Jonty Winch described the planning, 'Transvaal officials of SACBOC – notably Rashid Varachia, A.M. 'Checker' Jassat [his name was actually Abdul Haq, A.H.] and 'Bree' Bulbulia – arranged for a West Indian team led by Frank Worrell to tour in November and December 1959. Varachia contacted the Minister of the Interior, Dr. Eben Donges, in order to obtain permission and in early January 1959, he was able to announce that he had received a letter from the minister stating that he had "agreed in principle to the admission of the West Indies cricket team". Varachia made it clear from the outset that arrangements were made strictly in accordance with government requirements. "The West Indies," he said, "are fully acquainted with the conditions

Four faces of Frank. Top: undated, from the MCC Library; from the press announcement that he was about to lead his side against England in 1963.
Bottom: a previously unseen photo of Worrell, at the age of 38, on tour in England in 1963; in England in April 1963.

Top: West Indies beat England at Lord's in 1950 and a
legend is born.
Middle: Kenneth Rickards, Frank Worrell, Clyde Walcott,
Roy Marshall and Everton Weekes about to set off for
Australia in 1951.
Right: Returning by ship to the Caribbean: Frank with
Velda, Lana, Sonny Ramadhin and Dattu Phadkar at the
end of 1952.

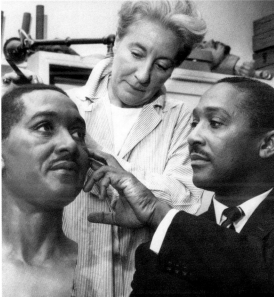

Top: August 1963 with Peter West and Ted Dexter on *Sporstview.*
Bottom: Denis Atkinson's letter from the 1954 WICBC files; Madame Tussauds in 1963.

Top: A farewell wave on the Oval balcony on 26 August 1963 (see page 19); Another farewell wave a month later as Worrell leaves the Waldorf Hotel to head back home to the West Indies.
Bottom: Worrell and Weekes walk out at Trent Bridge in 1950 to complete their demolition of England.

Top: Worrell celebrating his double hundred at Trent Bridge in 1950, an innings he did not consider among his best.
Above: In *Cavalcade* magazine in 1945.
Right: Walking out to bat with Jeff Stollmeyer against England at Georgetown in 1954.

Top: The original Frank Worrell comic; the reprint of the comic; a brochure for the Commonwealth tour to Pakistan 1949.

Middle: the Manchester University student register.

Bottom: the 1963 West Indies team – back row George Duckworth (scorer), Willie Rodriguez, Seymour Nurse, Joey Carew, Charlie Griffith, Lester King, Easton McMorris, Lance Gibbs, Basil Butcher, William Pye (physio); middle row: Berkeley Gaskin (mangaer), Rohan Kanhai, Conrad Hunte, Frank Worrell (captain), Wes Hall, Garfield Sobers, Alf Valentine, H Burnett (assistant manager); front row: Deryck Murray, Joe Solomon, David Allan.

Top: The last act of the tie at Brisbane in 1960-61 – Worrell is at the bowler's end as Joe Solomon runs out Ian Meckiff.

Botom: Gerry Gomez, tour manager in 1960-61, and Worrell on the team's motorcade through Melbourne before they headed home.

Top: Frank Worrell, Everton Weekes, Sonny Ramadhin and Clyde Walcott, in 1957.
Middle: Worrell watching West Indies bat at the Madras Cricket Ground in January 1967.
Bottom: Two scenes from Punjab University in 1967 where Worrell received his honorary doctorate (photos courtesy of Bhushan Mahajan).

here and are prepared to accept them". He explained that "they are keen to encourage non-white cricket in South Africa."'

They met Worrell in London in late 1958, and it seems he readily agreed. He wrote privately to the WICBC secretary, Cyril Merry, telling him about it and asking for confirmation of the scheduled tour by the MCC at the end of 1959 so there would be no clash of dates. Merry responded that it was too early for specific dates to have been arranged as the itinerary was not yet finalised. There was no discussion of the political implications of making this trip.

Months later, as events unfolded and the WICBC tried to unravel the details, K. Lindsay Grant wrote to Kenneth Wishart on 29 June, copying Board members Cyril Merry, Cecil Marley and Tom Peirce.

'Cyril Merry has informed me that Worrell wrote him and he replied, but he understood they were personal letters and that no one knew in November 1958 what the M.C.C. Tour programme was likely to be. We feel that ALL the professionals should be here by 31st December 1959, and those playing for Barbados should arrive earlier.'

At that stage in 1958, there did not seem to be any doubt in Worrell's mind about going, or any concern about the political implications. His primary interest was in earning income. Although he had been studying at the University of Manchester since 1956, in an environment where racial inequities were prominent – especially for Africans and West Indians – and he was involved in groups where it was high on the agenda, he did not see the proposed tour as contradicting his principles.

The year before, an MCC team had toured South Africa. In fact, there had already been five tours to South Africa under apartheid: England had visited in the 1948-49 season and again in 1956-1957. ('England off-spinner, Jim Laker, wrote of the MCC's priorities when touring South Africa in 1956-57. "Before we left England," he said, "we were given the usual preliminary briefing by the President of MCC. He reminded us of South Africa's problems, and told us that colour, as a topic of conversation, was strictly out. It was something never to be mentioned," wrote Winch.)

Australia had been there in the 1949-1950 and 1957-58 seasons, and New Zealand had toured in 1953-54. As late as October 1959, a Commonwealth XI had toured South Africa, playing three first-class matches. The team had been led by Denis Compton and included Tom Graveney, Brian Close, Bert Sutcliffe, Frank Tyson, Godfrey Evans, Roy Marshall, Bob Simpson and Ian Craig. These were white teams, and the conditions were vastly different from what Worrell might have imagined for his entourage.

Winch wrote, 'Jassat travelled to London to confirm arrangements, later recalling the emergence of a "strange twist". Worrell, he said, wanted to bring the best West Indian team and that meant it would be all black. It suggested no restrictions were placed on Worrell in his choice of players. It was also a revealing reflection of West Indian cricket rather than a racial issue – Worrell was said to have more white than coloured friends.'

His list of potential players was thought to have included Tom Dewdney, Andy Ganteaume, Conrad Hunte, Frank King, Ralph Legall, Ivan Madray, Manny Martindale, Sonny Ramadhin, Donald Ramsamooj, Collie Smith, Garfield Sobers, Alf Valentine, Everton Weekes and Chester Watson.

Plans seemed to have been fairly advanced before the WICBC became aware, when a letter arrived from SACBOC thanking them for allowing the tour to go ahead. At its March 1959 AGM, Sir Errol dos Santos led the proceedings for the last time as president, and the issue was raised. After the formalities, the second item on the agenda was Worrell's tour of South Africa.

'The Secretary [Clarence Edghill] outlined the position in regard to this projected Tour: that he had no intimation whatever from Mr. Worrell, nor, until rather late in the proceedings, from the non-white South African Cricket Board of Control who had written to thank the Board for sanctioning the Tour (of which he knew nothing), and that he had received a considerable collection of protests from other non-white sporting bodies, including the South African Sports Association and the South African Congress requesting the Board to do all they could to prevent the Tour.'

A letter from George 'Jackie' Grant (the former West Indies captain who had led them to their first Test series win in 1934-35, and who had subsequently become a missionary in South Africa) was read. It strongly advised against the tour, and the Board asked Edghill to write to Worrell, 'indicating to him that the Board was not in favour of the projected Tour and would urge him to cancel it in the interest of the game generally and in the interest of West Indies cricket specifically, whose non-white players would be open to indignities.'

The meeting proceeded with other matters, which included the election of officers. Sir Errol thanked the Board for his seven years as President (1952-1959). 'He thought the time had come for the seat of the Board to be transferred to another territory,' and nominated John Dare of British Guiana as his successor. The Barbados members indicated that they had wanted Tom Peirce, but would go along with Sir Errol's recommendation. Dare was then unanimously installed until March 1961. Kenneth Wishart, also of BG, was elected to the position of Honorary Secretary, replacing Edghill, who, like Sir Errol, was from Trinidad.

A caricature of Sir Errol might portray him in a safari suit, cracking a whip; a grimly clenched pipe wafting a perfectly rendered ring of smoke past the bushy eyebrows up into his white hair. The artist might include prostrate figures cringing at his feet, obsequious smiles stretched across their features. These would not be cricketers though – Sir Errol would not deign to speak directly to them – these would be the administrators of West Indies cricket, who quaked under his control.

Born in 1890, Errol Lionel dos Santos was a Trinidadian of Portuguese descent, who attended the prestigious St. Mary's College. He'd started his career in the government service, quickly rising to the most influential and powerful positions. On 28 December 1946, the *New York Times* reported that he had been appointed Colonial Secretary. He was also Financial Secretary and acted as Governor. He had been appointed CBE in 1939 and was knighted in 1946.

In one way or another, he was heavily involved in the business and political affairs of Trinidad and Tobago. He was Governor of the Imperial College of Tropical Agriculture (which became The UWI), Commissioner of Currency, Income Tax and Estate Duties, chairman of the Civil Service, Widows and Orphans Pension Scheme; he also served on the Public Officers' Guarantee Fund, Local Industries Development Committee, the Agricultural Bank, the Cocoa Subsidy Board, the Cane Farmers Price Control Committee and was a member of the Housing Committee, and the Banana Board.

'A firm disciplinarian who was accustomed to getting his way,' the Queen's Park Cricket Club's Hall of Fame citation noted also that, 'Many of the members would have experienced his leadership role as de facto President from 1943 to 1980, during which time he acted as a one-man committee, personally supervising the construction of new stands and other development work at the ground.'

He was actually vice-president of the club from 1943 to 1962 when he took over the presidency until 1980. He then emigrated to the UK where he spent the rest of his centenarian life. His *Wisden* obituary called him a 'fervent Anglophile'.

He presided over meetings – whether or not he officially sat in the chair – and his word held sway. WICBC meetings, official ones and the unofficial 'conversations' where decisions were made, generally reflected his opinions. QPCC members referred to him as 'The Great White Lord'.

The March minutes also recorded that the WICBC had decided to again write to the South African Cricket Board of Control to inform them 'as to the Board's attitude towards the projected "Worrell Tour" during the continuance of the South African policy of racial segregation.'

On 3 April 1959, Edghill wrote to Worrell at his Radcliffe home as requested. He informed him of communications received from South African groups, representing white and non-white views, and noted that the Board knew he had also had similar letters.

He quoted from Grant's letter which said that the tour would simply serve to confirm the declared policy of the Government. 'Moreover, in sending a team, the W.I. Board will not quicken but delay the breaking down of the barriers which are so part and parcel of the present policy. Again, a visit from a W.I. team is likely to perpetuate colour discrimination, rather than eliminate it. And of course, I am sure that no West Indian will readily welcome being treated as a 2nd class or even 3rd class visitor as far as travel facilities, hotel accommodation, social amenities etc. are concerned. I strongly advise against the acceptance of the invitation, and you are at liberty to make my point of view known with appropriate discretion,' Grant had written.

Wishart told Worrell that as long as the policy of segregation continued, the Board 'is not disposed to undertake a tour to South Africa'. He said that the previous year they had declined a similar invitation as 'it was not considered to be in the best interests of either the West Indian or the non white section of the South African community.'

Worrell and his team members, he said, would 'be subjected not only to considerable inconvenience and embarrassment but also to indignities which we are certain are not within your experience.' Reminding him that the MCC tour of the West Indies came immediately after, he said the efficiency of the players could be impaired.

'In all these circumstances it is the feeling of my Board that any tour of South Africa by a team of West Indian players, at this time with conditions as they are, would be most unwise and they cannot too strongly urge you to give every consideration to the cancellation of the tour,' he ended.

While these communications were taking place between the WICBC and Worrell, a more public debate had begun once word of the tour got out.

John Collins, appointed Canon of St. Paul's Cathedral in London in 1948 – the year apartheid officially began in South Africa – had become an active opponent of the regime. By 1956, he was involved in raising funds to support defence campaigns for activists who had been accused of treason in South Africa. He would later be instrumental in having the tour cancelled. He wrote to Learie Constantine, urging him to step in. The letter was published on 28 February, in the *Nation*, where C.L.R. James was editor.

My Dear Learie,

I have been asked by Alan Paton to try to persuade Worrell not to take his team to South Africa on the terms at present agreed. Alan Paton and many others who are working for better race relations in South Africa, feel that a visit by the West Indies team under such terms would seem to be an acceptance of the policy of apartheid, and would certainly be taken as such by the South African Government and the African National Congress. They believe, therefore that the visit would do great harm.

If you agree with this judgement – as I do – would you very kindly do anything you feel might be useful in the matter.

Yours ever

J.C.

Three weeks later, on 20 March 1959, in the People's Forum section of the paper, a member of the Hyads Club in Belmont, P. Philip, commented, 'Worrell is not going as a party to a quarrel, but as an exponent of the game of cricket.' He questioned whether Canon Collins would deny a call to preach the gospel in South Africa, and he argued that there would be 'more good all round' from Worrell's visit. 'Worrell and his team of cricketers would do more for the South African cause than all the Patons and Collinses. Why interfere?'

Another letter, from George C. Ramdial of San Fernando, declared Worrell a god, but he cautioned against the visit. 'Although Worrell's intentions of taking a team of coloured wizards to this territory are primarily on those grounds, intricate political implications could very well result. His purpose of letting his unfortunate brothers see for themselves that their own are on par with the rest of the world, could be lost in the dark clouds of racial antagonism.'

The following week (27 March), Andy Ganteaume, whose name had been included for the proposed touring party, added his voice to the letters. 'I think the West Indies should go because it is a private venture despite the publicity which has been given to it. It is an invitation from the Coloured Association in South Africa which is a recognised body. While we all deplore apartheid, I don't think that by going we are subscribing to it, and this venture could possibly open a way for bigger opportunities to the African in the future. What is more, it will be an education as well. It would provide us with an opportunity for seeing things in that country at first hand.'

Others appearing on that date included Joseph Soanes of Group 6, Siparia, Trinidad and Tobago, who wrote such a cryptic letter that his position was unclear until he delivered his verdict at the end: 'By all means go.'

L.G. Richards said it would have a moral effect. 'It has been suggested that carrying his team under such terms is an acceptance of the policy of the apartheid. The policy of the apartheid is a challenge not only to the South African Negro but the Negroes all over the world. Whenever a challenge is issued to an opponent, the worthy, noble and courageous opponent does not side-step, but accepts the challenge and proceeds to deal with it by way of counter. It is time that the challenge is of a political nature. Though it is not possible for Worrell to lead a political army into South Africa, nevertheless he can convert the energy into some other form of energy and the best energy is the one he seeks to employ, the field of Art. Art rather than Politics plays the dominant role in shaping a people's destiny.'

Constantine, who was then Minister of Communication and Works in Trinidad and Tobago, also lost no time in airing his position, and James readily published it on 24 April as the rationale for his opposition.

'Should Worrell take his team to South Africa? My answer is an unequivocal "no",' began Constantine stridently. He examined the policy of apartheid, 'Dr. Donges, Minister of the Interior, has stated that it is the Government's intention to introduce apartheid to its fullest possible measure so that not only shall Europeans be separated from non-Europeans but coloured should be separated from Bantu, and in this sense I believe Bantu describes all native born Negroes.'

He referred to Canon Collins' letter, saying it was clear that there had been prior consultation with the South African Government before closing the deal with Worrell. 'The South African Government agreed with the tour but laid down certain conditions: (a) that the Association should make private arrangements for transporting players; (b) that it should have separate seating accommodations on the grounds for whites with their separate entrance; (c) that non-Europeans should not be allowed to use that accommodation nor the entrance.'

If any good could possibly come out of the tour, he said, it would be nullified by the conditions imposed, as the visiting players would be accepting South Africa's racial policy.

'The acceptance of the tour by the South African Government is part of the policy of convincing world opinion that the Negro can live a "full" life in his ghetto. He is not allowed to get out of the country and the citizens of other countries who have gone into the Union and endeavoured to raise one finger of objection to this disastrous state of affairs are soon deemed prohibited immigrants. Ask Rev. Michael Scott, Alan Paton, or Canon John Collins, to name only a few.'

While he conceded that there might be an 'uplift both psychological and real' for the non-Europeans, he thought it would not help the greater cause. 'Would it help them in their battle to defeat apartheid? My answer is again an unequivocal "no".'

But James thought Constantine's position would play right into the hands of the supporters of apartheid. He ran his rebuttal three weeks later in the paper and invited readers to send in their views. He thought the dominant issue concerned the African cricketers and the African people. They were stifling in a prison from which they wished to be freed, he said, and they wanted to know how they compared with international players. That, he said, was paramount to him.

He said he knew that Canon Collins, Alan Paton 'and others of that way of thought,' meant well, but, 'They are dominated by opposition to the South African government and apartheid. That struggle they want to keep pure. They are holding high a banner of principle. This means more to them than the living struggle of living people.' He knew the attitude well, he said; their argument was that by accepting the conditions, you accept the apartheid.

'Do the Africans who live under apartheid thereby accept it? If Africans play West Indians under apartheid conditions, do the Africans accept apartheid? Surely that is absurd. Do our boys accept it? I cannot see that at all.' He cited his experience organising a strike of sharecroppers for six months in the US. 'I was kicked around as usual, eating in kitchens when I travelled, sitting in the rear seats of buses, etc. Did I "accept" segregation? Did I help to strengthen it? The facts are that I did exactly the opposite. The sharecroppers whom I worked with had a larger objective.'

He returned to the political value of the tour. 'You want proof the tour is a brilliant political step?' He said that even before it began, it had created a stir internationally, and that was good enough for him, even if there were those who said the South African government was in favour of it. 'Are they? Put yourself in their position when they received the application. Could they say no? The whole policy is that the Africans can have all privileges, as long as they are by themselves. They therefore laid down the most stringent apartheid conditions. I haven't the slightest doubts that some of them hoped to kill the tour. They failed, at least so far. Furthermore, if they had said no, they would have created a storm of anger: you wouldn't let them play with you, you wouldn't let them play by themselves.'

He said he would be delighted to see the players compete against each other, and the headlines it would make around the world. 'Think of what it will mean to the African masses, their pride, their joy, their contact with the world outside, and their anger at this first proof, before the whole world, of the shameful suppression to which they are subjected.' Whatever the agenda of the South African government, he believed it would 'live to curse that this project was ever put forward'.

He added a postscript, saying that while he called the trip political, Worrell would probably deny it was so. 'In fact, he would be wise to do so. I go further. He may have had no such motive in mind. But it is already clear that this is a political bombshell. That is another reason why I am in favour. I want it to go on exploding and exploding. The only people who can be hurt are the South African jailers. I want them hurt and plenty. My personal belief is that they will try to stop the tour without coming out openly and saying so.'

James had spoken long and often with Worrell on cricket matters. He had written copiously on him, referring to their conversations and how impressed he had been with Worrell's intellect. While he may have discussed the matter persuasively with Worrell, the postscript of his article suggests that he was aware of Worrell's deciding rationale and was providing a strategic explanation for it by declaring that Worrell would be better off denying any political dimension to the tour. He obviously knew that Worrell saw the tour as a chance for cricketers to sell their services at a profitable rate, whatever the politics involved.

With the public debate continuing, the WICBC still remained uncertain of the circumstances. On 1 June 1959, Honorary Secretary, Kenneth Wishart had written to members, mentioning that a press release had been issued. 'In this Release, the President [John Dare] has sought to make clear this Board's position as regards this Tour, and I have also written to Frank setting out the facts and stressing that we are still to receive the letter which he claims was written to us more than six months ago.' (This may have been the personal letter to Cyril Merry.)

On 6 June, Wishart updated members on the MCC tour, writing as well, 'Incidentally, I am still to hear anything official from Frank Worrell on the South Africa tour, although I wrote him on May 19'.

An excerpt of a letter sent a month later (19 June) to all Board members from Wishart, eventually outlined Worrell's position. Worrell's actual letter could not be found.

'We have had a long letter from Frank on the South African Tour, the gist of which is that he and the other professionals are left little option but to sell their, what he terms "specialised services" in a market that desires them, and take the chance on the consequence of the Tour. He stresses that the professionals cannot obtain any routine jobs at home during the off season, and are keenly disposed to the idea of earning a little in South Africa. In this connection, Berkeley [Gaskin] says that they have been offered substantial sums, and I believe that he mentioned that Worrell's fee would be £1,000.'

He said that Frank had reminded him that he had written to Cyril Merry the year before, informing him of the tour to avoid a clash in schedules. He had indicated that he did not wish to offend the Board, and had no intention of jeopardising the chances against England, and had arranged for all players to be available.

'He says that when he spoke to Berkeley in London, he was wavering a bit afterwards, but a few days later, representatives of the South African Board produced some equally impressive arguments which made up his mind for him that he should go through with the Tour,' wrote Wishart.

The tour had been proposed for the end of the year, in between West Indies' tour of India and Pakistan, and the MCC visit which would begin immediately afterwards.

Worrell was completing his final year at Manchester University whilst these discussions were going on. He had written to the WICBC in May 1958 declining the captaincy and participation in the 1958-59 tour of India and Pakistan on account of his studies.

Edghill informed the Board members and sent them the press release he had prepared for publication. 'It is with the greatest regret that the Board have to announce that the Captain-elect for the India/Pakistan Tour, Mr. F.M. Worrell, has found it impossible to undertake the tour. Mr. Worrell, who is more than halfway through his degree course at the University of Manchester, has been advised by his Tutors that to break his studies now would seriously endanger and might even jeopardise his University career.' The tutors had also written to the Board asking that their assessment be accepted.

This had taken place before Worrell had been approached by the SACBOC officials. It appears that by the time the offer came, with its expected tour dates coming tightly squeezed between West Indies commitments, he was as concerned with his 'own future' as the WICBC declared itself to be.

He would not have played any international cricket during his period of matriculation, except for the 1957 tour in England, where he had been outstanding. He had struggled to keep as fit as he once was, and he was concerned about his capacity to earn an income that could support his lifestyle, especially as Lana was approaching the age where the level of schooling Worrell wanted for her was expected to be costly. When the offer came from South Africa in 1958, he was influenced mainly by the prospect of a profitable tour.

In *South Africa's Greatest Bowlers: Past and Present*, authors Ali Bacher (who was responsible for the 1982-83 and 1983-84 rebel tours) and David Williams, wrote that Worrell had agreed to 'a tour fee of £5000' which was to be shared by the players. Berkeley Gaskin had reported that Worrell's personal fee was £1,000.

For the purpose of comparison, the WICBC correspondence regarding payments for players for the MCC tour which was to follow immediately, offers an insight into the existing remuneration packages.

The WICBC had been debating whether it was better to offer a flat sum for each tour, or whether payments should be made on a match-by-match basis. Part of the argument had been that players misrepresented their fitness levels so that they would not miss out on games (for which they had been earning £75 each). The feeling was that it would make them less anxious and more reliable if they knew precisely what their income level would be for each tour. After much debate, the WICBC eventually decided on flat sums, but then there was further discussion over the different fees for amateurs and professionals. Consideration was also given to where players lived. In the case of the MCC tour of 1959-60, it was felt that since Worrell and Ramadhin lived in the UK, they would be paid a flat sum of £450 each.

On 24 July 1959, President John Dare asked Wishart to put out his proposed solution, 'Each professional to be paid a flat sum of £300, plus £30 per Test Match, plus £15 for the Colony Match. This, assuming each one plays in all the Tests, will give a total remuneration of £465 and you are asked to note particularly that no weekly allowances will be payable under this proposal.'

This was the range within which players were being paid. They were concerned about their capacity to earn steady incomes, and confided their anxieties to Worrell. How much of it influenced his decision to accept the offer to tour South Africa is simply speculation. The political implications would have been pressed upon him by two vociferous and influential camps.

C.L.R. James had publicly declared his desire for international exposure to be brought to South Africa's discrimination policies through whatever means. He would have communicated directly with Worrell to share his views. The SACBOC officials had also represented their case more than once, visiting Worrell in London to follow up on their letter of invitation.

Worrell had indicated that Berkeley Gaskin had caused him to waver when he spoke to him in London on the team's return voyage from Pakistan (where they had also discussed payment terms generally), but then he said he found SACBOC's arguments more compelling.

He had even sought the counsel of his older brother, Livingstone, in New York. Livingstone, a pan-Africanist, had advised that he only go if he could be guaranteed that they would play solely in integrated environments.

WICBC correspondence indicates that the South African Sports Association and the South African Congress had written to them, and presumably they had also communicated directly with Worrell. The arguments for and against were persuasive.

According to Bacher and Williams, 'The South African government did not object to the tour as long as the matches involved blacks only. The tourists were to be billeted in private homes as few quality hotels for blacks were in existence. Since they did not have any decent turf facilities, SACBOC negotiated for matches to be played at Kingsmead, Newlands and the Wanderers.'

Winch wrote that the organisers had raised £5,000 to guarantee expenses. 'Travel was to be by air, coaches and private cars, there were to be sight-seeing trips including a game reserve and, where suitable high-class hotels were not available, then the tourists would stay in private homes. SACBOC also hoped to make provision for separate seating so that whites could attend all matches.'

The requisite visas had been procured, and the itinerary had been set. It was already somewhere around July and plans were proceeding apace. Worrell, it seemed, had ordered a collection of ties, blazers, badges and bow ties. According to Tennant, he had them done in the colours used by his good friend Vic Lewis for his team. During his Radcliffe days, Worrell had met Lewis, who led a jazz band and was a cricket fan. They became friends and Worrell would play for his showbiz XI when he could.

'It was Lewis who helped to quash Worrell's plans to take a West Indian side to South Africa in 1959 at the invitation of non-white South Africans. Worrell had readily accepted, feeling it would help to break down apartheid: he had been promised matches would be arranged against multi-racial teams. He organised a scratch side, had ties made in the same colours as Lewis had for his XI – mauve, green and blue – and ordered long and short sleeve sweaters,' wrote Tennant.

There is no evidence to support the claim that Worrell changed his mind about the tour, but there is evidence that the colourful uniforms had been made. In fact, the return date for the team was set for 29 December 1959.

During the West Indies tour of South Africa in 2014, an article appeared in the online version of the *Johannesburg Mail & Guardian* on 18 December, headlined 'Why Axe fell on 1959 Cricket Tour.' Written by an unnamed staff reporter, its opening paragraph suggested how incredible the whole idea seemed over 50 years later.

'If you were to confide in a passer-by at SuperSport Park this weekend that Frank Worrell was once on the cusp of bringing a black West Indian cricket side to apartheid South Africa, they wouldn't believe you,' it said.

The author declared that proof existed in 'a framed collection of tour artefacts' hanging at the back of an insurance broker's office in Fordsburg. The artefacts were made by a Fordsburg tailor and comprised 'a tie, blazer, badge and bow tie,' the last physical remnants of the tour's existence.

The article went on to quote Mohamed Mayet, in whose company offices the objects hung. 'It was very late in the day,' he said, of the tour's cancellation. Mohamed had 'inherited the firm and its artefacts from his uncle, "Chummy" Mayet in the 1990s.' Unfortunately, as with many of the records regarding Worrell and the WICBC, his archives were lost in a flood.

It turned out that M.S. Mayet had been a businessman and sports enthusiast, who had been friendly with men such as Rashid Varachia, Bob Pavadai, W.J. Warnasuriya, and 'Checker' Jassat.

They were part of a sport association responsible for developing the Natalspruit ground which had been used primarily by the Indian community in Johannesburg. Matches on the Kenya tour of 1958 had been played there and it is easy to see the connection Mayet would have had with the 'Worrell tour' as it was commonly called.

Despite objections, there were no official attempts to stop the tour. Minutes of the meeting of the Imperial Cricket Conference (ICC) held at Lord's on 15 July 1959, indicated that the tour had come up for discussion. Under the item of Correspondence, the following was recorded: '(a) A letter from Mr. D.A. Brutus, Hon. Secretary of the South African Sports Association [one of the tour objectors] sending information regarding the nature of the work and scope of his Association was noted.'

Another letter advising of the names of the newly elected officers of the WICBC was also noted, and then the WICBC representative, B.K. Castor, 'reported that the projected tour to South Africa by Mr. F.M. Worrell was a private venture with which the West Indies Board had no connection. Mr. A.H. Coy (South Africa) reported that this tour was a private venture and unofficial as far as the South African Cricket Association was concerned.'

WICBC documents up to July show that the Board had accepted that the tour was going to happen although they continued to hope it would be called off.

Internal correspondence suggested that members had become testy with each other. Cecil Marley had written to Wishart on 30 June about the tour, referring to Wishart's letter of the 19th, and his of the 18th. Grumbling that he had already dealt with the matter, he did not see how the latest missive would change his views.

'If I know for a fact that Worrell had received the letter from the Board mentioned under the heading Minutes in my letter of the 18th instant I would come to the conclusion, without much trouble, that he was determined to carry through the tour regardless, money being the only consideration. I am quite certain that he has not been properly informed as to the conditions he will meet in South Africa or advised what to expect, and I frankly feel that no good can come from a tour of this nature,' he wrote.

He said that Worrell's reference to correspondence with Merry indicated that there had been no official Board communication, and if that were so, then the 'Board may once again find itself at the receiving end of the stick. What a difference had the letter been sent in March or early April as was the intention of the Board at the last meeting!' (The letter he referred to was sent to Worrell after the AGM and was dated 3 April.)

Cyril Merry wrote to Wishart on 13 July about Marley's letter, which had been forwarded to him by Lindsay Grant. Regarding Worrell, he noted, 'I don't quite know what all this relates to but I presume someone was to have written him and did not. I seem to remember having heard somewhere lately that an advance of £5,000 had already been made to him by the South African people and I can see the difficulty, if some of that money has already been spent, of calling off the tour at this late moment. I fear, however, that our players are going to get the shock of their lives if they go to South Africa as I understand things there are even worse than they were when I was over in 1946 – and they were bad then.'

It is not clear when the South Africa tour was cancelled; from August, the WICBC appeared to be completely focused on arrangements for the tour to India and Pakistan and then the visit of MCC, including booking travel and accommodation, and no mention of it was found in correspondence.

What seems clear is that the tour was not aborted because Worrell changed his mind about going; the pressure in South Africa became too much for the organisers, and they backed away.

Bacher and Williams wrote that '… anti-apartheid activists, including a youthful Dennis Brutus and Hassan Howa, vehemently denounced the tour because it was racially segregated. In the 1980s "Checker" Jassat, SACBOC's secretary at the time, recalled to highly respected journalist Ameen Akhalwaya how "ANC officials, Nelson Mandela and Walter Sisulu, and Indian Congress members, including Dr AB Kazi, visited us. When it became clear that they would organise demonstrators to disrupt our matches by sitting on the pitches, we decided to abandon the tour."'

175

Mandela made two significant interventions in West Indies cricket during his lifetime. The first was in his capacity as a member of the ANC, when he objected to the Worrell tour. The second came nearly 40 years later, when, as President of the Republic of South Africa, a letter bearing his signature was presented to each member of the team, asking that they reconsider the decision not to proceed with the 1998 tour of his country over a pay dispute. The team, led by Brian Lara, with Carl Hooper as vice-captain, had been at odds with Pat Rousseau's West Indies Cricket Board (the word 'Control' had been dropped from its name in 1996) over several issues, including tour fees that were reportedly as high as £35,000 each. Mandela's letter was instrumental in enabling the ill-fated tour to proceed.

Whether Worrell should have considered going to South Africa at all remains hanging over his history.

CHAPTER 21

SOUTH AFRICA – THE AFTERMATH

As international pressure against apartheid mounted, South Africa opted to become a republic on 31 May 1961, and was no longer deemed a part of the Commonwealth. Whether it could remain a part of the ICC was scheduled to be discussed at a meeting at Lord's on 19 July 1961.

The WICBC sought to establish its position beforehand. At the end of April, the Board was given a memo prepared by President John Dare, outlining his thoughts on the future Test-match status of South Africa, as a form of briefing their representatives. He doubted that anything definite would be decided and didn't think South Africa would even send representatives. But he did not think the ICC could retain SA in the Test framework, unless the rules were changed, specifically Rules 2, 3 and 5.

Rule 2 dealt with the constitution: 'The Governing Bodies of Cricket in countries within the British Commonwealth having been duly elected, shall be entitled to send not more than two representatives to a meeting of the Conference.' Rule 3 dealt with membership: 'The original members of the Conference, M.C.C., Australia and S. Africa, will be known and recognised as "Foundation Members",' it said, and, 'Membership shall be restricted to recognised Governing Bodies of countries of the British Commonwealth of which the representative teams are accepted as qualified to play official Test matches.' Rule 5 pertained to the cessation of foundation membership: 'Foundation Membership, Membership or Associated Membership of the Conference shall cease, (i) should the country concerned cease to be a part of the British Commonwealth.'

Was the present 'problem' sufficient cause for alterations? Dare did not think so. 'It might be different if there were other "break-aways" involved, threatening the Conference and representative cricket generally. It is just thoroughly unfortunate, and particularly cricket-wise, that the S. African situation has developed out of such unhappy and, to our way of thinking, unnecessary reasons.' He said that the WICBC had already communicated its position to South Africa, 'that while apartheid exists we could not send an official team to S. Africa nor could we entertain any visit from them.' He conceded that there might be a chance if their teams were allowed to become multi-racial, but thought that was unlikely. In any case there would still be the issue of South Africa being a part of the Commonwealth. 'Of course, unofficial tours could probably be continued with countries willing to do so, but they would have a much diminished popular appeal,' he ended.

Having read the President's memo, and at the request of Lindsay Grant, Gomez, Stollmeyer, and Merry met to discuss it and communicated their thoughts to Wishart on May 13.

'Unanimously, we are of the opinion that South Africa's leaving the Test-match Countries would mean the end of cricket in that Country and much as we deplore their attitude towards people of colour, we feel this would be tragic and that every possible effort should be made to ensure the continuance of cricket there,' they wrote.

Saying West Indies were in the unique position of being the only multi-racial Test-playing nation, its delegates, Jeffrey Stollmeyer and E. Scott Johnston, should urge the ICC to 'leave no possible avenue unexplored in an effort to retain South Africa amongst the cricket playing Countries of the World, if that is possible.'

They further emphasised that they did not mean the currently constituted South Africa, 'but a South Africa Board of more generous outlook towards pigmentation and we are of the opinion that our Delegates should not be hamstrung in this effort with hard and fast directives from the Board on this matter but should be given a free hand to try to get the Conference to do everything possible, even to altering the Rules, to keep cricket alive in that unhappy Country.'

Even if it seemed a naïve hope, they concluded that they would prefer not to help to kill cricket in South Africa.

At the ICC meeting, the issue was tabled as Item No. 4: South African Cricket Association (all white). The minutes provide a sense of the tenor of the discussions. (See Appendix)

At the end, South Africa was not re-admitted to the ICC. The voting was split with West Indies, India and Pakistan voting for exclusion, and England, Australia and New Zealand voting that their scheduled matches should not be cancelled. *Wisden* reported that at the Imperial Cricket Conference at Lord's in July 1962, 'it was agreed there was nothing to prevent matches played by South Africa being called Tests, though these were not recognised as official by the Conference.' New Zealand had just played five matches against them and these had been sanctioned as Tests.

Southern Africa was still accepting cricketers who would abide by its government's policy.

Gerry Gomez said they had no objection to playing in southern Africa at that time. The team, wrote Winch, had been invited to Rhodesia in 1960-61 after the Australia tour (where Gomez was manager), but some of the team had other commitments. 'Otherwise,' said Gomez, 'we would certainly have gone.'

'With the Southern Rhodesian Government publicising the racial character of its sport, a cricket journalist, Ron Roberts, seized the opportunity to arrange a tour in February-March 1962. He selected a star-studded team that included two West Indian players who had earlier hoped to visit South Africa – Everton Weekes and Sonny Ramadhin – as well as Basil D'Oliveira and leading cricketers from India, Pakistan, Australia and England. It was the first time black cricketers had been allowed to play first-class cricket in southern Africa,' wrote Winch.

He noted that they were denied permission to use the facilities at Queens Sports Club in Bulawayo, and so they played at the Showground. The Commonwealth XI beat Rhodesia by six wickets. 'On his thirty-seventh birthday, Everton Weekes won the game "with a glorious straight drive off [Joe] Partridge for four". Splashed across the sports page of the *Bulawayo Chronicle* was the headline, "BIRTHDAY BOY A WINNER",' with the newspaper recording that 'one had the unique sight of seeing a former West Indian star walk straight across to former South African opening bat Tony Pithey and shake hands on the field,' wrote Winch.

However, he said, the front page the following day told a different tale. 'Weekes was refused a drink at the Midlands Hotel, Gwelo, on his way to the tour party's fixture at Que Que. It was mistakenly thought that he was a "freedom sitter". According to Roberts in a letter to his friend, E.W. Swanton, there were a 'few incidents of Europeans refusing to serve our non-Europeans – Ramadhin a hair-cut, Weekes a drink – but these little set-backs have been accepted philosophically.'

Winch reported that a second tour had also been arranged by Roberts, this one including West Indian players Wes Hall, Rohan

Kanhai and Chester Watson, alongside D'Oliveira and players from India, Pakistan, England and South Africa. 'With reference to the latter trip, D'Oliveira said that Kanhai was upset by incidents and wanted to fly home, but "by this time, it was getting laughable, so Rohan decided to see the funny side of it and called off his decision."'

Is there a comparison to be made between Worrell's cancelled tour of 1959 and the 1980s rebel tours of South Africa that resulted in lifetime bans for the West Indian players who had consented to being 'honorary whites' for the duration of their stay?

While there are striking similarities in the arguments surrounding both the 1959 tour and the rebel tours nearly 25 years later, there are also distinctions.

In June 1977, Commonwealth heads of government met in Scotland and took a position on sporting contact with South Africa, which came to be known as the Gleneagles Agreement. Its statement declared that member countries 'have long recognised racial prejudice and discrimination as a dangerous sickness and an unmitigated evil,' and that 'they accepted it as the urgent duty of each of their Governments vigorously to combat the evil of apartheid by withholding any form of support for, and by taking every practical step to discourage contact or competition by their nationals with sporting organisations, teams or sportsmen from South Africa or from any other country where sports are organised on the basis of race, colour or ethnic origin.'

In Worrell's time, although Jamaica had activated a trade embargo on South Africa in 1957, there was no official policy on relations with the state of apartheid.

In 1970, the ICC finally banned South Africa from international cricket and for more than two decades their players were isolated. In the early 1980s, the two heads of the South Africa Cricket Union, CEO Ali Bacher and President Joe Pamensky, devised a strategy to revive the country's fortunes by paying large sums to cricketers from outside to play within the banned nation.

First English players, then Sri Lankans went, earning money but also bans – three years for the former, 25 for the latter – for defying the international code. In 1983, West Indians were approached and 18 of them, led by Lawrence Rowe, made two visits to the country, earning lifetime bans in the process. The English penalty seemed more of a mild reprimand. Indeed, Graham Gooch, one of the players, later returned as captain of the England team and even led a tour of the West Indies in the 1989-90 season.

Unlike the offer to Worrell in 1959, the approaches were made under extraordinarily secret conditions, and players were under no illusion that this was an enterprise that would be widely excoriated. Preparations were made under subterfuge, decoys were employed to throw journalists off the scent, denials and lies hung like a shameful shroud as cricketers departed their homelands. There were no dilemmas of conscience.

Those rebel tours have been the subject of several debates; many of the participants have aired their rationales. And one of the common reasons is that they felt that they would be helping the cause of black and coloured players in South Africa by allowing them to benchmark themselves against international players who looked like them.

It was the same perspective that C.L.R. James had brought up in encouraging Worrell to go. Although apartheid was officially dismantled in South Africa in the 1990s, there is no substantial evidence to link these visits in the Eighties to the end of an inevitably doomed policy. Additionally, the lives of every one of the West Indian players, and the other 'rebels,' were severely damaged by their visits.

At varying levels, they defended their choices on the ground of earning a livelihood – they had no guaranteed income or future from West Indies cricket, and the money was enough to allow them to look after their families. It came down to seeing themselves with only their cricketing services to offer commercially in a world whose political state was of no concern to them as they struggled to make ends meet.

It is an echo of the case Worrell had made when he said that he and the other professionals had little option but to sell their specialised services to a market that wanted them, even if they had to face the consequences.

In the end, the decision to tour was taken out of Worrell's hands, but had it not been, would he and his band have shared the fate of the rebels of nearly 25 years later?

CHAPTER 22

1957-60

END OF THE THREE Ws

Several events during this period would have profound effects on the Three Ws in their careers and in their personal relationships.

Worrell may have been influenced to keep his distance after the vice-captaincy discord during the 1954-55 Australia visit. He would have undoubtedly known what had taken place behind the WICBC's closed doors (and the open cable offices). As the Board planned for the tour to England in 1957, members met to select the captain. After much debate about the two prospects – Allan Rae (who was a director of the WICBC then) and John Goddard (Test player) – Sir Errol threw his weight behind Goddard, though he thought he had been 'soured' after his previous captaincy experience. Goddard was chosen by a majority vote, under Sir Errol's influence. Stollmeyer, who thought he was the incumbent, had envisioned leading on that tour as his final ambition. At the inter-colonial tournament in BG, he learned from Cecil de Caires that Sir Errol had gone to Barbados to ask Goddard to return. He was stunned. 'Cecil, I have played my last first-class match,' he said.

That evening at the airport in Trinidad, Stollmeyer told a reporter that he was retiring from first-class cricket as he considered himself too prone to injury. He would be turning his attention to the family business. That was the end of his playing days, but he later became President of the WICBC from 1974 to 1981.

At the same Board meeting, a stalemate ensued over the selection of a manager. To bypass it, Tom Peirce and Cecil de Caires were jointly chosen, with equal status but clearly demarcated areas of responsibility. Many, including Worrell, would say that the tour failed as early as on the voyage to England because appointing two managers was a mistake, and the administrative arrangements were poor.

In 1956, Worrell had written to the Board saying he was trying to fit three terms' work into two so he could be free for the tour. He had expected to be named vice-captain, but was not chosen. Instead, on the voyage to England, Walcott was announced as Goddard's second in command.

The question of the vice-captaincy had also become a contentious one at Board level. Minutes of a meeting held in February 1957 (at which seven members were present) show that it was agreed to accept the selection committee's proposal that no vice-captain be appointed and that the Tour Control Committee 'should be given the responsibility of appointing a captain for each game in which John Goddard would not be playing.'

Later, at the October AGM, the official post-mortem got underway. Edgar Marsden asked whether Walcott had put 'pressure' on the Tour Committee, as his appointment was 'entirely contrary to a firm decision taken by the Board.' Peirce explained that there was uncertainty among the players, and they felt, as Goddard did, that it was best to announce Walcott as vice-captain to the press, and that although it had turned out 'most unfortunately' it was done in good faith.

The two managers presented separate reports because 'they did not agree on certain aspects' of the tour, particularly regarding a press statement by de Caires that neither Weekes nor Walcott was fit nor had they made any attempt to get fit.

Pace bowler Roy Gilchrist's 'violent temper' had come up, and the managers disagreed on the question of whether Weekes had provoked him too much. De Caires thought that Weekes should have known better, especially when he saw that his 'teasing' had provoked more than one player to the point of tears. He believed that his behaviour 'made for disharmony' within the team.

De Caires said that additionally Weekes and Walcott avoided the nets, and that Goddard agreed with him that they showed 'definite reluctance' to train. Peirce disagreed. Walcott had been in good form, but after he was injured, he 'developed a complex'. Weekes had not found his form and this upset him, but he was also suffering from 'double vision' caused by his sinusitis.

De Caires persisted, saying their attitude was 'most disappointing, the more so when compared with the wonderful team work of Worrell'.

The discussion went on to Walcott's 'attitude' towards his teammates. Here, the tour managers found something to agree on in his unexpected behaviour: 'He had indeed earned the sobriquet of Colonel Nasser and that even Frank Worrell had been displeased.'

This was a few months after the Suez crisis. In July 1956, Egyptian President Gamal Abdel Nasser had nationalised the Suez Canal, prompting an invasion first by Israel, then the UK and France. By November, the three invaders retreated, after political pressure from the US, the Soviet Union and the UN. Nasser's name had come to be associated with despotic traits.

None of the Three Ws ever publicly confirmed the flying rumours that the selection of Walcott as vice-captain had upset Worrell, or that he was displeased by Walcott's reportedly high-handed conduct.

Sir Garfield Sobers refers to the discord in his autobiography, saying that while Walcott was a selector, Worrell was asked to be an observer. 'He told me that he used to observe, they would pick the team and then talk to Frank, with Clyde reminding him that he was not to pick the team, only to offer advice.'

Worrell resented this. In one instance, where a choice had to be made between Andy Ganteaume and Nyron Asgarali, Worrell opted for Asgarali, 'but he knew damn well he was wrong and did it deliberately,' said Sobers. 'His justification was that he was not to tell them whom to select, only to advise.' It is a reminder of how Worrell had responded to Goddard's snub in Australia, when he decided to withhold his advice.

Walcott had written that his leg injury had damaged his confidence, but denied that he was negligent about his fitness and training, and blamed the press for 'wildly fantastic' stories that suggested rifts among team members.

He and Weekes laughed, he said, at the story that Everton had asked him, 'Since when have you been a world-beater?' He dismissed the 'rumour' that Collie Smith and Denis Atkinson had fought and that was why Atkinson had hurt his neck. He scoffed at the story that the only reason Goddard had played in all the Tests was that Worrell had refused to play under his (Walcott's) captaincy. 'It was certainly news to me,' he wrote. He was 'not sure' what the writer meant when he said the Leeds Test was lost because of his lack of support for Goddard. In each of these protestations he raises, but does not directly deny, any of the allegations. Even as he praises Worrell for preserving 'our cricket reputation,' he points out that he had examinations early in the tour and was studying for them and was 'perhaps something less than his usual energetic self.'

Yet Worrell managed a feat of pure stamina in the third Test at Trent Bridge. After bowling 21 overs and fielding during England's first innings of 619 for six declared, he then batted through the innings for a score of 191 not out, before West Indies were asked to follow on. Within minutes of walking into the pavilion, he had returned to open the batting once more. *Wisden* described his 20.5 hours on the field as 'probably the longest time any cricketer has endured.' While it has been one of his most celebrated innings, he never expressed anything but contempt for it as a batting accomplishment.

He wrote that it was proof of how 'valueless to cricket statistics are.' He criticised the superlatives it had invoked as his 'best-ever' innings. To him it had no right to go down in history as a fine performance. 'How can you describe a knock of 191 by an experienced batsman as a good innings at Trent Bridge? You can only play a good innings when conditions are fair for both sides, and conditions are not fair for both sides at Trent Bridge.'

There is a vehemence in the manner he describes this innings that earned him so much acclaim. Writing that he was not proud of it at all, he said it was boring and unsatisfying because he did not have to fight for the runs. It was simply a defensive battle, fought to achieve a draw.

He presses forward his analysis and immediately one can see this is not polite modesty. This had been the crux of his cricket: passion instead of plodding. It exasperated him that his essence had not been recognised; that the acclaim negated his quest. Worse, it was an affirmation by commentators of the stance of Peter May and Colin Cowdrey in the first Test at Edgbaston when they played with their pads to negate and psychologically demolish Sonny Ramadhin. BBC radio commentator, Rex Alston, would say, 'The marathon Cowdrey-May partnership was not easy to commentate on. There are only so many ways of describing exactly the same shot or delivery. Keeping the dialogue fresh was a great challenge.'

Worrell's tirade was not a self-effacing response to praise; this was a snarl at the mediocre. He protested the comments made by 'colleagues,' who said he must have been tired when he got out early in his second innings. He said he had never felt tired during the long first innings, and although only minutes separated the two, tiredness was not the deciding factor.

'They said that I played like a man mentally tired and that I played my shot in a lethargic manner when I got out. My only reply is that I didn't feel tired, either mentally or physically, and the ball from Brian Statham was a beautiful one, coming back at me appreciably.'

He seemed to have been very stung by the comments, and insisted that Statham's ball would have got him out even in the first innings. It is very likely that the stinging comments had come from Walcott.

Defeat at Nottingham put West Indies 2-0 down, and there was no way back. They had begun the series in the ascendancy, bowling England out for 186 on the opening day at Edgbaston (Ramadhin seven for 49), then establishing a first-innings lead of 288. Worrell hit 81 and shared a sixth-wicket partnership of 190 with Collie Smith. But May and Cowdrey's fourth-wicket stand of 411 in England's second innings, during which they nullified Ramadhin by thrusting their pads at almost every delivery, turned the match around. With Worrell off the field and unable to bowl, the West Indies attack was underpowered and Ramadhin was kept on for an extraordinary 98 overs, still a Test record. On the final day, West Indies were reduced to 72 for seven and briefly seemed set to lose a match they had dominated for three days.

At Lord's there were no doubts. After winning the toss, West Indies were hustled out for 127 and the match was done and dusted in three days, England winning by an innings and 36 runs. There was another humiliation at Headingley, England strolling to an innings and five-run victory.

By the time West Indies returned to London for the final Test at The Oval, West Indies were ravaged by injuries and cut a demoralised and dispirited sight. They duly suffered a third innings defeat of the summer.

Cricket Punch, which was mostly devoted to this tour, was published in 1959, a year after Walcott's *Island Cricketers*. Worrell would have read it, and although he does not comment on any of the internal strife that was being reported, he devoted just over four pages to a chapter called 'The Three W's.' Here, he writes that they had known each other from youth and offered personality portraits that were brief but typically incisive. He described them both as light-hearted lovers of fun and jokes, and praised their superb sense of timing and their powerful hitting. Whereas he restricted himself to these categories in describing Walcott, he acknowledged that Weekes could be blunt, 'the frankest of men' who never refused to say what he thought. But, he contended, those were the qualities that made him a fine friend.

'If you have Everton Weekes as a friend you have a true pal who will stick by you and defend you through each and every crisis.' He did not refer to any such friendship in describing Walcott, who, remember, had later said he was not a pall bearer at Worrell's funeral because, 'I was not asked.'

Michael Walcott, Clyde's elder son, said that when the three played together they were very close, but as they got older, there was a rift that 'developed because of jealousy' after they stopped playing.

Yet, he had found a letter from Worrell to Walcott, asking him to join him in Australia at the end of 1960 as vice-captain. He said his impression was that his father refused because of work commitments 'and it was important for him to look after the welfare of his family at that point because he had already retired.' Although he was still playing local and regional cricket, 'his focus was not on the cricket.' He believed there was still a connection between them. 'Obviously Frank would not have written him in such a personal way about doing something like that if there wasn't.'

Michael had also observed the widening gap between his father and Weekes, who had once been regular visitors to each other's homes. From the 1970s, with the Walcott family back in Barbados, 'I'd never seen Everton visit the house or anything like that, or my dad going to his house. That seemed to have stopped.'

He didn't know why, because older people wouldn't talk about those things. 'There was some animosity that I know about. Lil bit of jealousy as well, but I think all of those things are normal in life, you know? Because one person may be doing better than the other or getting through this way and the other gets jealous. But I think the most important thing in their relationship is how they got on while they were playing, and I think that while they were playing they were very close.'

Whether or not they acknowledged it – in his final years, Weekes conceded that things had not been particularly warm between them because there may have been some jealousy – it is clear that the bond that had been formed from the Forties, had been fractured.

On the outside, other forces were unwittingly coalescing to break it all apart. Recriminations after the England tour aside, at the same extraordinary general meeting, the Board turned to the imminent tour by Pakistan and the following one to India and Pakistan.

The WICBC had offered the captaincy to Worrell for both tours. The minutes showed the Selection Committee's recommendation that 'every effort be made to secure the services of Frank Worrell as Captain.'

'It was decided to cable Worrell indicating to him that the Board considered his captaincy of the West Indies against Pakistan to be of paramount importance to the cause of W.I. cricket, provided that his presence in 1957/58 would not preclude his making the Tour to India in 1958/59.' Should Worrell respond negatively, they decided they would ask Franz (Gerry) Alexander to lead the team.

Worrell declined, explaining that he needed to focus on his studies at Manchester. Sir Errol accepted that the WICBC should not do anything to affect Worrell's career. Merry lamented that it would take more than one person to replace him. 'He was on the Team as so many things; possible opening bowler; possible opening bat; middle-of-the-order batsman and sheet anchor...'

He also mentioned that there was 'some talk of asking Clyde to re-consider his decision to retire if Frank did not go,' but he did not think it was prudent to ask him to come back for one tour. He recommended that no vice-captain be named if Worrell was not there, and the position should be rotated if necessary to give selectors a chance to assess candidates.

At the October 1957 meeting, they decided to inform Walcott that he would revert to amateur status because of his employment in British Guiana. There had been protracted discussions about whether the nature of Walcott's employment with the British Guiana Sugar Producers' Association qualified him to earn the higher fees that professionals commanded. He and his employers had been asked to submit a range of documents defining his work, and had done so. But coming after the accusations over his fitness in England, and with his employers showing every intention of investing in his development – they had paid for him to stay on in England to do courses with the Industrial Welfare Society – he was reconsidering his role as a West Indian cricketer.

Walcott had approached the Secretary, Clarence Edghill, in January 1958 to discuss his amateur status, especially as he felt it would affect his income. He had been writing articles for the press and appearing in commercials, in addition to his work with the Sugar Producers' Association. He was most concerned, he said, about the timing of any announcement, coming as it did with the statements in the press about him and Weekes.

Edghill reported to the Board that Walcott had 'admitted that the team members had thought that his appointment as Vice-Captain had gone to his head,' but he was surprised by this as he was 'never conscious of acting in a dictatorial manner.' He told Edghill about an incident on the ship when Valentine had made a 'quip' to which he responded, 'you should know I can send you home,' but said it was done in a jocular fashion and he was sure Valentine understood this, and perhaps other members did not.

Edghill indicated to him that discussions about his amateur status had taken place before the tour and had no bearing on the decision, but agreed to place his point of view before the Board. It was not enough. Walcott declared that he was retiring from West Indies cricket after the home series against Pakistan in March 1958.

Meanwhile, Weekes had responded differently to the allegation that he had been unfit and unwilling to train and that he had displayed public disaffection with the WICBC. He had been advised to take legal action against the WICBC. Things had become 'too ridiculous' for him to continue and, as Walcott left the stage, he played his final Test match against Pakistan.

Worrell's relationship with the WICBC had become more mutually respectful, and his opinion was sought on several matters regarding players; often he was asked to liaise with them to arrange terms and conditions. He was now highly regarded as a senior player whose knowledge of the players was intimate, and whose understanding of the game was unsurpassed. Whatever the term used then, he was recognised as someone with the kind of emotional intelligence required in the face of adversity.

In the wee hours of 7 September 1959, the talented Jamaican cricketer, O'Neil 'Collie' Smith was involved in a car accident in Staffordshire that claimed his life. The 26-year-old was on his way to a charity match with Tom Dewdney and Sobers, who was driving.

Just before five o' clock, the car ran into a truck, and Smith, asleep in the back, was thrown forward, damaging his spine. He went into a coma and died on 9 September. Sobers was found guilty of careless driving, his licence was suspended for a month and he was fined.

Sobers was devastated, and trying to numb the pain, he turned to alcohol. Soon he was drinking heavily, abandoning everything as he wallowed in depression. He began spending his days at the tracks, gambling, and his nights wrapped in the careless arms of booze. He was only 23, and the guilt and desolation consumed him. After Smith's death, the WICBC cabled Worrell, asking him to help Sobers deal with the tragedy. Although they had sent official condolences, they knew that Worrell could provide the compassion and support Sobers needed in his despondent hours. Lindsay Grant told his fellow directors, 'It is now up to all of us to do our bit to help this youngster to overcome the terrible shock and aftermath'. Sobers would later say that, from then, he felt he had to play for his friend as well: it was the only way he could think to pay tribute to Collie, and the only way he could motivate himself to keep going.

Smith died just a couple of months before the West Indies players were due to gather in the Caribbean for the home series against MCC. With the proposed tour to South Africa cancelled, Worrell was asked to sort out the logistical arrangements with players based in England: Ramadhin, Valentine and Sobers.

Gerry Alexander was to be the captain for the series. He had been captain for the previous two Test series – when Pakistan had visited the Caribbean and immediately after when West Indies had toured India and Pakistan – because Worrell had said he was not available. There had been widespread criticism of Alexander's selection, seen as a continuance of the white leadership policy, especially because Walcott and Weekes were not considered.

It had not helped that he had been held responsible for the termination of Roy Gilchrist's Test career. Gilchrist had been sent home by Alexander during the tour of India for aggressive behaviour. Alexander was reported to have been arrogant and high-handed in his treatment of Gilchrist and had summarily decided to send him packing. Two elements of that story have not been sufficiently examined and explained. One is that the decision to send him home arose after considerable discussions between the team and the committee on the scene. The second is that Gilchrist was not automatically expelled from West Indies cricket. The WICBC correspondence for the period shows intense and prolonged debates, including efforts to seek psychological counselling for him, and that Worrell was asked for his views on more than one occasion. The evidence is that Alexander was not the reason Gilchrist's Test career ended.

However, Alexander's choice for the MCC tour, despite Worrell's availability, stirred already inflamed passions and triggered a prolonged campaign by C.L.R. James. 'Alexander must go,' was one of his headlines in the *Nation* newspaper. While he made the legitimate point that Worrell was best suited for the position, his rapier thrusts demonised Alexander in a way that was unfair to Alexander's skills and character. Later, James would admit that he admired Alexander but was determined to make his point that Worrell was being discriminated against, whatever it took.

'I put my scruples aside and I think that for the first, and I hope the last, time in reporting cricket I was not fair,' he wrote in *Beyond a Boundary*. Alexander was not as eager for the position as Denis Atkinson had been in his time. He too was aware that Worrell was best suited; he respected him, and was happy to serve as his vice-captain for the following tour to Australia. He had written to the Board saying that he was not comfortable with the idea of being captain of a team when Worrell was the obvious leader.

The minutes of the WICBC's AGM on 16 and 17 March 1960 in British Guiana, recorded the captaincy vote for the 1960-61 tour of Australia. 'Mr. Gaskin reported that the Selection Committee of the Board recommended the appointment of Mr. F.M. Worrell and this was unanimously confirmed on the motion of Mr. Peirce, seconded by Mr. Grant.

'It was also agreed to record the fact that Mr. Alexander had expressed the desire to be relieved of the captaincy in view of his responsibilities as wicket-keeper and the availability of Mr. Worrell.

'Discussion then followed as to what publicity, if any, should be given to the request made by Mr. Alexander, some members feeling that it was desirable to make it public on account of the campaign carried on against him in a section of the Trinidad press. It was finally decided that a bare statement announcing the appointment of Mr. Worrell would be made.'

In his book, *Calypso Summer*, Mike Coward reported that Alexander said, 'I had always felt I was only a stand-in for Frank until his studies were completed at Manchester University. Who was I have to an altercation with Frank? I was tremendously delighted when he was finally appointed captain. I thought the great injustice of my appointment against Pakistan in 1957-58 was not primarily to Frank Worrell but to Clyde Walcott and Everton Weekes. When I was made captain Clyde and Everton came to me and said there was a fine set of youngsters who wished to play under me, because they would never let the public say that because Gerry Alexander was captain of the West Indies team they didn't wish to play. They also said, "Let me tell you, at the end of the Pakistan tour, we will retire." And in fact they did.'

In light of the fact that Worrell had been asked to serve as captain before, it is puzzling that the Board had turned to Alexander for the visit of England – even if one attributed it to discrimination. Ivo Tennant said that Alexander had surmised that the Board may have wanted to publicly endorse his previous success and his handling of Roy Gilchrist, a touchy affair. That Alexander accepted the captaincy is equally perplexing. He had no driving ambition in the realm of cricket, or captaincy. His interest lay in pursuing his profession as a veterinarian, for which he had studied at Cambridge. It is possible that some external pressure pushed him to accept the position. Although the first West Indian Test captain was Karl Nunes, a Jamaican, and George Headley had captained one match in 1948, no other Jamaican had been asked to lead West Indies since – that had been the province of Barbadians and Trinidadians. Was he persuaded to accept to keep the Jamaican flag flying?

Worrell, for his part, did not seem to have any disdain for Alexander, rather he held him in high esteem, and he was also looking forward to the chance to finally play in a Test series now that his arduous university days were behind him.

He had contacted the WICBC, telling them that he wanted to fly out of the UK earlier than scheduled to go directly to Jamaica for personal reasons. The Board agreed to pay the additional cost, calculating that it would be balanced out by them not having to pay hotel expenses for him as he would be staying at the home of his 'godfather,' Ruel Vaz.

However, Gerry Gomez and Lindsay Grant speculated that he would possibly arrive in a physically unfit state. John Goddard said he would take charge of ensuring that Worrell and Ramadhin had physical training. On 30 October, Grant wrote, 'I understand, that of the Three Ws, Frank was the one who was fittest in England in 1957, and I believe he will react favourably to gentle persuasion, but we must make sure that he does.'

On 4 December, Grant wrote to Wishart with some relief. 'I am glad to report that he has arrived and I understand that he looks extremely fit and well and I gather that the reason for this is that he has been playing quite a bit of soccer.'

It turned out to be yet another eventful series. The three top run-scorers for West Indies were Sobers, Kanhai and Worrell. Sobers had started off in Barbados with 226, then 147 in Kingston, 145 in BG and 92 in Port of Spain. He was indeed playing for two.

Worrell played in four of the matches, with his highest score being 197 not out in the first Test in Barbados, where he established a record fourth-wicket partnership with Sobers. He ended the fifth day of the six not out on 177 and, according to Tennant, he batted and boozed from Saturday to Monday and was in a 'stupor' that Tuesday morning. 'He managed only 20 runs in two hours ten minutes,' and so Alexander declared the innings with him three short of his double century. It had been his first Test century at Kensington, in front of the crowd that had cheered him the day before. His extreme alcoholic intake was perhaps a sign of the demons he still battled when on home ground. It was exacerbated when he was booed by spectators. Even with six days allotted there was never any prospect of a result; just 42 overs of England's second innings had been bowled when time ran out.

The following day, nine members of the team travelled to Port of Spain for the second Test, Worrell arrived on the Friday, and Sobers and Hall on the Sunday.

The *Trinidad Guardian* of Thursday 4 January 1960, carried several comments and reports on the drawn first Test.

Brunell Jones rose to Worrell's defence. 'Here they go again putting Frank Worrell on the West Indies cricket whipping post. Happily for Worrell, he must by now have become accustomed to being blamed for anything that goes wrong with the West Indies team.'

Cricket reporter, Gordon Punch, noted that Gerry Alexander defended Worrell, saying that Peter May's bowlers were not giving anything away, and that Worrell got most of his runs in front of the wicket and 'was by no means a slugger, which meant it was far more difficult for him to get the ball through the tight field.'

But when the chartered plane carrying the nine players arrived in Trinidad, Punch noted that 'not one cricket official was on hand' to welcome them. When the English players arrived two hours later, 'not only was the crowd much thicker; but there were West Indies and Trinidad cricket officials on hand to greet them.' He commented that the English 'looked none the worst after their experiences in the sun during the 14 hours the West Indies batted on the Kensington wicket.'

The paper's sports editor was less inclined to be charitable. The hero had fallen from grace on the final day, he said, comparing it with the 'mysteries of a Fu-Manchu serial.' Wondering why Worrell had not been asked to explain, he speculated whether he was tired, whether he wanted to grind the English into the turf, whether he was afraid of reaching 200, or whether the bowling had indeed restricted him. 'Only Worrell knows the answer it seems,' he concluded, vowing to ask him if he got half a chance.

The English press were also critical, with the *Daily Mail* saying his tactics, 'make a mockery of cricket.'

Tennant's observation was confirmed by Sobers.

'I remember we were staying at the Marine Hotel in those days, and we were batting and Frank would get in around three o'clock in the morning, or four and I would sit and wait for him. And we would go by the bar and have a drink and then go and lie down on the bed and then he and I put on 411 runs together. If I got in before him I would wait for him, if he got in before me he would wait for me. I remember when I got 226 and he got 197 and people were saying he was stalling because Gerry Alexander was captain and he wanted to be captain, and he's doing this as a revenge, and it wasn't that. Frank, when he came in he said to me, I am so bleddy [bloody] tired if they had let me bat for another hour, I still wouldn't a got those three runs,' said Sobers.

Letters to the editor, appearing in the *Trinidad Guardian* of 24 January, just four days before the second Test, suggest that public mood was divided. This was the environment Worrell endured in those intervening weeks.

One writer, Rousseau Anatole, praised him and said the response of the English press was reminiscent of the 1953-54 tour. 'That these writers should have turned their invectives on Frankie Worrell after a heroic performance by this illustrious batsman is as amusing as it is preposterous. Their actions can be termed nothing else than "Colonialism in Cricket,"' he said.

Another writer, identifying himself as 'No Ball', demanded that Worrell be dropped. 'His disgraceful batting on the 5th and 6th days of the first Test was, in my opinion, a perfect example of selfishness, lack of discipline, disloyalty to his team and disobedience to his captain. It makes him unfit for selection to the team again, let alone captain, it seems to me.'

Walcott, who was still in British Guiana representing the colony, and still seething over the slights he had felt at the hands of the Board, would come out of retirement for the final two Tests – in BG and Trinidad. The WICBC offered him £50 per match. He scored nine in BG (WI batted only once), and 53 and 22 in the final. They would be his last Tests for West Indies.

England had seized the advantage in Trinidad, winning by 256 runs (Worrell nine and nought), and the remaining three matches were all drawn. With Walcott and Weekes gone, there would no longer be the Three Ws who had excited the cricket world for ten years. Each would continue to play major roles in the development of the game, but from different corners of the field.

PART FOUR

CHAPTER 23

THE CROSSING

'You like that shot? Keep playing it then.'

How on earth could the sarcasm be missed? Yet Garfield Sobers considered it evidence of Frank Worrell's diplomacy.

'He won't tell you to cut it out. He'd say, if you like that shot, keep playing it. You getting out with it, but you don't want to stop playing it. Keep playing it! See how far it will get you. He'd never say don't play that stupid shot. He'd find a way to tell you without offending you.'

It is a measure of the harshness usually directed at players for thoughtless swipes. There was no holding back. Language was coarse and scorching, like a fiery pepper sauce, and they would not care who overheard the expletives. 'But he would find something else to say which he thought would not offend them. It's not what you say, it's how you say it,' recalled Sobers with a wry smile after his bout of laughter.

Although he could be sharp, Worrell was not an autocrat, said Ainsworth Harewood, who captained the University team at Mona when Worrell was there. 'He would give you gentle suggestions. He had a way of getting across his point by using anecdotes. He talked about what some fellow did and did not do and how he fared and so forth. And you had to be a fool not to realise that what he is telling you is you have to change your approach,' he said. 'But he never dictated to you.'

By the time he graduated from Manchester in 1959, Worrell's knowledge of human interactions had grown in a more formal sense. He had often said that he had been most interested in social anthropology (where he had his highest marks) and sociology, out of all the courses he took. Those were subjects exploring the human condition, cultural differences and trying to fathom behaviours.

He had nurtured and mentored peers from as far back as the 1940s when he had tried to persuade Weekes to leave Barbados. On several occasions in interviews about him, people said that even if they had just met, he made them feel that he was completely focused on their words, and that everyone else could wait; so attentively did he listen.

It calls to mind a profile of the former US President, Bill Clinton, by Gabriel García Márquez, who had evidently fallen under his spell. Clinton's 'sharp intelligence' made you feel you could talk to him about anything, and he had 'the seductive power' of making you feel, 'from the first moment of meeting, that he is someone you know well.' Márquez said that one of Clinton's detractors had told him that Clinton used those gifts 'to make you feel that nothing could interest him more than what you are saying to him.' Clinton was a masterful politician; Worrell was no less savvy about how to weave his magic on those around him.

That 'gift' had been sharpened by his university training which served to deepen insights into his colleagues. He was genuinely intrigued by the lives of others, the core of his noted empathy.

His easy manner was still evident, but he was firmer now about training, fitness and discipline – an iron fist in a velvet glove. Wes Hall said that in Australia, Worrell told them 'no longer must you go out to practise with a laissez-faire attitude, you must train with the same intensity as if it were a game,' and he insisted on it.

Jamaican academic, John Figueroa, noted that Worrell was 'much more of a disciplinarian' as captain. At a reception at Sabina Park, Worrell had described a situation with a member of the team in Australia.

'Frank felt that this player was not treating practice in a sensible and serious fashion. Moreover, he was sapping the confidence of one of the bowlers by simply hitting him all over the place. Frank had a quiet word with the gentleman in question, suggesting that a run around the track would be better exercise if it were merely exercise that he required. The indiscriminate hitting continued: the player was removed from the nets.' He was firm but fair, he thought. Worrell invited Figueroa to the West Indies dressing room at Birmingham in 1963 and during lunch, 'Frank prepared [Wes] Hall for the fact that he was not going to get the new ball when it became due soon after. The captain had decided that Sobers should have it but he did not wait until all were on the field simply to throw the ball to Sobers, leaving Hall disappointed. He very subtly warned Hall.'

Such emotional intelligence was rare then, and Worrell was exceptional in the way he was able to coax the best out of talented alpha males. Tom Graveney had observed that Frank might not have been tactically brilliant. 'He was sound without being superb, but he is the one [West Indies] captain I have seen who could get the other ten players pulling and working in the same direction with one common aim – victory.'

C.L.R. James said he 'was amazed to find that his main judgment of an individual player was whether he was a good team-man or not. It seemed that he worked on the principle that if a man was a good team-man it brought the best out of him as an individual player.'

In Worrell's obituary, James wrote that he seemed poised to apply his powers to bring about unity and self-realisation for West Indians. 'Not a man whom one slapped on the shoulder, he was nevertheless to the West Indian population an authentic national hero.' James enrobed him in the mantle of leadership, saying that he had 'shown the West Indian mastery of what Western civilization had to teach.' Yet James was defaulting to the code he had learned growing up, positioning Worrell within the context of a superior Western civilization, even as he hailed his 'audacity of perspective'.

Worrell had never been one for raucous displays in public; he stood outside the boisterous circle of his teammates. More reserved than aloof as captain, he adopted an avuncular role. It would not have been difficult. On the team that toured Australia under his captaincy, nearly all of the players were from a later generation. Apart from vice-captain, Gerry Alexander, who was born in 1928, and Joe Solomon, Sonny Ramadhin and Alf Valentine, born in 1930, the others could hardly be his buddies. They would have been teenagers when he was already an international star. It must have been overwhelming to find themselves in such proximity to a childhood hero. They were ready to do his every bidding, even off the field.

Alexander felt that Frank 'enjoyed the full and absolute confidence of everyone in the side. If Frank said move to your right you simply asked how far to the right.' The team trusted his judgements and believed that whatever he did was in their best interests. 'This was a remarkable support to feel on the field,' he said.

Wes Hall recalled how Worrell took charge of his career by proposing a ten-year plan. 'I did not understand what this man was doing,' he said, 'but I was delighted.' Young, hyperactive, and totally inexperienced, he was simply drifting along. Before the Australia tour, he had given up his job at Cable & Wireless to turn professional at Accrington CC in the Lancashire League. Afterwards, Frank told him he should spend another two years there. He then advised him to go to Australia to play in the Sheffield Shield as no West Indians had yet participated in that competition. Rohan Kanhai was going to play for Western Australia and Garfield Sobers for South Australia – on Worrell's advice. Hall played from 1961 to 1963, competing in 16 matches for Queensland. He was contracted to also carry out coaching clinics for children throughout the State, while he worked in the public relations department of the oil company, Esso.

Brisbane, capital of Queensland, had been the venue of the famous tied Test, and Hall was a celebrity everywhere he went. He was enjoying himself while learning about different pitch conditions and how to modify his bowling to suit them. Then Worrell told him that he didn't want him to return to Queensland; it was time to go to Jamaica. 'You've proven that you guys can work internationally, but people have to start giving you a job down here.' So he went to Jamaica and did the coaching rounds again for two years. Hall said that Great Chell CC in the Staffordshire League were interested in him and when West Indies were playing at Lord's in 1963, Worrell got them to come to interview him at the ground.

'But they interviewed him instead,' he said. 'When I heard Frank explaining my virtues, I didn't know who he was talking about.' He guffawed at the memory. He left Accrington in 1964 for Great Chell, and got married as well that year. 'Frank gave me away,' he said, to his Barbadian belle, Shurla.

But then Frank told him he should return to Australia. No way! he said, but Worrell explained that it was not for competition. 'Your job is to look at the system there.' Worrell wanted him to learn about the structure of cricket and pass on his knowledge to him so that it could be modified for the West Indies. Then, during the 1966 tour of India, Worrell told him he wanted him to go to Trinidad to play and coach. Hall had just signed up with Haslington CC, but with Frank's intervention, the club agreed to release him once he could find a suitable substitute. He recommended Clive Lloyd. All the while, Worrell was arranging things in Trinidad. He was now based at the St. Augustine campus of The UWI and he arranged with

Jeffrey Stollmeyer for Hall to get a job at the West Indian Tobacco Company. From there, he coached children based on the Australian system, in what became known as the Wes Hall League. Sadly, by the time the arrangements had been put in place, Worrell was dead. But from 1960, he had consistently and strategically steered the giddy youngster towards seeing a career path that included mentoring youth through structured systems. Hall would spend three years in Trinidad, joining with Fr. Gerry Pantin in his Servol programme, which was based on the same principles. Sobers had also been part of the Trinidad sojourn.

'So here was a man who deserved a Nobel prize. He had a vision,' said Hall. 'I had these visions of what would have happened had he lived, in terms of West Indies cricket. He spent a long time shaping the lives of young men.'

Worrell had decanted years of experience. He understood what it meant to have been footloose, to disregard rules, and to have confidence that overrode caution. The teenager who had abhorred the tyrannies of authority had worked out how to get what he wanted out of players without breaking spirits, the way his had been shattered at Combermere.

He knew what it was like to be young and fit without structured training. That had not been a substantive part of match preparation in his time. As young men constantly engaged in all manner of sport, they lived fast and energetically; in daylight, and under the cover of night. But it had been done almost unconsciously, without purpose, and Worrell knew that in a fiercely competitive arena, this would not be sustainable.

A composite drawn from the reminiscences of cricketers – stories of their youthful lifestyles – might create a rough profile suggesting that their bond was based on cricket and a similar social outlook. Their experiences with women, outside of the matriarchal ones with relatives, were hardly intimate, hardly enduring, and almost never on equal terms. Women were objects, either prizes or pastimes; dalliances were frequent and more inclined to be associated with bouts of carousing, an accompaniment to partying and drinking. Their greatest concern was being caught out by other female 'interested parties'. The lifestyle was crudely simple. Cricket, practice, and afterwards, nights out. They might play card games or dominoes, or go to rum shops, maybe dance halls; drinks were always present, and women were casually available. These were no more than superficial relationships, they were liaisons that rarely extended for any lengthy period. Yet, the idea of marriage represented a rite of passage into adulthood. It was a declaration of manhood and an assertion that a man was now in a position to look after a wife and family. It affixed a veneer of respectability that did not necessarily require relinquishing the previous range of activities.

These bands of players were learning that the skills they had acquired on the streets and pastures could take them to places they'd never imagined coming from their backgrounds. They were often inclined to give primacy to one set of activities over the other.

Frank understood that it was not enough to be talented: there had to be structure, training, and a commitment to the team. He'd encountered the leadership styles of men from various cultures, and he applied whatever he thought relevant to his cause. Ever the intent observer, the man hungry for knowledge – recall his determination to know everything about freemasonry – he was not content to just watch, he had to set the course.

The series against England in 1959-60 were his last Tests under anyone else's captaincy. The time had come to put on his stripes. His career had come to a satisfying juncture. He'd accepted two offers from West Indian institutions. He would be captain of the West Indies team, and would take up the position of Warden (the equivalent of a director of student affairs) at the University College of the West Indies – soon to be renamed The University of the West Indies.

Heading to Australia, he was full of confidence, ready to samba.

CHAPTER 24

1960-61

AUSTRALIA AND THE BEAUTIFUL GAME

If football is the beautiful game, then it is Brazil that has made it so. Flair, passion, mastery, rhythm; you could say Brazilians have been perpetually romancing the ball. From childhood, they had learnt the art of courtship, wooing the ball with lithe caresses. They could make the ball dance and sway off every part of their bodies, from head to toe – neck, back, torso, thighs, ankles; it is a sensual spectacle.

This distinctive style had its origins in a culture steeped in the musical traditions of Samba and Ginga (pronounced jeenga) with its Capoeira roots. 'We want to Ginga,' Pelé was reported to have said. 'Football is not about fighting to the death. You have to play beautifully.'

Yet the dazzling way Brazilians played earned both plaudits and criticism internationally. The football world, mostly European and South American, was conditioned to a structured formula: technique and discipline, like line and length. Yes, they were dazzling; yes, they were virtuosos: but were they too often swept away by capricious moments? They should construct their game more appropriately within approved standards, snorted the fundamentalists, they should follow the rules we made.

The red flags of disapproval did not acknowledge the training regimes Brazil had adopted after hosting the World Cup in 1950, although fitness and technique were apparent. Superstars such as Pelé and Garrincha roused spectators to delirium. If football had grown a little staid, Brazil was a defibrillator.

'Out of a muddy pond,' sang the West Indian poet, David Rudder, celebrating the birth of the steel pan. 'Out of a muddy pond, ten thousand flowers bloom.' So in the land of Samba, as muddy and impoverished as its Caribbean neighbours, did these flowers blossom and sway to a praise song for life. And just as Brazilian football pulsed to a rhythm that was its lifeblood, so too did West Indians rejoice in the tempo that was a visceral soundtrack from birth. 'Is nine months meh mudder make me check out she heartbeat,' declared Rudder.

There is an undeniable affinity between the two cultures, not only in temperament, but in the nature of their journeys. Faced with the kind of initial rejection that only true innovation brings, Brazilian mavericks juggled and dribbled their way into the international arena, enchanting the world into playing *joga bonito*, the beautiful game. Brazil was the soul of football.

Football had come to the South Americans the same way cricket had come to their Caribbean neighbours. A game for the elite, it trickled down into villages where only improvisation could provide gear and spaces. Anywhere there was flat terrain: alleys, streets, fields, beaches, you could hear the thud of body on ball. For West Indians, cricket had come via the English, but the circumstances were essentially the same. The history has been almost identical. Music and dance have been the pounding heartbeat of both cultures – Samba, Soca, Reggae, Chutney – rendering a percussive anthem to otherwise mundane lives.

The emergence of star players from the ranks of the social underclass is as much a part of the Brazilian football story as it is for West Indian cricket. In the personal stories of major West Indian cricketers, two common pastimes recur: dancing and football. Many played football well enough to represent their countries, and only gave it up because it conflicted with the call of cricket. The love for dancing was almost a given – even a staid Englishman such as Pelham Warner had rejoiced in the charms that the Three Ws embraced.

Flair, passion, mastery, rhythm; the words just as aptly describe the way West Indians played. And just as it had further stiffened stiff upper lips on the football field, so too did it bring derisory remarks about calypso cricketers and their collapso cricket from disapproving critics. Even the besotted Neville Cardus referred to 'that hint of primitive impulse which has usually marked even the most civilised of West Indian batsmen' in his Worrell obituary. Objectors had frowned on that freedom to play the game with gusto while international cricket was slowly grinding itself into a stupor, loitering pathetically in the doldrums. Recall the Rex Alston complaint that it was not easy for commentary. 'There are only so many ways of describing exactly the same shot or delivery,' he'd said.

Reporting on the MCC tour to the West Indies in 1959-60, Wisden had grumbled about time-wasting, short-pitched bowling and throwing.

'England must take the biggest share of responsibility, for after winning the second Test they realised that only under exceptional circumstances would they repeat the victory. Therefore, they set themselves the objective of ensuring against defeat, and by partly negative cricket and at times overdone time-wasting they succeeded.'

Worrell had grumbled that he'd not been proud of his high score on the featherbed wicket at Trent Bridge because it was a stodgy innings, the kind he abhorred. This was the defensiveness the MCC had brought to the Caribbean in the previous series, and it was fresh in his mind as he faced the upcoming tour of Australia.

As captain in Australia, he was determined to lay on a spectacular feast. Richie Benaud, in whom he'd met his match, was just as game to make sport. As a journalist with the Sydney *Sun* newspaper, Benaud was assigned to interview Worrell at Sydney Airport. It turned out to be more of a photo opportunity and chat between the two captains, but it provided a brief interlude for them to feel each other out. As they parted, with Worrell about to board the Lockheed Electra which was to take him to Perth for the first three tour matches, Benaud, who could not play because of a broken finger, called out, 'I hope it's a great summer!' Worrell halted in his tracks and took a few steps back, smiling, 'We'll have a lot of fun, anyway.'

Of that historic tour, much has been recorded in print and video, and the statistics are readily available online. Two books by Australian journalists: *With the West Indies in Australia* by Johnny Moyes, and *Calypso Summer* by Mike Coward, offer comprehensive details. Moyes travelled with the teams from beginning to end and summarised each match insightfully. Coward's book emerged from a television documentary of the same name. He interviewed the players years later and the story is told mainly from their recollections.

While the tour resulted in the first tied Test in cricket history, that is not the only reason it has been deemed one of the best series ever played. It was entertaining and sportsmanlike, a far cry from the Ashes series of that era. Fiercely patriotic Australians warmed to the West Indians, who were truly ambassadorial. Apart from turning out cheerfully for scheduled matches, they attended coaching clinics and charitable events, in addition to fulfilling their social obligations. Worrell, always one for dignified conduct in public, continuously reminded players that they were ambassadors, and had laid out what that entailed.

'He told us we were not just flannel(led) fools, not just cricketers, but statesmen,' said Conrad Hunte. They were expected to establish a West Indian identity that would be respected and admired, and so it depended on them, 'not just as players but as diplomats to make that image permanent.'

Apart from the conviviality, that series claimed several outcomes for the future – entertaining cricket, the formation of a genuinely unified West Indies team, and a greater focus on fitness, training and discipline within its camp. Nearly all accounts of the series have concentrated on the Tests, but the work that Worrell did with his team had been painstakingly constructed during the tour matches. Therein lies the story of Worrell's legacy from Australia.

He was determined to play attractive, competitive and sporting cricket and this earned Australian admiration. He pulled the team together from a band of talented individuals into a spirited unit. They would learn to put everything into every match, fighting right down to the last ball. Even before he had been appointed captain, Worrell had the devotion of his team. He had been hero, mentor and enabler for them and they were prepared to do whatever he asked. Yet they had not learnt how to play together as a team.

'Frank clearly understood that we were a bunch of good individual cricketers, and his dream was the West Indies should be known as a cohesive force. He thought Australia was a good place to do it,' said Wes Hall. When they arrived in Perth, Hunte recalled that he had told them how he intended to achieve it. 'Gentlemen, on previous tours I have noted we easily segregate into little cliques within the team. I want none of that on this tour. I want us to play as a team on the field and live as a family off the field.' He organised the squad into 'cell groups' and appointed Hunte, Gerry Alexander and Alf Valentine as leaders. Unlike Benaud, he did not favour regular team meetings, and so encouraged players to approach their group leaders with any issues. He would always be available should they need his direct counsel.

At the beginning, while the West Indians were enthusiastic, their fielding was often sloppy; the bowling erratic, and the batting could either sparkle or sputter. The inconsistencies, Worrell thought, were due to the generally excitable temperament of the players (perhaps what Cardus had discerned). Coward noted that privately, 'he spoke openly about his belief that West Indian players generally were given to a state of nervous anxiety and high emotionalism, especially at tense times in matches.' Worrell played a key role as a tranquilizer during the frequent episodes of high noon.

Moyes' match reports provide the kind of detail that traces how the team began to coalesce, how they endeared themselves to their hosts, and how they gradually sparkled more than they sputtered.

Their first match was a two-day second-class game in Bunbury against a Western Australia country side in late October. They won by an innings and 94 runs, but despite a half-holiday, attendance was only around 2,000. The following day, play began in a four-day first-class match against Western Australia at the WACA in Perth. 'Many of them played far too light-heartedly,' wrote Moyes. 'They forgot they had not become used to the light; they did not wait to survey the height and pace of the pitch. They waved their bats at the ball and they paid the penalty.' The first innings was a disaster – 97 all out – but they fought back in the second. Sobers hit a superb 119: Moyes rhapsodised over his driving and cutting in the period after lunch. 'This portion of his innings provided some of the most gorgeous batting seen for years and Sobers in that period certainly wore the purple robes as one of the kings of the batting art. Such stroke-play and such amazing power combined gave many people a new conception of what batsmanship could be.' Despite Sobers' efforts, the match was lost by 94 runs.

The next game was also at the WACA, against an Australian XI. After their previous performance, West Indies were expected to be hard pressed, but instead they outplayed a strong side until the final day when their fielding broke down. After 'scintillating' play, they wilted in the last two or three hours and again looked a very ordinary team. They had to settle for a draw as the Australian XI finished eight wickets down.

Sobers had been crowned by Moyes for the previous match; this time it was Kanhai's turn. There had been speculation that the two stars did not have the appropriate chemistry for a productive partnership. The undercurrent of competition between them was said to be the reason Worrell later separated them in the batting line-up, moving Sobers to number six during the tour.

Boundaries were coming regularly, said Moyes, and then, 'just as Sobers seemed likely to let loose all his power and artistry, he was run out. Kanhai played the ball to third man and instead of watching his partner, kept his eye on the moving ball. Sobers, whose call it was, went through and the two batsmen were at the same end. It was a shockingly bad piece of cricket.' Moyes added that a member of the touring party later said that Kanhai should have been down on his knees asking for forgiveness. However, with Sobers gone for 20, Kanhai, went on to make a splendid 103, playing 'any number of beautiful shots.' Then it was Worrell's turn to impress. This distinguished player, wrote Moyes, 'gave a magnificent exhibition of stroke-play which was text-book stuff,' as he drove and cut with 'glorious ease and certainty.'

If Worrell's unbeaten 65 in the first innings impressed, his 68 not out in the second produced an emotional passage from Moyes. 'His driving was so majestic that even the fielders stood there and applauded. It had been said that he did not sight the faster bowlers as in his days of plenty, but this could not have been entirely true because he drove them straight and through the covers with a grace and superb power that made one's heart leap in loyalty to a man who had reached back over the years to give us again cricket of a rich and fragrant brand.'

Still, the match fizzled out, ending with a 'poor effort,' which suggested that some 'tightening up was essential.'

Rain washed away two of the four days allocated for their next game against South Australia at the Adelaide Oval. One the second day of actual play, 'the West Indies gave a deplorable display for such a talented band,' wrote Moyes. 'Altogether it was a disappointing match from every standpoint, but from the West Indies point of view the shocking misdemeanours in the field must have caused some heartburnings. This was their biggest problem, because no side could hope to win Test matches when good batsmen were given a second and sometimes a third opportunity, and when returns to the wicket were so haphazard.'

Next was the match against Victoria at Melbourne. West Indies dominated throughout, wrapping up victory inside three days. Ramadhin took ten wickets in the match, and Kanhai became the first West Indian to pass 200 in Australia.

'This impertinent little batsman with all the strokes and the urge to play them, with a tremendous gift of timing and placement, ran to 252 before he was caught at mid-on from rather a tired stroke, and those who saw the innings will never forget it. The sight of this smallish man driving Meckiff straight down the ground was sheer joy, but he cut and hooked with equal venom and certainty, while he was never afraid to lift the ball into the open spaces in a spirit of adventure that captivated the crowd,' wrote Moyes.

He praised Worrell's 'charm and skill' and singled out a 'perfect cut' above his superb driving in his total of 82.

'More than 41,000 people watched the game during the three days and the West Indies players made a tremendous impression on them. Word of their brilliant play quickly spread and they left behind them a reputation for skill, brilliance and audacity.'

Richie Benaud was fit for the next tour match against New South Wales at the SCG, taking six wickets, five in the second innings, where he bowled Sobers for a first-ball duck. It was a portentous return. Moyes warned that Benaud would be a big danger in the Tests as West Indies slumped to an innings defeat.

The final match before the first Test was against Queensland, with Worrell sitting it out after hurting his leg in the first innings of the previous match. This game was also affected by rain, and was drawn.

'In the total of 254 there were 34 hits to the fence and one over it, a most exhilarating display that roused the enthusiasm of the crowd in no uncertain manner. They had not seen anything like this in former years and they loved every minute of it,' wrote Moyes.

In the six weeks and seven matches that led up to the historic first Test, they had gone from a team getting 2,000 spectators on a half-holiday to one that was attracting more than 40,000, excited by the prospect of seeing these dazzlers. They had even hurdled longstanding barriers. Australian cricketer, Colin McDonald, felt the West Indians had brushed aside many prejudices, although the White Australia Policy still existed, and racial discrimination persisted at various levels. 'They didn't look at the colour of their skins – the Australian people loved the West Indians because of the way they played cricket.'

Although Worrell never tried to alter style, he was adamant that they tighten up training and fitness regimes. Knowing he had the players' respect and trust, he mentored rather than bullied them, and he offered sweeteners when asking for extras. Little perks – a fancy suite at a hotel, a rest from a tour match, permission to go to the races – these customised treats made the men feel specially recognised and appreciated. He did not impose curfews, yet he made it clear that players were responsible for their performances and he expected them to adhere to reasonable time-keeping. He discouraged card-playing at nights, based on his theory that the short-range focus could affect vision on the field, a result of his year of studying Optics.

Inevitably, there were numerous dalliances with women, who found the players exotically alluring. An Alf Batchelder photograph of the magnificently built Wes Hall walking on to the Melbourne Cricket Ground is striking for what stands in his wake. Through his mostly unbuttoned shirt one can see the famous cross dangling on his chest. He is rubbing the back of his head with his left hand, seemingly oblivious to the appreciative eyes of the five women he has just passed. This was during the fifth Test in February. In the five months on Australian soil, Hall was not the only one who had warmed the cockles of many hearts. Worrell simply asked for discretion.

He was not all sugar and spice though; more like carrots and sticks. 'You like that shot? Keep playing it. See how far it will get you.' He would not raise his voice, but was known for cutting remarks, dripping sarcasm. He did not resort to loud remonstrations; a quiet word or a glare would suffice. If he felt his methods had not been effective, a player could either have his training requirements increased, or find himself sitting out a match.

His consciousness of public image was always uppermost and although they zestfully fraternised with their hard-drinking Australian mates, they tried to keep their activities off the public radar. His primary concern was that they respected their professional obligation to perform.

Affection had grown within the teams as well and players mixed freely. After you came off the field everybody got together, said Valentine. Hunte said they were in and out of each other's dressing rooms all the time. Hall and Cammie Smith would often take off with Alan Davidson to the race tracks. Unlike the cold English encounter of the mid-Fifties, Worrell and Benaud treated each other with obvious respect, courtesy and genuine admiration. Their teams followed their friendly example. Lindsay Kline said that even 'the press picked it up too; and the public did. They could feel something special.'

Winning the hearts of the Australians was one aspect of Worrell's determination that the West Indians should always represent the finest elements of human behaviour. Under Benaud, the Australians found it easy to reciprocate. By the time they took the field at Brisbane for the first Test on 9 December, everyone expected a splendid encounter. No one could have imagined the extraordinary spectacle that would unfold.

Although it is obvious when you think about what a tied match means, it seems odd to see the figures. In this case, it meant each team had scored 737; that's 1474 runs in five days. When Moyes carted out the overall statistics, the parity made the finish all the more scintillating. 'The West Indies batsmen hit 87 fours and one six; the Australians 67 fours and two sixes. The West Indies batted for 846 minutes. In the first innings they scored approximately 4.5 runs an over and in the second, approximately 3 an over. The Australians batted for 891 minutes, scoring approximately 3.8 runs an over in the first innings, and approximately 3.4 an over in the second innings. The Australians averaged 4.37 minutes for each over bowled, and the West Indies 4.42. Thus there was little difference in the average scoring rate, but the best West Indies batsmen were faster than the best Australians, and their ability to get the ball to the fence was extraordinary.'

It is impossible to write about this Test match without referring to what must still rank as the most eventful eight-ball over to end a game. Seven deliveries, six runs to get – and everything unexpected happened at the Gabba. Hall sends the first ball flying into Grout's stomach, but Benaud calls for a run. Hall bowls a bumper and Benaud goes for a hook which finds Alexander's gloves. Ball three was the only breather, as Meckiff sent it to mid-off and they ran a single. Ball four could have seen a run-out except Hall's wild throw cost runs. Ball five could have been safely caught by Kanhai, except that Hall, adrenaline spouting from every pore, charged in and deflected the effort, dropping the ball in the process and conceding another precious run. There were three

211

balls left and three runs to get. Meckiff hit hard and they ran for three, but Hunte's return throw to Alexander saw Grout skidding along in vain. The scores were now level. Two deliveries left. Hall to Kline. A stroke to square-leg and they set off for the winning run. Using his mango-pelting skills, Solomon took aim at the single stump in his line of vision and sent it clattering. Pandemonium broke out, said Hall. In all the excitement, Worrell's knees buckled.

The following day, *The Age* newspaper reported on how the match turned.

'The Australians seemed in an impregnable position ten minutes before stumps when they needed only seven runs to win. At that time captain Richie Benaud and fast bowler Alan Davidson were together in a sixth-wicket partnership which had yielded 134 runs. Then disaster struck. Starting with the dismissal of Davidson, four wickets fell in 13 balls. Davidson, Wally Grout and Ian Meckiff were all run out.'

It was an improbable end to an extraordinary encounter. Worrell was happy, Benaud was not. He complained to Bradman that their performance was ridiculous, 'three run-outs in that short space of time and we had it there for the taking.' Bradman was sanguine, telling him that the tie would turn out to be 'the greatest thing that has ever happened to the game of cricket.'

The tourists played 22 matches in all, counting the one-day affair against a Prime Minister's XI (contrived to finish in a 288-run each tie), after the fifth Test at Melbourne. They'd lost the second Test (also at Melbourne). It might be wildly speculative to connect the low scoring there to the New Year's holiday revelries that fell in the middle of the game – Solomon made 0 and 4, Sobers 9 and 0, Worrell 0 and 0. Overall scores were nowhere near the previous Test's: Australia 348 and 70; West Indies 181 and 233; a grand total of 832, just over half of the first Test. On the Monday, the festive attendance was 65,372.

West Indies bounced back to win the third Test at Sydney by 222 runs. A brilliant innings by Sobers illuminated the first day. He batted cautiously at first but went on the offensive after lunch, putting on 63 with Worrell and 128 with Seymour Nurse. After West Indies posted 339, their spinners, Lance Gibbs and Alf Valentine, hustled Australia out for 202. As they set out in search of a decisive lead,

Alan Davidson reduced West Indies to 22 for three, but Worrell (82) and Smith (55) reasserted their supremacy. 'For sheer brilliance of stroke-play, this innings of Worrell's was one of his best ever,' wrote L.D. Roberts in his book *Cricket's Brightest Summer*. He looked set for a century until adjudged lbw to Benaud ten minutes from the close: to most observers it seemed clear the ball was going over the stumps. It was Worrell's vice-captain, Gerry Alexander, who put West Indies in an impregnable position on the fourth day with 108 before he was last man out. Alexander had admirable support from the tail to set Australia an unlikely 464. When Neil Harvey and Norm O'Neill put on 108 for the third wicket, they entertained hopes of pulling off a remarkable victory but once a limping Harvey was superbly caught in the covers by Sobers off Gibbs, it was a stroll for West Indies. Gibbs and Valentine took nine wickets between them.

The fourth Test at Adelaide was another thriller, featuring a hundred in each innings by Kanhai, and a hat-trick by Gibbs. But it ended in controversy with West Indies being denied the wicket that would have given them victory and a 2-1 lead going into the final match. They were thwarted by Australia's tenth-wicket pair of Ken Mackay and Lindsay Kline, who batted for 100 minutes and added 66. But West Indies were convinced Mackay was out when he was caught by Sobers at silly mid-off off Worrell. The West Indies players were celebrating and schoolboys were running on to the outfield when umpire Col Egar ruled that it was a bump ball. 'I thought it was plainly a catch,' Worrell said. 'Nine of us who were in a position to see it thought it was a catch, but umpire Egar disallowed the catch. It was just one of those things,' he concluded diplomatically.

The fifth and final match at Melbourne broke two world records off the field. The *Sydney Morning Herald* of 12 February 1961 reported that, 'The attendance of 90,800 and gate takings of A$16,416, were the greatest ever in international cricket.' This was for the second day alone; on the final day, 41,186 attended. Overall, the attendance reached 274,404 for that match; more than a quarter of a million people spent A$48,749, enabling the West Indians to take away A$30,000 (roughly equivalent to A$521,425 in current times) at the end of the tour.

Australia won by two wickets, but it was a closely fought contest with another tense finish. It was marred at the end by a decision

Wisden deemed 'debatable' involving Grout, dislodged bails and a not-out decision. Coward wrote that Peter Lashley 'sagged to the ground in an overt show of disappointment until reproved by Frank Worrell.' Moyes was less specific about the dissent, 'One or two sat on the ground until Worrell brought them to their feet.' He asserted, however, that, 'most people realised later on that Grout was out bowled.' As an indicator of the spirit in which the series was played, Grout had begun to walk, but was waved back in by Mackay. He then swung suicidally at Valentine and was caught – a premeditated shot was the general opinion. Apart from that incident, it was 'a magnificent climax' to the series, wrote *Wisden*. 'That Worrell and Benaud were the leaders cannot be stressed too much. Upon their insistence on attractive, sensible cricket was laid the foundations of a true demonstration of this great game.'

At the conclusion, the huge crowd, having stormed the field, waited patiently as the players showered and changed into formal wear for the presentation ceremony. Sir Donald Bradman, who had been named chairman of the Australian Board of Control for International Cricket only two months before the start of the series, credited the 'great revival' to 'our West Indian guests' and thanked them for the 'superb cricket.' He praised 'Richie and his boys' for their equal contribution to its grandeur. He announced that in commemoration of the series and particularly the tied Test, the Board had created a trophy for permanent competition between the two teams. The trophy, designed by a former player, Ernie McCormick, was topped by one of the balls from the Brisbane Test. Although it was Sir Donald's idea to name it the Frank Worrell Trophy, there was unanimous agreement, and when he revealed its name, the crowd burst into sustained applause. Handing over the trophy to Worrell to present it to Benaud, he declared him a 'grand sportsman,' and a 'very gallant loser.'

All the while, Worrell, could be heard clearing his throat repeatedly, which he did all through his response. He barely uttered the words, 'Mr. Chairman,' before he was interrupted by the spectators bellowing, 'For he's a jolly good fellow,' and sending up resounding cheers that visibly choked him. In a voice rendered even huskier by the moment, he delivered the famous speech that demonstrated the grace that was his hallmark.

'This is indeed a very sad and happy occasion, because the drawing of stumps this afternoon marked the end of the most sensational, interesting and enjoyable series that any West Indies team has ever been engaged in. It also marks the culmination of a very enjoyable stay in your country, and we would like to thank all those people for their very kindly letters and all of you for the lavish hospitality. We are also sad to think that we shan't be taking this back with us [raising the trophy]. Judging from the standard of the batting today, well, I think I'm left with the duty of explaining to our people at home what this trophy looks like, what it feels like, and I shall be able to tell them where it is and where it is likely to stay until we meet you again. We've had a very enjoyable tour, and if fortune decrees that this trophy should stay in Australia, we have got to congratulate Richie and his men for their wonderful fightback in Adelaide and for dominating the scene here in this match. And we are looking forward to seeing this trophy in the West Indies, where we shall try to wrest it from you in the same friendly and exciting manner as it has been won during this series. I've got two duties to perform. I've got to present this trophy and congratulate him and his men for the wonderful cricket. Secondly, I've got a little token which I should like to present to him also. Firstly, Richie, congratulations to you and the boys [he hands over the trophy]. And finally, ladies and gentlemen, we've got a symbol here of a scalp [his cap]. Secondly, you can have my neck [his tie]. And you can have the upper half of my body [his blazer]. I shall refrain from offering the lower half of my body because the knees wouldn't stand him in any stead. Thank you all.'

Worrell's presentations were constantly interrupted by laughter, cheers and applause as the crowd lapped up the graceful theatrics.

Benaud's response was equally gracious.

'Frank was kind enough to say that he was offering me a scalp, and his neck and the upper half of his body, but I'm quite certain that you will all agree with me that he himself will remain in the hearts of cricket lovers in this country for many a long day.'

The applause was so sustained that it took him a while to continue his presentation, which ended with the sentimental sound of the country's unofficial anthem, 'Waltzing Matilda', capturing the emotional mood. Even from time's distance, it is impossible, in the face of such unrestrained affection and the gracious responses, not to feel the magnificence of the moment.

It would have been doubly resonant for those who were gathered as witnesses, and who may have seen it televised later. It may well have been the catalyst for the spontaneous gathering of thousands to bid farewell to the team as they were driven through the streets of Melbourne on 20 February, five days later. It was the first and perhaps the only time that any opposing team had been so publicly celebrated by a home crowd. As Worrell and Gomez absorbed the surreal scenes around them, they were so choked by the outpouring that tears streamed down their faces, partially hidden by their dark sunglasses. Other members of the team later admitted that it was the same for them all. Just as nothing could have prepared anyone for the Test that was tied at Brisbane, no one could have imagined the tour coming to such a gloriously loving end.

The tributes to Worrell for his role in creating that environment – although it was not solely his doing – say much for the impact he had made. Fast bowler, Ian Meckiff, expressed it simply and succinctly.

'He was just one of those beautiful men.'

CHAPTER 25

1961-67

INSIDE ACADEMIA

The WICBC was elated at the success of the Australian tour. Two weeks after the series, the Board held its AGM in Georgetown, and members unanimously supported President John Dare's appreciation 'to the Captain, Mr. Frank Worrell, and the Manager, Mr. G.E. Gomez, for the wonderful performance of the team, which had surpassed all previous efforts.'

Dare wished particularly to 'acclaim the captaincy of Mr. Worrell and suggested on behalf of the Board he should write to each member of the touring party expressing our appreciation and admiration for all they had done for West Indies cricket.'

Members agreed on bonuses for all. The captain and the manager were to get BWI $1200 (£250) each; the rest of the touring party received BWI $720 (£150) each.

Gomez wrote to the Board on the day of the reported 500,000-strong turnout to bid the team farewell in Melbourne. His letter, the first section of which was written with Worrell, was presented at the meeting. Apart from making the case for increased payments, in the second section he 'strongly' recommended that the Board President make 'overtures to the right Government quarters to have appropriate honours bestowed on Frank Worrell for the great service which he has done, not only to the West Indies, but to the cricket world in general. He, above all, has had the most profound effect on this team and is easily the greatest single factor in the outstanding success of this tour.'

When he went to Jamaica, where he planned to spend a week, Gomez intended to 'obtain an interview with Mr. Norman Manley and put the suggestion to him that Frank Worrell be considered as an outstanding prospect for a knighthood.' In a postscript added the following day, he reported that as he saw Lance Gibbs and Joe Solomon off, they met the Australian Prime Minister, Robert Menzies, who was travelling on the same flight. 'He invited Frank and I to have drinks with him in his private rest room and at an appropriate moment I took up with him the matter of having suitable honours bestowed on Frank. As a great admirer of Frank he was most interested and promised me that he would make a point of seeing Mr. McLeod [Iain Macleod], the Colonial Secretary on the matter. I did not specify Knighthood but suggested the highest honours and he waxed quite enthusiastic.'

The award of the key to the City of Kingston in Jamaica, a State reception in Barbados, a benefit match from his former club, Norton, a street named after him in Radcliffe; the honours rolled in from all quarters.

The Prime Minister of the West Indies Federation, Grantley Adams, sent his congratulations on behalf of the ten member states. One year later they would be federating no more, leaving Mr. Trinidad and Tobago, Dr. Eric Williams, to say bitterly, 'One from ten leaves nought,' in reference to Jamaica's withdrawal.

During the short-lived political union (1958-1962), a second campus was added in 1960 to the University College of the West Indies initially established in Mona, Jamaica in 1948; this new campus was located at St. Augustine, Trinidad, and would become the second home for Worrell in a few years. It evolved from a merger with ICTA, the Imperial College of Tropical Agriculture.

Less than a month after leaving Australia, Worrell received his letter of appointment on 17 March 1961, as a Warden of Irvine Hall at the Mona campus. Arthur Lewis, principal of the UCWI – and the first Vice-Chancellor when the transformation to The University of the West Indies came in 1962 – would have been instrumental in this appointment. He had come to the UCWI in 1959, the same year Worrell graduated from Manchester University.

Frank and Velda moved into the Warden's three-bedroom official residence on the campus (Lana would visit on boarding-school holidays) and he assumed his responsibilities for the students at the beginning of the new semester in September. Apart from trying to ensure their needs and wants were reasonably met, he also dealt with the routine shenanigans of student life: girls entertaining boys in their newly constructed dorm rooms, spats, over-indulgence in alcohol (and other substances), aggression, and so on. He also looked after the facilities, including the kitchen and the dining area, where dinners were served at seven.

218

Irvine Hall had grown to accommodate around 700 students, and close to 250 were female. It was the first co-ed Hall at Mona, and a block had been reserved for them, but the arrangement was still in its fledgling stages. Eventually, another block was added to accommodate an additional 120 students, but on the condition that after the first two years, they would find other quarters. The growing population demanded a full-time Warden, and because of the simultaneous clamour for assistance with sporting activities, Worrell was an easy choice for the position.

Although he was involved with general sporting activities, he took a particular interest in the cricket team and, naturally, this was reciprocated. His reputation alone invoked just as much, if not more, of the adulation he'd had from his young team in Australia. After all, these were students for whom he had been a remote idol. Frank had experienced this already from his days at Manchester where, apart from being an international star, he was also far older than the average student.

He soon became the de facto coach and mentor of the campus team, a role he enjoyed. He even organised training sessions, for other sports – football was another of his passions – and he would attend regularly.

In his first few months at Mona, he was largely based at the campus, getting to know the ropes. He had declined to take part in the regional cricket tournament scheduled for October 1961, but his time was frequently broken up. He was still captain of West Indies and it meant absences for long spells during the Test series with India in 1962 and then his final one in England in 1963. As a selector, too, he attended WICBC meetings. Apart from this, he travelled often throughout the region. Visiting the smaller, neglected Leeward and Windward islands, he looked at their cricket structures and offered administrative, coaching and mentoring advice.

Despite the absences, he managed to initiate a significant number of changes at Mona. One of his notable interventions was the redesign of the cricket field, which he had personally helped to complete with the clay dirt that he transported in his white Jaguar.

He worked with architects on the plans for the Students' Union building and a new pavilion. He was determined to build a sporting culture within the university. His generosity, a source of exasperation for Velda, often extended to giving items of his kit to the Boys' Town community. He had supplied the two netball teams in the Jamaica Association with gear and uniforms and even paid their fees. He kept abreast of their progress – one led the local tournaments for the entire 1962-63 season – and he continued to dip into his pockets for these causes. On 10 August 1967, a few months after his death, the bursar wrote to the Guild of Undergraduates noting that he had obtained a stock of jerseys valued at $81.40 for the rugger and soccer students. The debt stood in his name and the bursar thought it would be a shame if the expense went to his estate. It had been a typical Worrell gesture.

After a cricket match, he might invite the team to the Warden's residence, where he would treat them to food, drink, music and conversation, or they might congregate at the Students' Union. Anything involving home-cooked food was welcomed by the youngsters, living off routine fare that more often than not meant bun and cheese – a Jamaican sweet bread with cheese in the middle – heavy, filling and cheap, perfectly suited for the budget, if not the palate.

It might not have been lavish, but it was free, and the sessions were convivial, cherished as an occasion to sit at the feet of the 'great man,' as one student recalled. So maybe once a month, Velda would offer up something hot from the kitchen, Frank would pour some drinks and the evening would go by pleasantly.

Although Frank loved entertaining, and was quite the party animal, these occasions maintained their decorum, especially as Velda appeared now and then to make sure none of her protocols were breached. Her worldly air, her sharp wit and her perceptive eyes intimidated the students. While she was as socially skilled as Frank, she had become wary of these male gatherings, suspicious that they might be opportunities to plan activities that did not meet her approval. She was not as inclined to see human frailty with compassion or patience, said one of the students who attended these events. A disapproving manner seems far removed from the gregarious nature that her sister, Olwen, described, and perhaps might have stemmed from Velda's growing distaste for Frank's capacity for excess.

Knowing Frank's proclivity for social affairs, the students surmised that Velda tolerated these gatherings at her home rather than having the 'limes' taking place out of her sight. Although they did not talk about it openly, it was common knowledge that stealthy dalliances took place. 'He was a very handsome fella,' said one, women chased after him. Not wanting to say it openly, he admitted that although Frank was so discreet, there was talk about liaisons scattered across the islands.

In the Worrell home at the campus residence, they were careful to maintain appropriate standards of behaviour, and even imposed their own code of discipline. Ainsworth Harewood, the Trinidadian captain of the Mona team, said that if one of the group was saying something inappropriate, 'I wouldn't let him continue, I would kick him on the ankle, very hard too.'

Jamaica had a strong culture of first-class and championship cricket, and there was an accompanying social element where teams would fraternise after games. Many had their own grounds, club houses, and bars. It was common to find players still unwinding after matches at midnight. The university team was not as well-off as their opponents and so at home matches they would scramble to provide enough food and drink for their guests. Understanding this, Frank would happily fill the breach, and so the Warden's residence became a social centre, though Velda would not let events stretch past the midnight hours.

Some members became regulars at his campus home. Harewood said the conversations ranged from cricket to politics, and never descended to 'locker-room' levels. 'So these limes, a lot came out of it: discussions about things in Jamaica, what happened in other places in the region, and so on. Because in each of the teams you had one or two players who played international cricket and had experiences of what happened.'

Frank enjoyed these sessions, said Harewood, because he would inveigle them to come over when he needed company by enticing them with the prospect of food. If the students demurred on account of preparing for exams, he would persist. 'He'd say, you should have no fear of not doing well because you miss one night. You could miss a weekend and still pass and pass well, and besides, ten years from now you think anyone is going to ask whether you got a first class or second class? And he'd say, "and by the way we are having so and so to eat tonight."'

Alva Anderson, a Jamaican who was also on the cricket team, felt that although the environment was always informal, they were continually being schooled. 'His main message was to think before you act and don't get flustered. Keep your head on at all times and do what you think is the best. That's how he was. You wondered how he was always so cool and poised,' he said. 'He was very open. Quiet, but very open.'

Harewood, who captained the Jamaica Colts team which played against the Indians in 1962, said Worrell always favoured a psychological approach to strategy. 'Never let your opposing captain be able to read your feelings based on your approaches and mannerisms,' he said. 'Everybody knew it was Frank running the side, and who was captain? Me. Nobody was able to discern how much he guided me on the field. Because we fielded relatively close to each other or made sure we passed each other at the end of the over, and he'd whisper to me, what about so and so?' said Harewood, insisting that it was all subtly done.

Another element of his nurturing and mentoring, said Harewood, was that Frank would help out struggling batters. 'The ball would pop up every now and then, so Frank says, make sure you hit the next ball behind the guy, get it in a space, either with the bat or with your body and run, otherwise you will be run-out because I will be down there. And so said, so done, by the time I was able to block the ball, Frank was down there. And by the time they collected it, I had a chance to get down there and Frank played out that fellow. I hardly faced that fella afterwards. I didn't have a problem with the guy coming in and sometime after that I read that that is normal in league cricket, where the professionals take care of the junior players.'

Harewood was struck by Worrell's self-discipline. 'He was inclined to put on weight, so off-season, even though he would play football, because Frank was a good footballer, he would put on ten pounds.' With a tour approaching, he said, it would be a different Frank. 'He ain't inviting you to have a drink or anything like that. Frank is waking up early every morning to go and run, and that is in Mona. He would pack up in the car about five of us. We would go to a place called the Mineral Baths, that is Ocean View just before Palisadoes.' Three times a week they would run and swim and study, and then attend practice sessions on afternoons. 'You would see Frank peeling off that weight, so by the time he is ready to move into the Test space, he would have lost at least ten pounds and you could see the mental and physical fitness developing.' He instilled that in them, said Harewood, 'that you have to do certain things to achieve your desired goals. So much we learned from him by example and that's the point I wanted to make.'

Worrell encouraged students to see a life beyond street corners. 'He always inspired the guys to shoot as high as possible. He encouraged you not only to do the best at cricket, but first and foremost, what you came out here to do which was study,' said Harewood, who served as Governor of the Central Bank of Trinidad and Tobago during the Nineties.

Baldwin Mootoo, who was in Jamaica finishing his Master's degree in chemistry, had returned home to Trinidad while he awaited his results and was pondering what to do next. He had played cricket with Worrell at Mona. In mid-June 1962, Worrell turned up with the Mona team for matches with Trinidad, and then British Guiana. Mootoo got involved in organising the matches, and in the course of conversation, Frank asked about his plans for the future. He was considering accepting a Commonwealth scholarship to India to do his PhD, but he was inclined to do the programme at Mona because he had met his future wife, Joyce, there. As he outlined his options, Worrell shook his head and said, 'You're going to Mona.' He wanted Mootoo to stay in the region so he could 'give back,' and as a sweetener, he promised to make him a sub-warden on the campus. It was a life-changing experience for Mootoo, but it was also part of the Worrell plan to bring sport-minded people to the campus.

Frank was determined to instill that sporting culture among the students, from whom he felt there was a lackadaisical approach. During the Sixties, the *Pelican Annual*, a campus magazine, was a popular forum for staff and students. Laying out what would become a template for his frequent discourses to students, Worrell contributed a forthright article titled, 'Gentlemen, the University.' His remarks were directed particularly to the Chancellor Hall males.

Telling them that he was personally disappointed that in a male student population of 600, there was such little interest in 'health preserving games,' he compared performances with those of the regional clubs. He insisted that the 'University sportsman needs a new orientation,' as he defined the current status.

'He displays a lack of purpose and devotion to his sports. Many of the undergraduate sportsmen are lazy; others are yet to be convinced that a mean can be struck between their mental and physical exertions. I cannot see that anything which is likely to make the individual healthier can fail to make him better; others are so orientated towards that bit of paper that they spend their three or more years convincing themselves that they cannot find the time from reading to spend six hours a week on the playing fields.'

In 1962, although the university had expanded to include a new campus located in Trinidad, its student population was still small. It had been established in 1948 as the UCWI, but Caribbean students had traditionally gone via either scholarship or family funding to institutions in the UK, as Commonwealth citizens, or to the USA. Access to tertiary-level education was only now opening up to the wider population.

Worrell felt that the global expectation was that leadership would come from university graduates, and he urged them to mould themselves for those roles by seeing their education from a holistic perspective, suggesting that sport be the 'first avenue' towards developing it.

'There are far too many youngsters around us who are thinking only of receiving and not giving. Their government gives them scholarships which they accept as a right, the lecturers impart the desired knowledge which they regard as an obligation, services are provided in the Halls of Residence which they consider they are entitled to. The scholarship, tuition and service they get will in due course enable them to earn a living for their families. Have they ever stopped to ask themselves what they have given in return? I doubt it.'

He waded into the overblown egos of the Chancellorites from Chancellor Hall. 'I find the bragging of these young men particularly galling,' he said, cautioning them that they were heedless of their standings in relation to the city teams. He also raised another of his peeves about insularity. Chiding them for celebrating their Halls but not supporting the university's football team, he said he was 'at a loss to understand what purpose this hall football serves,' if it was not seen as a step towards representing the university.

He had been upset that the laxity of the students had brought them close to expulsion from the Senior Cup competition, and although as a member of the Jamaica Board of Control, he managed to prevent it, he tried vainly at first to encourage greater participation. In 1964, with the support of the new Vice-Chancellor, Philip Sherlock, Worrell introduced a system for awarding university colours in sports.

On his return to Jamaica, he had chosen to play with one of the more downtrodden clubs in Kingston, Boys' Town. The boys were poor, from impoverished backgrounds. 'It was rough and crude,' said Anderson.

The founder of the club, Rev. Hugh Sherlock (brother of Philip), had persuaded Frank that his mentoring could make more of a difference there than at other clubs. Seeing the struggle of the youngsters through all manner of adversity had heightened his displeasure at the entitled airs of the university students.

The leitmotifs of giving back, eradicating insularity, seeing sport as a major component of overall good health, discipline and focus would become the foundation of his public speeches for the rest of his life.

In August 1962, Jamaica had become an independent country, with the flamboyant Alexander Bustamante as its first Prime Minister. Worrell had been selected to serve as a senator in the new parliament in December. The following year, he would tell English journalist Ian Wooldridge, that initially he had not realised that he was 'being used by a political party.' He attended the senatorial sittings, but only made two contributions, and in April 1964, he gave up the position. He had decided that politics was not for him, and his public service would take another form, chiefly, mentoring young people.

A knighthood was bestowed upon him by Queen Elizabeth II at the beginning of 1964. Typically, he made no announcement, preferring to show rather than tell. He invited friends over to his home for lunch, where Lana was present as she was on school vacation. One of the guests was Baldwin Mootoo, who recalled that he never said a word until the announcement came over the radio.

His relationship with the Trinidad and Tobago Government was more than cordial – he was invited to attend independence celebrations in 1962 – so it was not surprising that in February, following his knighthood, the cabinet formally requested that he be seconded to that newly independent nation 'to advise the

Government on its Better Village Programme for one year in the first instance.'

Three weeks later, on 20 March, the Finance & General Purposes Committee approved the request – a mere formality – and Frank and his family packed up and moved to a Government house at 10 Barbados Road in Federation Park, the north-western side of Trinidad, where most of the diplomatic community had offices and residences. It was during this posting that he encouraged Wes Hall to be part of community coaching that developed into the Wes Hall Youth Cricket League in Trinidad. He had also persuaded Sobers to join them in the developmental work.

The Chronicle of the West India Committee of 1964 heralded their arrival in a clip headed 'Sports impetus,' part of a cluster of news items.

'Sport is also in the forefront of the news, with a Trinidad & Tobago team back from the Olympic Games in Tokyo, and the redoubtable Sir Frank Worrell, the former West Indies cricket captain, and Garfield Sobers, the new captain-elect, arriving in Port-of-Spain to take up appointments with the Government which are expected to encourage and enthuse young minds in the schools and villages, and perhaps others not so young. The disciplines of sport, as well as its recreational value, appear to have been much in the Government's mind when it engaged Sobers and Worrell. Sir Frank has already begun work in the Community Development Ministry, and there has been talk of him and Sobers advising on the erection of a national stadium, to be financed (and this from the Prime Minister himself) from a national lottery to be run by the Ministry of Finance. With Worrell here, can a national stadium be far behind? And will he help to end the long winter of our discontent with the low standard of Trinidad cricket?' The national stadium, later renamed the Hasely Crawford Stadium, was opened in June 1982, 18 years later.

Unlike his first visit in the late Forties, Worrell enjoyed Trinidad, forming many friendships, such as with Andy Ganteaume, at whose home he was a regular guest. He visited several cricket leagues, helping them to devise management systems and offering coaching and training advice. Still, he was often travelling. Although no longer captain of West Indies, he had become an integral part of the WICBC. He was a selector and was manager of the team in 1965. He saw it as service, not only to the Better Village programme, but in a sense, service to better West Indies cricket.

As his formal relationship with the T&T Government was approaching its end, he requested that he be seconded to the St. Augustine campus. On 26 March 1965, the campus bursar wrote to him, advising that the Appointments Committee had approved his transfer to the post of Warden, Milner Hall and Dean of Students for one year, beginning 1 August 1965. His contractual terms remained unchanged, according to the minutes of the meeting. He still received an annual salary of £2290, with a child allowance of £150 and an entertainment allowance of £200.

The University would usually pay the cost of transporting 'household effects,' up to £300. In Frank's case, the cost was £506 and the F&GPC (Finance & General Purposes Committee) had to approve the additional amount.

Although he was soon settled at the St. Augustine campus, there were some moments of acute distress over finances, as he had taken a £5,000 loan (at seven per cent per annum) from the University to buy a house, 'Welches' in Barbados in October 1964. He was mistaken about the terms of repayment, assuming inaccurately that interest payments were not due until the end of one year. The tone of the deputy bursar, Hugh Holness, in the chain of correspondence regarding this matter is curiously stiff, although that may have simply been the officious standard of the time.

On 18 August, Holness wrote, asking what arrangements had been made to pay the accumulated interest of £320.16. A week later, Frank sent him a handwritten response saying he thought repayment was not due until one year after the loan's date. 'You can either deduct the sum from my annuity (if this is constitutional) or from the year's salary, whichever is convenient to you. I would rather it be taken from the annuity if it is possible.'

Holness responded three weeks later. 'I am afraid that I can do very little to assist you in repayment of the interest of £350 and the Sinking Fund of £250, making a total of £600, which is outstanding for the first year. I do not understand what you mean by repayment from your Annuity. If you are referring to your F.S.S.U. [Federated Superannuation System for Universities, the pension plan], this is not permissible. As I see it, the £350 outstanding interest should be settled immediately and you should arrange with the bursar at St. Augustine to deduct monthly the repayment of interest and Sinking Fund.'

On the same day, Holness wrote to Carlton Morrison, the bursar, attaching his letter to Worrell. 'He must arrange to pay immediately the outstanding interest for the first year of the loan. You should tie him down to a fixed arrangement for the monthly payment of the interest and Sinking Fund, and advise me what arrangements you have made with him.'

On 17 September, Morrison wrote to Holness saying he had spoken with Frank: 'As of September 1965, £50 ($240.00) per month will be deducted for the second and subsequent years' repayments. If you let me know the date on which the loan was made, I would be in a position to determine whether $240.00 should be deducted from September or earlier on account of the second year. He is contemplating the payment of £600, one year's arrears in a lump sum. I have not yet had a firm date on this payment but will advise you as early as possible.'

Five days later, Holness asked Morrison for an update. A stream of letters and memos between Holness and Morrison ensued and on 13 December, he wrote again to Frank.

'Further to previous correspondence ending with my letter of 15th November, I should be grateful if you would let me have a reply as early as possible regarding payment of the outstanding amount of £600 on the first year's mortgage. No doubt this letter has been overlooked. Please treat as very urgent.'

In another handwritten letter dated 16 December, Frank tried to sort out the matter. Uncharacteristically, he admitted that it had brought him considerable stress and had worn him out.

'There are two suggestions I can make (1) sell the house and repay the loan or (2) give you permission to withhold all or any part of my salary that you think necessary. I have burnt up the maximum nervous energy trying to raise the money and failed to do so. The suggestions are desperate ones and I leave it to you to decide what course you think necessary,' he wrote.

Eventually his mortgage loan was repaid and an advice circulated that no further deductions should be made after the end of December 1966.

This unpleasant chain of correspondence began barely two weeks after his official transfer to St. Augustine, yet Worrell continued his quest to improve the sporting facilities and increase student participation. He was instrumental in the creation of a playing field that was later known as the Sir Frank Worrell ground. After his death, Sidney Martin, Principal of the Cave Hill campus in Barbados which had been set up as the College of Arts & Science in 1963, issued a circular, which linked him to the cricket ground on that campus.

'It may not be widely known that Sir Frank gave willingly of his advice and experience to our new campus last year. He consulted with our Architect, Captain [Kenneth] Tomlin, and myself on the laying out of the Playing Field and Sports pavilion at the Cave Hill campus. He further advised on the first plans that were drawn by the Architects. Thus it is a fact that Sir Frank played a role on each of the three University campuses.'

In October 1966, the editor of the *Pelican Annual*, mourned another version of the break-up of the West Indian Federation.

'The last issue of the "Pelican Annual" which marked the first joint effort of the three campuses, promised to initiate a tradition of co-operation. Mona has since opted out of this "federalist" venture. St. Augustine has thus decided to go it alone leaving little Cave Hill to fend for itself. The West Indian mentality!' This was the opening of the editorial that noted that the campus, 'having awakened from its idyllic lethargy and apathy, is now seething with activity'.

On the following page, was an article headed, 'The Dean of Students Speaks,' by Sir Frank Worrell. He enumerated their sporting facilities.

'The University Games Committee is comprised of the ten recognised West Indian sports; these are Football, Tennis, Cricket, Rugger, Athletics, Hockey, Volley Ball, Netball as outdoor sports, with Billiards and Table Tennis as indoor games.'

The university's student population was 699 males and 211 females, he said, adding that 'with the necessary dedication and coaching these young ladies and men should have their University at the top of every sports table in the country'.

He repeated his observations from Mona that the students were participating negligibly in sport, and while he tactfully conceded that 'one can advance a thousand-and-one theories on this disappointing state of affairs,' such as the opinion of parents and teachers that recreational activities threatened academic success, he questioned its 'wisdom'.

He said the University's offerings provided ample opportunity for 'moulding the well balanced individual; one who could be well versed in the humanities with a working knowledge of the sciences and the sports' but in their academic competitiveness, students were ignoring recreational activities.

'It is unbelievable that in the majority of cases the absence from the playing field by the players with the potential is not reflected in the quality of the degree they finally achieved. One comes to the conclusion that the period between 4 p.m. and 6 p.m. is spent in idle and non-creative small talk at a time when the University and the students themselves stand to benefit from their attendance at games of their choice.'

It was the university's task to get the students 'to think in terms of making a contribution not only to the University itself, but to the people of their respective countries and, indeed, the people of the West Indies. The only thing that an undergraduate has to give at the moment is his services, but he has to be cultivated, and this will take time.'

Time would be the one factor in short supply for Worrell. Within six months, his life was over.

CHAPTER 26

1962

INDIA AND A MIXED BAG

Barely four months had passed since he took up his responsibility as Warden of Irvine Hall at the Mona campus when Worrell officially requested leave to 'assist' the WICBC during the Indian tour of the Caribbean. He had again been named captain of West Indies, and his leave was granted, with pay, for the duration of the Test series.

In early February the Indian squad arrived via the wintry conditions of London and New York to land in Trinidad for a two-day match against a Trinidad Colts side beginning the next day.

Planning for the tour had been complicated by scheduling conflicts with India's other matches, the availability of the West Indies' professionals based on their club contracts, and even the possibility of rain affecting games. It had become so difficult to arrange that at one time abandoning the tour was considered. Secretary Wishart wrote to Board members on 15 April 1961, saying it was too late to cancel.

'There are strong reasons why we should not call off the Indian tour. It is an international matter and we have already invited them and notified M.C.C. An important point that has been made is that the racial element in Trinidad and British Guiana cannot be overlooked and that to turn back now may be inviting public resentment.'

So the tour came to pass, although the timing was tight. Following draws against the Colts and in a four-day game against Trinidad, the teams readied themselves for the first Test, from February 16-20 at Queen's Park Oval. This was Worrell's second series as captain, and his team won all five Tests, completely dominating the Indians. Polly Umrigar (445 runs at 49.44 and nine wickets) was outstanding, as was Sobers (424 runs at 70.66 and 23 wickets). Wes Hall was fierce, taking six for 49 in the second Test, three for 64 in the third, and five for 20 in the fourth.

But it was Charlie Griffith who inflicted the most damage. A controversial and almost fatal ball struck the Indian captain, Nari Contractor, a sickening blow to the head during a tour match against Barbados. It was a moment that altered the careers of both men. For Contractor, it brought an end to his Test cricket, although there was a point when he felt he had recovered well enough to return to the game. For Griffith, it brought a kind of notoriety, and accusations of being a chucker – he was called later in that same match for throwing.

The incident linked Worrell with Contractor in cricket history, although they never met afterwards. When Contractor was rushed to the hospital, Worrell was one of a few who immediately followed and donated blood on his behalf. His condition was so serious that a neurosurgeon from Trinidad, Samuel Ghouralal, was flown in by helicopter to attend to him. He was later transferred to a hospital in New York, where a plate was inserted into his head.

At his home in Mumbai after hip surgery in October 2018, Contractor haltingly described the events, the years of rehabilitation and the ultimate disappointment of feeling that he was ready to return, but was not given the chance. His deepest pain came not from being hit in the head (he had already had broken ribs from Brian Statham in 1959), but from feeling that despite the years of hard work to rebuild himself, he never played the one more Test he craved.

As he shared his memory of that fateful day in March 1962, he said apart from teammates, Chandu Borde, Bapu Nadkarni and Polly Umrigar, Worrell and a journalist, K.N. Prabhu, had turned up at the hospital. It seems they all donated blood.

Frank, he said, had a 'great heart,' and always had a smile on his face. 'It was a pleasure playing with him. Honestly.' It is one of the quiet ironies associated with Worrell's short life that the gesture of his blood donation is commemorated annually, both in the Caribbean and India, and that the man whose life it was intended to save, was still alive 60 years later.

Contractor said he had heard that later at a dinner in Barbados, Worrell had denounced illegal bowling and had declared that he would not want Griffith on any of his teams. 'But I don't know,' he said, 'that was somebody telling me this.' The somebody was evidently the respected Indian journalist, K.N. Prabhu, who was following the team, and whose account of the tour, 'Havoc in the Caribbean,' appeared in the *Wisden India Almanack* of 2016.

Eric and Denis Atkinson had collected him from the airport and took pleasure in warning them of the bowling. 'Eric, in that quaint

Bajan accent, kept telling us of Charlie Griffith and his deadly propensities. "He'll kill you, man, he'll send you to hospital," he kept repeating this at the reception next day,' he wrote.

'I shall never forget, to my dying day, the sickening blow that Nari took on his skull. There have been many versions of that incident, mainly to absolve Griffith of the charge of chucking and the deliberate charge of wanting to maim Contractor. But the facts are simple. The picture clearly shows that Contractor could not have ducked into the ball, for he seems as if, after settling into his stance, he had been brought down like a "sitting duck".

'As Contractor's feet buckled under him and he was virtually carried off the field, we sensed that the injury could be serious, for he was bleeding through the nose. Minutes later, Frank Worrell came to the press box, ashen-faced, shame-faced. That night at the reunion at Frank's Combermere school, he took Wesley Hall to task in front of us – for joining that "bitch" in bowling bouncers at the later batsmen, in being roused by the bloodthirst of the Bajans who shouted, "kill, kill, kill".

'Later Sir Frank declared that he would never lead a side with Griffith in it – but he was to make concessions for the coming series against England in which "no holds would be barred." And he joined Ghulam Ahmed in condemning chuckers, only to be denounced by his Board president as a "subversive influence in West Indies cricket."'

Nothing in the available WICBC records confirm that Worrell was branded as subversive, but it is not an improbable statement.

Griffith, who had made his Test debut during England's visit in 1960, when he took one wicket in the first match, did not play in any of the Tests against India. But in that Barbados match, he had sent down 12 overs in the first innings, bowling both the Nawab of Pataudi and Bapu Nadkarni for ducks. He took three wickets in the second innings, including the Nawab's, again for a duck. But after Contractor's injury in the first innings, Vijay Manjrekar also retired hurt. In the second, three Indian players were absent: Contractor and Erapalli Prasanna, hurt, and Polly Umrigar, ill. It was an unpleasant encounter from all accounts.

It turned out to be the beginning of a glittering career for the 21-year-old Nawab, Mansoor Ali Khan, who was vice-captain until the injury. He went on to captain India in 40 Test matches, winning nine, and earning the nickname, Tiger.

As an aside, the series also saw the WICBC take measures to ban the playing of portable radios at grounds. Circulating a report that had appeared in *The Times* of 24 June 1961, saying that after MCC members had complained of the 'noise nuisance' at Lord's 'in the bars, grandstands, and on the grass where people sit, the radios have been banned for the first time at a Test match'. WICBC members seemed pleased to institute the same ban for the India series.

Lindsay Grant of Trinidad wrote to Secretary Ken Wishart in BG, applauding the MCC decision. 'I intend to take the necessary steps here,' he wrote, adding, 'There have been so many complaints it is about time we took notice of them.' Wishart agreed to do the same in BG.

Earlier that month, on 8 June, Wishart had circulated the latest positions regarding the itinerary of the India tour, addressing each territory individually. He eventually came to an item headed: 'Matches against Local Indians: These have faded out of the picture for good and sufficient reason, but it might be as well to let members know that the B.G. Board has asked its representatives to suggest to the W.I. Board that such games be discontinued. The view taken is that these matches savour of racial bias and that there is really no need for them nowadays, particularly when we are trying to build a West Indian nation and forget race. I recall seeing a similar view expressed in the "Trinidad Guardian" recently and Lindsay has also referred to it in recent correspondence. I think it is a matter that might well be put down for discussion at the next General Meeting and have so noted it.'

The day before, Lindsay Grant had written to him about adopting the policy of one manager for an entire series, instead of one for each territory, and raised the issue of the behaviour of players.

'In regard to the supervision of W.I. players on home tours we strongly approve of something being done to correct slackness, etc. on the part of our players. I do not quite remember, but have a recollection that we were considering the appointment of a manager for the entire Tour instead of each territory appointing its own manager. Can you please advise me on this?'

The practice was soon adopted.

Apart from the catastrophic injury to Contractor, the series produced an emphatic victory for the West Indians and it was cause for celebration at the WICBC.

In the first Test at Port of Spain, Jackie Hendriks scored 64 on his debut. Worrell made a first-innings duck, but India collapsed to 98 all out in their second innings, and West Indies won by ten wickets.

At Sabina Park, they were equally dominant, although India's first-innings 395 should have been some insurance against a thrashing. But West Indies responded with 631 – centuries for Easton McMorris, Kanhai and Sobers – and after Hall took six second-innings wickets West Indies won by an innings and 18 runs. The third Test in Barbados followed the tour match in which Contractor was hurt, leaving the Indians understandably distracted. It was another crushing West Indies victory, won by an innings after substantial contributions from Joe Solomon, Kanhai and Worrell, and second-innings figures of eight for 38 from Gibbs.

The fourth Test returned to Port of Spain: India were forced to follow-on with a deficit of 247. Although they made a better fist of things second time around, with centuries for Salim Durani and Umrigar, West Indies still recorded a seven-wicket victory. The 5-0 clean sweep was completed in Jamaica, where Worrell was left marooned two short of his hundred at the end of West Indies second innings. Nevertheless, West Indies won by 123 runs.

Afterwards, Worrell returned to Mona and resumed his responsibilities as Irvine Hall Warden.

By the end of the year, he was readying himself for the England tour, his final one as captain of West Indies. On 31 January 1963, Sidney Martin, then acting registrar, notified him that his request for leave from 28 March to 30 September had been approved with pay. His good friend from the biochemistry department, E.V. Ellington, the sub-Warden, was appointed to act for him during his absence, as he would be during Worrell's many trips off the campus. Leave was also approved for him to attend the WICBC meeting in BG from March 10-16, just before they set off for the UK.

CHAPTER 27

1963

FAREWELL TO ENGLAND

England, Worrell's home for 12 years, offered the prospect of a lovely summer and a chance to end his Test career on a glorious note. Although West Indies had not won in Australia on his first tour as captain, the series had already become the benchmark for exceptional cricket. The home series against India had been a success, despite the scars. In the UK, his stature as a Test player, as a league professional and as part of the Commonwealth teams, meant he was a star wherever he went.

The English team had just returned from Australia where they had achieved a drably drawn series but not regained the Ashes, which the Australians held throughout Benaud's captaincy.

Despite anticipation for the series, opposition to Worrell's captaincy came from an unexpected source. C.L.R. James wrote a strident document on 7 March 1961, saying Worrell should not be captain and that Conrad Hunte was a better choice for the future of West Indies cricket.

'I am absolutely and militantly opposed to Frank Worrell being made captain of the 1963 team to England. Worrell has stated in the most unequivocal terms that his physique is no longer fit for Test cricket. West Indians who know say that the man for the post is Conrad Hunte. Let the English people see Hunte as captain in 1963. Worrell has shown what we are capable of. He had to wait a long time. The English people know all about Worrell now. He can add nothing to our and his reputation. But he can lose a lot of both. Confining myself strictly to play on the field, I say that if you send Worrell, and he does not immediately strike form, or obviously tires at the end of the day, you strike a serious blow at the morale of the whole team. The players will begin to wonder whether Frank wasn't right in saying that he didn't think he could stand the strain.'

Titled 'After Frank Worrell, What?' the document is largely concerned with the future of West Indies cricket, and although James disagrees with the choice of Worrell as captain, he pinpoints his role in the development of world cricket. This paragraph, which he typed in capital letters, exuberantly acclaims Worrell.

'All that the Australians and their Prime Minister are saying about our team and about Worrell was quite obvious for years. It was there for everyone to see. Ever since he first appeared here during the war and up to this day, there have been people who went to cricket grounds just to see Frank Worrell come in to bat or walk about the field. I have listened to tough, seasoned Everton Weekes and Andy Ganteaume and George Lamming talk about Frank. As for English and other journalists and writers, they have written words about Frank Worrell that they have not written about Don Bradman. I have never spoken to anyone on cricket who, like Frank Worrell, if it was only for five minutes, did not quite casually, make some profound observation that illuminated the topic, even though it might be on an aspect of cricket I had studied for years. His quality was there for all to see.'

The nearly 10,000-word essay was never published, although James ends with a declaration that it was 'ammunition' and 'should be printed and circulated in large numbers.' Worrell would not have known its contents. James had written this right after the Australia tour, while he was finishing his manuscript for *Beyond a Boundary*, which was finally published in 1963.

The concern James expressed for Worrell's reputation on the field was misplaced, simply because his stature had reached an impregnable plateau. In the first Test at Old Trafford, which West Indies won by ten wickets, he made 74 not out in a display that recalled all the elegance of his career. Not for 50 years, said *Wisden*, had there been such a 'graceful exhibition of late-cutting.' But off-spinner Lance Gibbs took most of the headlines with match figures of 11 for 157 as West Indies established a 1-0 lead. Worrell's batting never again reached such sublime heights during the tour – he had been having constant treatment for strains – but his captaincy earned the same extravagant praise from the report.

'Worrell's shrewd appraisement of the strength and weakness of the opposition, and his ice-cool control in all types of situation inspired his men and compelled them to give of their best including their last ounce of energy.'

Wes Hall's phenomenally protracted bowling spell on the last day of the second Test at Lord's was perhaps the best example of a man going way past his own capacity at the behest of his idol. Worrell had promised him a day to luxuriate in a hotel if he would keep going. Still, when Hall recalled the effort, he simply shook his head, not quite understanding where he had found the energy. Taking four wickets for 93, he bowled 40 overs unchanged for almost three and a half hours: with his long run-up and lengthy follow-through, that translates into miles.

Then, there was Worrell's management of Charlie Griffith, the subject of his ire in 1962. Paired with Hall, the two menaced the English batters throughout the series. 'Hall bowled as though he meant to take a wicket with every delivery,' reported *Wisden*, noting the 'weekly advancement' of Griffith's skills, especially his yorker. With Lester King, Lance Gibbs and Alf Valentine, supported by Willie Rodriguez, Sobers and Worrell himself, the bowling was superb.

The batting did not falter. Kanhai was described as a 'near batting genius,' Sobers was the 'strong man,' Hunte was a match-winner, Butcher was dependable; the cupboard sparkled with treasures. The young wicketkeeper, Deryck Murray captured a record 24 dismissals, 22 caught and two stumped. It was a record for any series in England at the time (since beaten), and remains a West Indies record for any series.

In his descriptive essay, 'The Test,' the writer V.S. Naipaul captured the gregarious musings as he milled about the ground, cheekily posing a question to Velda at the back of the pavilion.

'Did you enjoy the cricket, Mrs. Worrell?'

'All except Frank's duck.'

'A captain's privilege.'

At the end of the second day, when England were 244 for 7 in response to West Indies' 301 and Frank had taken two wickets, she was baited again.

'You can still bowl, then, Mrs. Worrell. You can still bowl.'

'Frank willed that, didn't he, Mrs. Worrell?'

'Both of us willed it.'

'So, Mrs. Worrell, the old man can still bowl.'

'Old man? You are referring to my father or my husband?'

(A clip of her being asked about how she thought the game would turn out, reveals a poised, sophisticated woman, tartly retorting that the answer was obvious.)

But on the third day, as things seemed to be tilting in England's favour, the West Indian mood became sombre and anxiety reared its head.

238

'Enter Worrell.' Naipaul recorded that the hope was for just 150 runs to keep West Indies in the game.

'And, incredibly in the slow hour after tea, this happens. Butcher and Worrell remain, and remaining, grow more aggressive. The latest of the Worrell late cuts. "The old man still sweet to watch, you know." The old man is Worrell, nearly 39.'

It was a match that thrilled down to the last ball. 'Day after day I have left Lord's emotionally drained,' said Naipaul. 'What other game could have stretched hope and anxiety over six days?'

What other game, yes, and, what other team?

'Worrell had an almost perfect side to lead,' said *Wisden*. No centuries were scored by an England batter during the Tests, although there were eight in the first-class matches, compared with four Test centuries and a tour total of 17 from West Indies.

And the side was as welcomed as they had been in Australia, drawing crowds that were more equally divided than they had ever been on English grounds. There could be no question that it was a resounding success for Worrell as captain. To seal it off, the five *Wisden* Cricketers of the Year for 1964 were Brian Close, Charlie Griffith, Garfield Sobers, Rohan Kanhai and Conrad Hunte.

In the end, they had won three of the five Tests, losing one and drawing the second. After the tension of the draw at Lord's – towards the conclusion of which all four results were still possible – England bounced back to win the third Test at Edgbaston by 217 runs. West Indies retook the lead at Headingley, with Sobers scoring a century and Griffith taking nine wickets in the match, before the closing encounter, Worrell's final Test, at The Oval. It was a hectic summer, with close to 40 matches, and it came to an emotional close, with spectators gathering to say a different kind of farewell to Worrell from the crowd at Melbourne, as it was his last season in international cricket.

West Indies won the final Test at The Oval by eight wickets. Worrell had scored only nine in the first innings, but chose not to promote himself in the order in the second innings to give spectators another chance to see him. Chasing 253 to win, West Indies eased home by eight wickets, meaning Worrell did not get his farewell appearance. Despite the disappointment, he was heartily cheered by the large crowd. 'Frankie, Take a Bow,' was the headline on a photograph taken on 26 August, as he waves from the balcony after the match.

Alan Ross painted a portrait of the end. 'Frank Worrell allowed himself few words but his smile, more expressive in its lazy geniality than any film-star's, was ample. For most of the summer he had displayed a sleepy air of non-committal relaxation, taking everything as it came, publicly unobtrusive to the point of indifference. He husbanded his resources as if he was 49 not 39. Thicker now all round, silkily languorous of movement, he performed as one whose mind had moved beyond the trivialities of cricket.'

This was the same impression Ian Wooldridge had formed – that he had made a transition from being a cricketer and was now focused on the years ahead. But Ross did not think that the apparent indifference reduced his contribution as captain nor his concern for his team. Footage of Worrell during one of the Tests reveal a stockier frame, slower in reflexes and a noticeable reduction in his trademark agility. Time may have taken its toll on his body, yet his mind remained sharply focused.

'But his presence, on or off the field, was as pervasive as the most lingering of scents. It might have appeared to the undiscerning, judging from the casualness of his approach, that he was merely the figurehead, a kindly father-figure dispensing soothing advice from behind the lines. Nothing could have been further from the truth. On the field, as captain, he kept gesture to a minimum, but his control, authority and astuteness were never in doubt. He had, it is true, all the weapons, but he deployed them with a single-mindedness and psychological subtlety that ensured they were never blunted,' said Ross.

Ross rated the Lord's Test as one of the greatest seen in England, and the public interest was evidence of its allure; attendance figures totalled 110,287. The match at Headingley, which lasted only four days, drew 106,938, and the final match at The Oval was watched by an attendance of 84,390. The five Tests together attracted 412,792 paying spectators.

After the final Test, it was on to Canterbury where West Indies were playing Kent, and where Wooldridge had tried to get Worrell to open up about his career and his future.

He had told Wooldridge about his battles with the WICBC, and had cited the tour to Australia as an example. 'Even before we left for our last trip to Australia we were offered terms that were completely unacceptable. I protested. I said that if the English players were worth £X in Australia then we were worth £X too. Those of us who protested got £X. Those who didn't got less.'

The letter signed by Gerry Gomez, which had been submitted for circulation at the WICBC AGM following the Australia tour, was written with Worrell.

They were aware that the Board had agreed in principle to compensate amateurs to the extent of 50 per cent of any income lost during the period. But they argued that this form of recompense would be inadequate in this case as home income generally related to standards of living there and the cost of items at home. On this tour, the amateurs were 'required to live in the standard of the environment of the cities and the hotels into which they are booked, and follow a pattern of life customary for the people with whom their touring activities bring them constantly into contact.'

They had checked the remuneration packages for Australian players: daily expense allowance, travelling, hotel accommodation, laundry, and so on, and their £85 per Test-match fee. 'We do not wish to insinuate that we consider the West Indies Board in a position to recompense their players at all times at the same level as Australian players,' they wrote.

'The evidence of this tour is that every member of the party has had to utilise other funds to meet expenditure which should normally be covered by the weekly out-of-pocket allowance. In many cases we have been able to help the amateurs particularly, by getting for them TV appearances for which they received TV fees. Some of the other amateurs in fact will need to draw on funds from home to meet a deficit.'

They contended that the Board should show its appreciation for the 'outstanding success' of the tour, which had enhanced the reputation of West Indian people as well as its cricketers.

'It is our view that in any consideration of this matter the amateurs should be first compensated to a level no less than the special allowance granted to the amateurs on the 1951-52 Tour of Australia (i.e. £350 sterling), this, of course, being instead of any broken-time payment allowance. We emphasize the need to compensate the amateurs at this level before awarding bonuses to the professionals, particularly because of the earnings of the amateurs at home, which in most cases are extremely small, whereas the amateur on this tour has played his full part along with the professionals in the tremendous success achieved from all points of view.'

This is what Worrell was referring to when he spoke to Wooldridge. While its tone is diplomatic, this was one of the occasions when he and Gomez felt compelled to campaign on behalf of the team, knowing that increasing the payments was not going to be a natural conclusion of the Board, despite the outcome of the series.

His relationship with Gomez had flourished over the years; a long way from the debut Test of 1948, when Gomez was upset that he turned up late for matches and was 'self-willed and erratic,' according to Tennant, who quoted Gomez as later saying, 'Frank told me later that the shock of being excluded from the touring party was the best thing that could have happened to him. He did all sorts of silly things in those days but he came to value discipline.'

Much had changed since then, but there were some elements of his personality that stuck. Easton McMorris, one of the players on the 1963 squad, said it was a confusing tour for him because he did not understand why he was not given a bigger role. He would only surmise cryptically, 'he takes things personally all the time.' He was reluctant to divulge instances, but it was a reminder of what Weekes had said of Worrell's very sensitive nature during childhood.

After England, it was back to Mona, where he would continue trotting around the Caribbean, helping with cricket development, especially in the smaller territories, and reminding students of their responsibilities towards building the region.

The series in England was the last of the three he had captained. He had led for 15 matches against Australia, India and England, won nine, lost three, tied one, and drawn two. It was a 60 per cent win record, as compared with Clive Lloyd's 48.6 per cent and Viv Richards' 54 per cent. In a short space of time he had altered international cricket and the way players saw it and themselves.

PART FIVE

CHAPTER 28

1964-66

BRINGING IN THE SHEAVES

Sowing in the sunshine

With a knighthood from Queen Elizabeth II at the beginning of 1964, he was now Sir Frank Worrell, acquiring a new status in the region. He resigned as a member of the Jamaican Senate in April, and set about diversifying his activities. At the end of January, he wrote to Vice-Chancellor Philip Sherlock, requesting study leave.

'I have been invited by the *London Evening News* to come to England and cover the Australian Tour this summer; this is an assignment which I would very much love to undertake. I gather there is a possibility of Irvine Hall being closed this Summer Vacation, and as I will have completed three years at the end of this academic year, I am wondering, (if I am entitled to study leave) whether this can be pre-empted by a few weeks to enable me to leave for England on or about the 15th of May.'

Sherlock approved his request as study leave, which entitled him to continued salary payments, as well as a grant for the period. A month later, on 26 February, he followed up with a letter to the accountant.

'I have been granted Study Leave by the University to take effect from the 15th of May this year, but there is a possibility that a spot of University business may make it necessary for me to proceed to England a fortnight earlier. My wife plans to leave on the 20th of April so as to spend a week with our daughter before she returns to school at the end of the Easter Vacation. I hereby apply to you for a pre-empted passage on my daughter's behalf as she came home for Christmas and only returned to England on the 11th of January 1964.'

In March, he wrote to the Mona bursar outlining the itinerary for a 'tour of the Windward Islands, etc in aid of the Princess Alice Appeal Fund'. With the prospect of full university status on the horizon, the fund was to help with an expected increase in enrollment. The 'spot of University business' he'd referred to was a version of the Princess Alice Appeal Fund in the UK.

The month-long tour began on 10 March, with five days in Barbados, where the Chancellor (Princess Alice) inspected the temporary quarters of the University. Included were stops in Trinidad, Grenada, St. Vincent, St. Lucia and Dominica.

He also made a trip to British Guiana to attend a WICBC meeting from 15-18 March, for which the WICBC would pay his passage and expenses. There were barely three weeks between the regional visits and his broadcasting assignment in the summer of 1964. The Administrator of Grenada, Ian Turbott, had written to the Vice-Chancellor, lamenting that Worrell had not visited the island earlier in the year as had been expected. 'Although his visit has been tied in with University affairs, the bulk of the public wanted to see him as a Cricket Captain, and were so very disappointed.' He asked Sherlock if he could arrange for Worrell to stop off in Grenada on his way back from the UK, so that he might meet the cricket enthusiasts in one or two schools and possibly join in a game. 'Sir Frank has done so much for the West Indies that I believe that every young West Indian should have an opportunity to meet him at this stage.' The Vice-Chancellor wrote to Frank, who was staying with his brother-in-law, Harold Brewster, at his High Commissioner's residence, asking him to facilitate.

He spent the summer doing commentary with Keith Miller and C.L.R. James when Australia retained the Ashes with a 1-0 win. He also found time to play about a dozen friendly matches, three of which were billed as 'Sir Frank Worrell's West Indies XI Tour 1964'. Ten of the players who had toured England the year before were on the team, as well as Cammie Smith and Roy Marshall. They played an England XI, captained in the first and third games by Trevor Bailey and Ted Dexter in the second. The first match at Scarborough was drawn; Worrell's XI won the second at Birmingham by 193 runs, and the final, at Lord's in September, was listed as drawn and not abandoned because of rain. It was his final first-class match.

The year buzzed along without his physical presence at Mona. The Trinidad and Tobago Government had written to the university in February requesting that he be seconded to them to advise on their Better Village Programme and the F&GPC had agreed to his transfer. He had known of this before he applied for the study leave, and had been aware that it meant he would not be returning to Mona to work.

His next move was to Federation Park in Trinidad until the secondment ended and he was transferred to the St. Augustine campus as Warden of Milner Hall and Dean of Students officially, from 1 August 1965. His remaining personal effects arrived on the Federal Palm on 19 April 1965, and because of the bulk had to be stored in a Port of Spain warehouse as he was waiting for the Warden's House to be completed before moving. His new post entitled him to free unfurnished housing, telephone and meals in the hall. He would pay for water, electricity, and housekeeping.

Still actively involved in the affairs of West Indies cricket, he was part of the planning for the visit of Australia in 1965. He managed the team for which Sobers was named captain at his recommendation, instead of Conrad Hunte.

'He didn't react too good to it,' said Sobers of Hunte. 'But he pulled his weight. He was a Christian type, because this thing moral rearmament (MR), he was very strong in that. So although he felt very let down and very disturbed about it, he still gave his hundred per cent, he was that kind of person.'

It was to be the first competition for the Frank Worrell Trophy since it had been so designated in Australia.

The Australians, led by Bobby Simpson, arrived in February and played the first Test in Jamaica in March, losing by 179 runs. The fifth Test ended at Port of Spain on 17 May, with Australia winning by ten wickets, their only victory in the series. The 2-1 victory was the first time West Indies had won a series against Australia. The series was marred by accusations that Charlie Griffith was throwing, though none of the umpires called him for the offence.

With that tour ended, Worrell was able to finally focus on responsibilities at the St. Augustine campus, including sorting out his loan payments with the zealous accountants.

In September, the Minister of Education, Health and Social Affairs in St. Lucia, H.J. Francois, wrote to the university saying that the St. Lucia Cricket Association wanted Worrell to come to do some coaching in October. Principal Dudley Huggins responded that he could not be spared then as the new academic term had just begun, but he could visit the following month. For two weeks in November, every day in St. Lucia was packed with activities. Apart from coaching sessions, there were luncheons, cocktail receptions and dinners, where he was the guest of honour. In January, the minister wrote to express his gratitude. 'His visit was a great success, and the coaching sessions much appreciated.'

In December, he requested leave to attend a meeting of selectors in Barbados for three days.

As 1966 rolled around, Sir Frank was keeping up with his range of itinerant duties. On 4 January, he wrote to Huggins saying he had been 'co-opted a member of the West Indies Cricket Selection Committee' for the England tour from April to September. Selectors were asked to see as many of the inter-territorial matches as possible. 'I would very much like to witness the Barbados vs. Islands match in St. Lucia from February 9-12, and afterwards apply for three weeks leave from February 17th to March 10th inclusive to watch the teams in Grenada, Barbados, and finally Kingston,' he wrote, adding that he was aware of the 'daily pressure on administration' but hoped the leave would be granted. Considering the request, the administration acknowledged that it was difficult either way, but chose to let him go.

On 28 February, Sherlock wrote to him confirming his oral agreement extending his St. Augustine assignment for a further two years from 1 August, 1966.

Worrell found time to make a cameo appearance in an Indian film, *Around the World*, released in 1967. Reportedly India's first 70mm film, it was not reviewed well – the musical score was said to be the best element. Worrell appeared as himself in cricket whites, outside the administration building of The UWI at St. Augustine, as he laughingly corrects the bumbling assumptions of the drunken Om Prakash. It was, indeed, a very brief and forgettable role.

Requests for him to visit the islands were frequent. In April, Grenada's Governor, Ian Turbott, who had been lobbying for him to visit since 1964 (which he did), wrote to ask if he could visit in the first two weeks of July 'to talk to the Youth Clubs and to foster the Duke of Edinburgh's Award Scheme and other Youth Projects'. Once the university agreed, a packed programme was set up for the week. This time, events were mostly set up around seminars, discussion fora and other activities related to the award scheme. Sir Frank was the feature speaker everywhere: St. George's Youth Groups, Birchgrove, St. James, La Digue, Byelands, St. Patrick's Youth Groups, clubs from Sauteurs, Chantimelle, La Mode, La Fortune, Snell Hall,

Levera, Morne Fendue, Grenville, La Fillette, Paraclete, Paradise, Mt. Horne, Boulogne and Belair. There was a radio broadcast, and a talk on community development, and of course, social events. The visits touched a broad range of communities and inspired the kind of attention usually associated with royalty.

At the end of May, Sherlock asked him to give the feature address at the Sports Colour Ceremony at the presentation of graduates on 18 June. He took the opportunity to do some additional work. 'I will spend Friday in discussion with Eric Frater on the Placements of University Graduates and vacation employment. I would also like to leave Jamaica on Sunday, overnight Barbados and have a look at the development of the playing fields to enable me to offer further advice if necessary,' he wrote as he made arrangements, which included two personal days beforehand (for which he paid his expenses).

Next, it was to the Bishop's High School in Tobago, and then Antigua. While he was at Mona's graduation ceremony, the Antigua Cricket Association had written asking for him to visit in mid-August. He accepted the invitation, telling the University in a memo, 'I have often been accused by the sportsmen of Leewards of partiality towards the Windwards as I have never really visited the Leewards since 1946. I gather that cricket has fallen to a new low in Antigua, and I would very much like to go and assist as I feel that if the standard of West Indies cricket is going to be maintained it will take some contribution from the Windwards and Leewards over the next decade.'

Having had another packed schedule in Antigua, in November he wrote to the Minister of Social Services, E.H. Lake, copying Chief Minister Vere Bird and the Cricket Association's President, H. Wallen, apologising for the delay in sending the coaching schedule he had promised. 'I trust that sports masters, players and administrators will do all in their power to pass on these instructions to the budding cricketers of the island.' He wrote separately to Sam Henry, the association's secretary, enclosing six copies of his suggestions and recommending that they be copied and distributed widely 'to anyone who is interested in assisting the Antigua Cricket Association in reviving interest in the game and putting Antigua in the forefront of West Indies cricket.'

The postscript demonstrates his detailed eye and nurturing instinct.

'What is young Challenger doing for a living? I think he has tremendous possibilities, and if there is anything I can do for him re: work in Trinidad where I can also supervise his cricket, do let me know soon.'

The young man he enquired about was Wesley Challenger, who went on to represent Antigua at both cricket and football, and was remembered at his death in March 2021 by Mervyn Richards (brother of Sir Vivian) as a talented all-rounder who also excelled in athletics, basketball and table tennis, and was one of the best goalkeepers in the country. Clearly, Worrell saw his potential, and just as he had told Ian Wooldridge in 1963, his interest was not in politics, but in helping students attain their dreams.

It would not be a far stretch to say that Worrell's encouragement of players in the Leewards and Windward islands paved the way for future legends such as Andy Roberts and Vivian Richards.

CHAPTER 29

1966-67

BRINGING IN THE SHEAVES

Sowing in the shadows

Contemptuous of politics, Worrell was annoyed by the announcement that a match had been scheduled for March 1967 between Barbados and a Rest of the World XI. The implications of the match reeked of conduct he deplored, and he spoke out publicly about it in the press in October 1966.

'This savours of bigotry, vanity and insularity,' he said. He invoked the concept of regional cooperation, which was dear to him, and complained that the move by Barbados suggested it felt it was bigger and better than the whole. He subsequently apologised to the incoming first Prime Minister of Barbados, Errol Barrow, for incorrectly assuming the match was being held at the government's expense, but he repeated his call for it to be cancelled.

Shortly after, on 3 November, he showed Dudley Huggins the invitation he had received from Muni Lal, the Indian High Commissioner in Trinidad, for him to undertake a six-week lecture tour to India beginning the following month. 'While it is not easy to spare you from the campus, especially during term time, I recognise that this mark of distinction is something which is good for you and for the West Indies as a whole,' was Huggins' response. Through its University Grants Commission, he would be a guest of the Indian Government and Lal made the arrangements.

The trip was scheduled to allow him to see the matches between India and West Indies. He missed the first Test in Bombay, but was present at the following two. He'd travelled on 26 December, and was expected to return in mid-February.

On his way to India, he stopped off in New York to spend a few days with his mother, Grace, and his beloved grandmother, Florence, who was now living with her daughter. It was the first time all his relatives were gathered in the same place: his two queens; his brother, Livingstone; his sister, Grace, and their children. Marilyn

Worrell, who turned 19 that Christmas Day, had gone to live with her grandmother in Brooklyn after graduating, and she remembered it being a very festive time.

'Uncle Frank had an incredible sense of humour. He was much fun even in that one visit when he was here and we were with him at Grandma's house. He was very personable and no matter how many people were in the room, when he was speaking to you, you were the focus of his attention.

'He was always joking around, and his mother would constantly be saying "Stop that!" because he would tease her in "the most outrageous way".'

A young man had called for her in her absence, and Frank had taken the phone call. When she returned, he made a great show of summoning her to have a 'private conversation,' which made her apprehensive. 'He made it sound like he was going into the Oval Office in terms of privacy,' she said, chuckling at the memory. 'It was all just to tell me that a young man had called and left a message.'

His drink at that festive time was the high-end Martell Cognac, a far cry from the bottles of beer that had stood like sentries outside the morning door when he first went to Radcliffe. Marilyn said that later, when she visited Barbados, she had been introduced to Cockspur Rum, which was Velda's favourite brew. It would be the last time Frank would see his family, and whether it was a trip inspired by the logistics of his travel, or a notion that it might be his last chance to be around his loved ones, it turned out to be a poignant reunion.

By the time he landed on Indian soil, Sobers and his team had already played the first of three Tests against the Nawab of Pataudi's men, and had won by six wickets. The West Indies won the series 2-0, but the second Test (where Bishan Bedi made his debut) at Eden Gardens was marred by a riot on the second day.

Bryan Davis, one of the youngsters on the squad, recalled that were it not for an intervention by Worrell, the team had already voted to abandon the match, despite pleas from officials. With tear gas still stinging their eyes, they were heading towards their bus, when it was surrounded by 'the mob' who began violently shaking it. The next day, the manager, Prior Jones, called a meeting to discuss whether they should proceed. He felt they should, but left the decision up to the players, who were then addressed by their captain. Sobers was adamant that they should abandon the series out of regard for their safety, and 12 of the 15 players agreed. At this point Jones told them that Worrell had asked if he could talk to them, should they decide against further play.

'He informed the team of exactly what their decision would do to relations between the governments of India and the West Indies. He explained how fractious it would be to cricket relations between the countries. He told of how embarrassing the incident was to the Indian people in general and the cricket fans in particular, that to walk away would only bring shame on them, the host country.' He reminded them of the ambassadorial roles they inhabited as cricketers representing the West Indies, 'our tiny region of different governments'. The players reversed their decision. 'I will never forget the lesson in diplomacy, self-respect and respect for others, especially one's hosts,' said Davis.

While Worrell was not officially affiliated with the West Indies team, his opinion still carried enough weight to shift the mood and reassure them by reminding them of their pedigree and purpose. Sobers had visited him in Calcutta, but was not aware of the nature of Worrell's trip to India, 'because he never talked about these things.

'He told me he wasn't feeling well. But nobody knew how bad or what it was. I mean, people don't feel well. It doesn't mean they're at that stage where they gonna die. He was just lying down. He was lying down when I went to his room and said he wasn't feeling well. There was no history of anything that you could tie it up with anything.' He said he had not lost weight, and there was nothing to suggest anything serious was wrong. 'It was really a shock to everybody. It was a surprise. Because whether he knew he had it or not, I don't think anybody else knew,' he said.

He might not have known the specifics of his cancer, the leukemia that took his life a few weeks later, but Worrell seemed aware that he was terminally ill. He had made a will, dated 28 September 1964, leaving his estate to Lady Velda and Frank Leo Gibbons as executors. Perhaps it was done in preparation for the loan he was taking to buy Welches, the house in Barbados, where he never lived.

Sir Everton Weekes said that even before he went to India, he had indicated that something was wrong. He surmised that Frank knew, or at least suspected, he had cancer about a year before he died. He said Frank had written to him that he had been to see a dentist in Barbados (a childhood friend), because of a toothache and there was no bleeding when the tooth was extracted. He'd asked Weekes to bring him some powder medication (he couldn't remember the name).

'When I brought the stuff he told me, I was sent to see a doctor to have some blood tests because I had this tooth removed and the doctor then told me that the signals are there that he'd got cancer. So I knew this before anybody else. Then he came through here going to India, that's the last time I saw him alive, and he called and said he was passing through, not to let anybody know, just you come, and I went to see him.'

Weekes vaguely remembered that they went to a bank and Frank told him he was hoping to come to Barbados for his last few sea baths, and he needed to see a tailor. But he asked Weekes not to tell anyone about his medical condition.

'He was sensible enough to know that he was dying. The next time I saw him, of course, he was in the coffin. I spoke with him at his bedside a couple of times because his wife was sitting there, apparently taking all his calls, because something had gone amiss with that relationship,' he said, refusing to elaborate because it would be 'controversial,' and he respected their privacy.

'It was sad. He was passing and my impression was that he was hoping to make a few things right, coming back here to make a few things right, because he left here in 1947 and didn't come back to play for Barbados,' said Weekes heavily. Sir Everton was only 41 when his best friend died. Despite his stoicism, it was clearly a loss that he felt acutely 50 years later.

Frank did have two suits made, according to a 14 November letter from University registrar Carl Jackman to the secretary at St. Augustine. The University was planning to charge £18 to Lady Worrell's account, and Jackman argued that she had nothing to do with this cost.

'Sir Frank, who was unaware of his impending death, whilst in hospital here, arranged for a tailor to measure him for two suits. He died on the day that these were completed. We buried him in one of them and the other I was able to sell and reimburse the tailor. The suit in which Sir Frank was buried would seem to me to be properly chargeable to his estate and not to Lady Worrell's account, since as far as I know, the payment of six months' salary to the widow of a staff member has no strings whatsoever attached and debts owed by the staff member cannot be deducted from it.'

On 8 February, Velda had been told by Frank's doctors that he was hospitalised there and that she should come. The F&GPC later agreed to pay the cost of her travel to Jamaica on 10 February. He had been scheduled to return to St. Augustine on 15 February, but had become so ill that he left India prematurely.

He had attended a New Year's Eve party at the home of the Phadkars. Their daughter, Lalita, believed that he had told them about his illness that night.

'My parents had Uncle Frankie and a few of the West Indian players over for dinner with a few of their friends,' she said. 'I can't remember who the players were, the only one apart from Sir Frank that I recall is Rohan Kanhai and that's because he spent time asking me about school and my 11-year-old world!

'My mother had taken one look at Sir Frank and, noting the grayish cast to his skin, had asked, "Frank what's wrong. Aren't you well?" He had brushed the query aside lightly at the time. Later however he followed her out of the sitting room into the kitchen and fell into conversation with her there. Some 20 minutes later, my father went to find them. He didn't come back either. The others sat around and chatted but the situation was getting awkward. Curious, I went to see where they were.

'I found all three of them sitting around the dining table, very close. My mother was crying a bit and both Uncle Frank and my father were looking very solemn. I heard my mother say, "Pray Frank, pray..." and then she saw me and fell silent. I retreated in confusion and they returned to the sitting room almost immediately after, as if nothing had happened. The next morning my mother only said, "Frankie is ill, very ill."'

Lalita emailed two photos of the night, showing Frank amid the guests, and another, with her father, Dattu, and her mother, Soudamini, at Eden Gardens during the Calcutta Test.

At the end of January, the University Grants Commission sent a cable to the UWI, advising them that Punjabi University was conferring an honorary degree of Doctor of Laws on him at its convocation ceremony on 4 February. 'Sir Frank has just ended a very successful lecture tour of many Indian universities,' it said. He had dutifully appeared at several universities, sharing with students the messages he had consistently delivered back in the region. Bishan Bedi, who was at Chandigarh when he spoke, said it was mainly an exhortation to use the knowledge they had acquired to empower their communities and to always keep in mind the concept of giving back. That was when Worrell, rising above the weakness and lassitude that was rapidly consuming him, had summoned Bedi to give him advice on English playing conditions.

In early 2021, C.D. Gopinath shared a memory of the last time he saw Frank during that India visit. He had invited Worrell to his home in Madras (now Chennai) to have dinner with him and his wife. 'That night he sat with us, nobody else was here, just us,' he said. Frank had told him he didn't know why he had been feeling so tired over the last few weeks; he just wasn't feeling well. Gopinath might have been mistaken, but he said the next morning Sir Frank left India to return to the West Indies. He had indeed ended up cutting short his trip as his condition deteriorated.

On the return voyage, he could only manage a telephone call to Lana during his stopover in England, telling her he couldn't visit as he was having sinus trouble. He had already decided to go instead to Jamaica, where he felt he could have a check-up at the University Hospital. He had hoped to also watch a Shell Shield match between Jamaica and Trinidad while there. It was not to be; still conscious of his image, he arranged a barber's visit that had to be abandoned half-way through. Instead he was admitted to the University College Hospital, where Dr. Rolf Richards diagnosed leukaemia. He told Carl Jackman to get Velda to come immediately and broke the grim news to her when she arrived.

For just over a month he struggled, a blood transfusion seemed to have helped, but it was too late. He saw visitors when he was able and took phone calls, but everything was under Velda's stern gaze, who was determined to ensure that he was able to rest.

At the St. Augustine campus, the cricket ground that he had worked on was declared open on 4 March, and named the Sir Frank Worrell Playing Fields. He would not live to see the project completed.

The end came at 10 o'clock on the morning of Monday 13 March, the day his new suits arrived from the tailor. You could practically hear the grief in the terse words of Jackman as he cabled Gibson, the secretary at St. Augustine, two hours later: 'Frank just died.'

As word of his death spread, condolences came pouring in from around the world. It was not only shocking because he was just 42, but because while in India he had attended many public events at which photographs were taken and there was nothing to suggest ill health. The 40 pounds he was said to have lost were shed within his last few weeks.

The university was so flooded with messages that they had to designate someone to manage them. The broad range from which they came reflected the number of lives he had touched. Scores came from the academic community within the UWI.

The Faculty of Economic and Social Studies at Manchester University cabled, 'We appreciate Frank as a great man in every way.' A separate one came from his friends there, signed, Max, Mary, John, Peter, Tim Gluckman. The universities he had just visited in India were stunned. The Senate of the Punjabi University, Patiala, which had conferred the honorary degree, issued a resolution, … 'Sir Frank Worrell occupied an important position in the University life of his country and in the wider sphere of human fellowship. The news of his premature death becomes all the more poignant in view of the fact that Sir Frank Worrell was in India early this year on the invitation of the University Grants Commission and participated only last month in the Convocation ceremonies at this University.'

The University of Bombay wrote to the registrar, 'The news of the sad and untimely demise of Sir Frank Worrell came to us as a great shock. It was only in January this year that he paid a visit to this University and captivated us all by his personality and charming disposition. We had fruitful discussions on University education. He did complain at that time of a slight indisposition for which he was given medical attention and he left us perfectly fit. His visit is so fresh in our mind that we can hardly believe that the cruel hand of death has snatched him from our midst.'

St. Xavier's College in Bombay also wrote to the registrar. 'The faculty and students of this College were enthralled by and enjoyed very much Sir Frank Worrell's visit to us on the 11th January, 1967. He spent about three hours with us. I had the impression that he liked being with us. We were all very shocked when we read of his untimely death. I am sure in Sir Frank's death your University has lost a very remarkable personality and a lovable person.'

The registrar of the University of Calcutta, G.C. Raychaudhuri, wrote to offer sympathies and a similar letter also came from Loyola College in Madras. Several went directly to the Indian High Commissioner asking him to pass on their condolences to Lady Worrell and Lana. The North Arcot District Cricket Association, the All India Council of Sport, the Urban Bank Recreation Club; there was even a cable from a B.L. Mathur in New Delhi. The High Commissioner eventually suggested that the university give him Lady Worrell's address so he could pass them on to her directly.

Within the region, the stream of condolences included missives to the press, and letters directed through the university to his family. The Ministry of Education in St. Lucia mourned the 'sad loss'. Letters came from Tobago County Council, the St. George County Council, the Tunapuna Community Welfare Council, the San Fernando Borough Council, the Trinidad Loyal Order of Harvest Reapers Friendly Society in La Brea and corporations like Texaco Trinidad and Fedchem.

Memorial services were held at all the university campuses. Flags flew at half-mast on many poles. At Mona, on the same day of his funeral in Barbados, Vice-Chancellor Sherlock gave the eulogy, and a collection was taken 'for the Frank Worrell Memorial Fund, which is being established in memory of Sir Frank to be applied for a special purpose at the University Hospital.' Carl Jackman, outside of his capacity as registrar, also officiated at one from the Sussex Lodge in Jamaica to which Sir Frank belonged. The Lodge in Trinidad, Eastern Star, also held a service.

His former club at Boys' Town sent a tribute, 'People young and old could be seen in little groups throughout the day, some with bowed heads almost near to tears as the reality of the situation came home to them.'

It was not only in the region that his loss was mourned. There was a memorial service at Norton where their flag was flown at half-mast, and at Radcliffe tributes poured in. A service was held at Westminster Abbey, more than a thousand people, dignitaries and diplomats, attended the first such ceremony to be observed for a sportsman at that venue. Queen Elizabeth II sent a telegram offering sympathies to his widow on 'the sad death'. Learie Constantine delivered a tribute on the BBC, George Headley wrote one for the *Jamaica Gleaner*. Cricketers and sportswriters wrote adoringly of him and sadly of his loss. If the world had been astonished by the nature and size of the spontaneous Melbourne farewell, it would be equally touched by the tributes that came from all over the planet. If he had lived in contemporary times where technology has given voice to billions, the number would have easily been in the millions.

Prime Minister of Barbados, Errol Barrow, barely four months in office, had arrived in Jamaica on the day Worrell died, and with Lady Worrell and members of the university community, it was decided that a State funeral would be held in Barbados. Vice-Chancellor Sherlock and Jackman organised a memorial service for the same day at the Mona chapel. His body was flown to Barbados – flying over Kensington Oval as scratch match between Barbados and a Rest of the World XI was just ending. The game he had criticised had ended earlier, with Barbados losing.

The funeral took place on Sunday 19 March, at 4pm at St. Michael's Cathedral, where he had enjoyed his choir days. The service, led by Rev. Gordon Hazlewood, Dean of Barbados, was broadcast by loudspeaker to the large crowds outside. The entire journey from the cathedral to the Cave Hill campus where he was buried (the Three Ws now rest there), was lined with mourners. His family had flown in from Brooklyn; for his mother and grandmother, it was the first and only time they came back to Barbados since they had left.

The casket was draped in the Barbados flag with a wreath shaped like a cricket bat, and watched by Velda, Lana, and the sombre group of mourners, Sir Frank was laid to rest. Gone, but not to be forgotten.

CHAPTER 30

FAMILY MATTERS

Velda and Lana were left devastated by Frank's sudden passing. Lana, just four months short of her 18th birthday, had lost the most important figure in her life – and unexpectedly at that. Velda went into a state of utter shock, inconsolable in her grief.

Lana had flown to Barbados from her boarding school in England and joined the rest of the family for the funeral. Afterwards, Velda left Trinidad and returned to England for a while. There, she stayed with her brother, Harold, and with close friends, Hugh Worrell Springer and his wife, Dorothy (who was a Gittens). Hugh had been registrar at The UWI in Jamaica until 1963 and became Governor General of Barbados in the Eighties. Velda had other friends there, who rallied around in her time of grief.

Her younger sister, Olwen, for whom she had been like a mother, remembered how hard it was for her to cope without her husband.

'Velda was gone. Velda was not there at all, because he was the caretaker sort of person; Velda was not. She really could not handle it,' said Olwen.

The house Frank had bought in Barbados, Welches, had been sold as she thought it was too big for her, and while she was in England, a new, more modestly sized one was constructed in St. Michael. This would be her home for the rest of her life.

She was still so shaken, said Olwen, that if it were not for the help of Sir Carlisle Burton and his wife, Lady Hyacinth, she didn't know how Velda would have fared. They remained close until her death.

As time passed, she donned her stately veneer and assumed duties of which she knew her husband would have approved. In 1974, she opened the Three Ws Stand at Kensington Oval, and she was the one who presented the Frank Worrell Trophy after West Indies-Australia encounters. She was made a life member of the Barbados Cricket Association.

Despite promises of financial support from the Tom Adams-led Barbados government, nothing ever materialised. Fortunately, friends were always ready to step up when the need arose. She also found work as a receptionist at the local Holiday Inn and took in students to meet her expenses. She lived fairly quietly, stepping out for the occasional public appearances when necessary.

Lana's grief took on a more defiant, rebellious nature. Her naturally effervescent disposition – a trait she was said to have shared with her father – reprogrammed itself into a devil-may-care veneer for Barbados society. She had returned grudgingly, sharing her father's distaste for its stuffy, prudish, judgmental nature, and it was difficult for her to settle. She had spent practically all her life in England, being indulged and living with a teenager's freedoms when she was forced to return to Barbados, and this, without her father's buffering presence.

Dr. Michael Walcott, son of Clyde, who later became her partner and husband, remembered the difficulty of the time.

'You talking about her as an English girl in the years where there were like Beatles and Rolling Stones and those kinds of things. She came down here wearing short mini-skirts and long eye-lashes,' he said, and Barbadian society made harsh remarks. He laughed at the memory and raised his tone a pitch higher. "What am I doing here?" she would say. Of course it was very difficult for her because life had changed. She'd lost the love of her life, who was her father.'

Like her father, she fled to Jamaica, marrying a white Jamaican artist she had met while in England. Swaby was his name, and she lived for a couple of years with him there, adopting his Rastafarian lifestyle. They had a son together, Jadau. She returned to Barbados for his birth on 11 November 1973. It seems the relationship had already fallen apart and she returned again to Barbados with her newborn, in 1974.

Her relationship with Velda began to improve as she settled in, trying to raise her son. Velda doted on Jadau.

Lana still found Barbados a difficult space. By then she had met Michael again (they had met as wee things in Lancashire), who saw that she was going through a difficult time, and they began spending time together. He became very attached to Jadau, and they developed a bond that was still strong in 2022. That closeness led to the relationship that eventually developed between Lana and Michael. In the late Eighties, she considered moving out of Barbados, and her half-sister, Heather, who lived in Canada, sponsored her emigration. Jadau, who has changed his name to Tiro, went to live there at the age of 14, never to live in Barbados again.

Lana worked at secretarial jobs, and then Michael, who had a thriving medical practice in Barbados, decided to join her. They got married in 1990 and settled in Canada. But he felt he would have a better chance at making a living with acupuncture in Barbados, and tried to persuade Lana to return as well. By then, her relationship with Velda had so improved that she wanted her to live with her in Canada.

It was not to be.

Velda died suddenly of a heart attack on 6 February 1991. She was 69. They had been planning a trip 'overseas,' said Olwen (she never named destinations, everything was 'overseas') and they didn't want to leave their mother, Esmé, in the care of their two brothers, as she was losing her memory. They put her in a senior citizens' home and every Tuesday the two of them would visit.

Velda never drove, so Olwen had gone to pick her up from a board meeting (she was a director at Caribbean Airways), and then they collected their brother, De Lisle, and made their visit. Olwen was planning to return to work that evening and Velda quarreled with her over the long hours she kept. Olwen decided not to go back to work. Velda cooked her a meal and she went home and was watching a television programme. At that time Velda had two young boarders from Martinique staying at the house. They rang Olwen and told her that Velda had fallen and they had called Lady Hyacinth Burton, who'd summoned an ambulance. Olwen drove to the hospital so fast that she missed the entrance. She hurried over to Lady Hyacinth asking what had happened.

'I just drop her home!' she said. 'Hyacinth told me, "the doctor wants to talk to you." He came out and he told me Lady Worrell has gone. I said, "Gone? Gone where?" She died. I screamed my head off because that was not in my mind, because all evening this woman was alive, cooking to make sure I get something to eat before I go back up to work, telling me that I had no right working so much and I should go home, and I could not believe that she had died. It was the hardest thing that I had to go through.'

Olwen was also the one who cared for Lana in her final days. She had not been feeling well and Olwen suggested that she come to Barbados and stay with her.

'But I couldn't get this girl to eat,' she said, her voice raising in anguish. 'She would say, Aunty Olwen, you know what I would eat?

And she would tell me and I would go and do it and when I bring it she could not eat it. So I called the doctor and I told her this child is not eating. She cannot live unless she eats.' The doctor referred her to another doctor who had her immediately admitted to hospital. On one of her daily visits, Olwen heard a clamour outside the room and the doctors stopped her from entering. Her doctor went to check. They had taken her for an x-ray and 'something went wrong,' so they moved her to the ICU. She went into a coma from which she never woke up.

She had already asked Olwen not to tell Tiro anything about her state. Tiro, still in Canada, had been worried because she was not answering his calls. He called Olwen who told him she was with her, and they spoke, but still Lana did not tell him the gravity of her situation. She implored Olwen to let Michael be the one to tell him. Tiro returned as soon as he knew, but by then she was in the ICU.

He was only 24 when his mother died on 25 February 1998, and it shook him deeply. She was not yet 49, taken in her forties, like her father. Tiro had been renting a room from a family friend in Toronto while at college, studying business computer systems; quite different from the career he eventually followed as a web designer. With his mother gone, 'I didn't even want to think about Barbados again.'

While Tiro and Michael had always been close, Lana's death strengthened their bond. Michael was his father in every way but the biological sense, and he would not make any major decisions without consulting him.

He had met his biological father when he was 11, but did not take to him. It was such a strong feeling that while previously he had been into drawing, he said, 'I didn't want to emulate him, so I never picked up a sketch pad after that point.' He reflected that he might have made a different choice had he been older, but that was how it was then. In any case, he had always considered Michael to be his father.

Speaking with him in 2018, from his home in Japan, Tiro sounds every bit the way his adoring Aunt Olwen and Michael had described him. He does not have the bubbly personality of the Brewsters; rather, there is something serene in his voice. He bears a striking physical resemblance to his grandfather, Frank, and maybe he carries something of his unflappable nature as well.

He had felt that without family in Toronto, he could travel around as he pleased. He felt his mother had died without fulfilling many of her dreams and he wanted to 'pick up where she left off,' and do the things he wanted while he could.

He wished he had paid more attention to the chatter of the household with visiting friends and relations when he was a child. 'When you're really young, you're not super-concerned with what happened before, but you know how sometimes you feel that you missed something?'

He recalled that there were many photographs of his grandfather on the walls and there were many conversations about him, vague in his memory. He could summarise that they were about his way of doing things, and how unique it seemed, how he never raised his voice, but if he told you to do something, you did it.

'They said that if they wanted to do something, like setting goals, he would train them to change their lives to get what they needed.' For instance, if his mum wanted to do something the next day, he would tell her, "Well, tomorrow morning you will wake up at 7am but don't set the clock, just tell yourself you will wake up at 7am and you will naturally wake up." He said his mother practised his concept of visioning. 'She never questioned him.'

After Lana's death, he decided that he would just follow his spirit. He went to Hawaii for a year and a half, then to Japan for six months. His schoolmates in Toronto were mainly Asian, he said, and he had connections to both places. For some time, he hopped back and forth between those two spaces, financing it with freelance work. He had met his Japanese wife in Toronto, and eventually they moved to Kyoto, where her family was. They have a daughter, Tamika. By 2021, they had separated, but he was still living in Kyoto. His sense of physical rootlessness fuelled the constant travel – he'd visited Australia and had started hopping over to Taiwan as well. He had found himself attracted to many elements of Japanese culture – anime, martial arts, movies – so it was not difficult for him to emigrate, he explained as I questioned the rationale for his choice. An interesting point, he added, was that many of the Japanese people he knew who had travelled throughout the Caribbean, had remarked that 'Barbados is the most Japan-like country in the Caribbean.' They had spoken of the industrious nature of Barbadians, 'people work hard in Barbados, they follow rules, Japan is like that. Very orderly, very safe,' he said. Is Toronto similar in that respect? 'Toronto is similar, but Japan is safe on a whole different level.'

The urge to travel may have stemmed from his loss of an anchor, but he was also looking for some stability in his life; a place that would be orderly, calm, uncomplicated and without the insidiousness of Barbados culture. It was also clear that there is something adventurous in his soul; perhaps the spirit of his mother and his grandfather. All it may have taken to unleash it was the catalyst of personal loss.

'It's the times when your feelings get hurt, when you are cut, that's when you change, like something inside of you has to change,' he said philosophically. 'If you remove all the sharp edges, you will not grow anymore.'

There is a poignant echo of Worrell in his grandson. Without an anchor, Tiro has found several homes outside of Barbados. Like Frank, he became a citizen of the world, cosmopolitan in outlook, devoid of insularity. He has not been afraid to take chances, to live with a spirit of adventure, knowing that without risk, there will be no growth. Observing the similarities, one cannot help but feel it is a shame they never met; they would have loved each other.

CHAPTER 31

ENCOMIUMS

In the months after Frank's death, tributes appeared in newspapers, magazines and books, as writers reached for every daub of eloquence to paint a Worrell canvas. The day after his death, John Samuel mourned in the Manchester Guardian, 'He had lived more than most in his 42 years. It does not make his death easier.' The following day, in the same paper, Neville Cardus wrote, he 'will be remembered as a cricketer of the highest attainments, as a great captain and not least as an outstanding citizen of the West Indies.' In May, C.L.R. James noted that he 'had already written his name imperishably in the annals of cricket.'

The West Indian Sports and Social Club in Manchester held a memorial service and took up collections at matches. They planned dances and concerts to raise funds to erect a recreational sports centre in his name. It does not appear to have materialised.

Tributes to his memory have been written on an almost annual basis for more than 50 years. It is the epitome of what constitutes immortality.

A year after his death, a committee was formed in the UK to set up a trust fund in his name. It was chaired by the Duke of Norfolk – Bernard Marmaduke Fitzalan-Howard – MCC President from 1956-1957 when the Three Ws were in their heyday. So avid a cricketer was he, that he had actually managed his own tour of the West Indies in the 1966-67 season with a Duke of Norfolk's XI.

It was called the Sir Frank Worrell Commonwealth Memorial Fund (SFWCMF) and was envisaged to have several units based throughout the Commonwealth. The UK Area Committee was to be the hub, managed by MCC, where Sir Frank had been recently named a member.

Its members included various High Commissioners: for Jamaica, Sir Laurence Lindo; for Trinidad and Tobago, Andrew Rose; for Barbados and Guyana, Sir Lionel Luckhoo; for the Eastern Caribbean, N.G.F. Taylor. It also included Sir Learie Constantine, Ted Dexter, the MCC Secretary S.C. (Billy) Griffith, Major-General Sir Francis de Guingand, J.C. King, Peter May, J. (Antony) Murray, Leonard

Smith, Dr. Hugh Springer, and E.W. Swanton. The committee hoped to begin raising funds during the 1968 cricket season. Declaring July 1968 as 'Worrell Month' donations were solicited from clubs and individuals.

Organising committees were proposed for England, Australia, New Zealand, India, Pakistan, Jamaica, Barbados, Trinidad and Tobago, Guyana, and the Associated States of the Windward and Leeward Islands. The plan was to start with a meeting in Trinidad and Tobago, under the chairmanship of Sir Hugh Wooding.

As they solicited donations, the UK Committee issued a flyer and circulated information regarding the intention of the fund. A general committee would be responsible for its administration and the fund would be applied to five purposes.

(i) Particularly in the fields of University life and sport with which he was associated.

(ii) To enable the youth of the Commonwealth countries to associate in sport and at Universities.

(iii) To ensure the maintenance and education of his family.

(iv) To provide facilities for training young people in the Commonwealth in sport.

(v) To offer postgraduate scholarships to Commonwealth students tenable at UWI.

From the UK, there was considerable interest in promoting schoolboy tours to the West Indies. In Trinidad and Tobago, there was a focus on erecting a pavilion at the grounds Frank had helped to design at St. Augustine.

The St. Augustine committee was to be chaired by Sir Hugh Wooding (a Lodge master since 1928), and was to include Dr. G. Bharath, George O'Farrell, Frank Blackburn, Gerry Gomez, Prior Jones, Angus Mackay, Gerald Montes de Oca, Bruce Procope, Jeffrey Stollmeyer, Ken Gordon, J. Sealy and Max Marshall. Ken Gordon recalled being named to the committee but did not know who had compiled the list. There was one meeting, he said, but nothing afterwards.

On 16 January 1968, Sir Hugh Wooding responded to an enquiry from MCC Secretary Billy Griffith to say that he could not provide answers as the Central Committee (which he was to chair) had not yet been constituted. Interest had been lukewarm.

'Despite the promotional efforts of the Australian Government Trade Commissioner in Trinidad, who was on vacation in Australia at the relevant time last year, a decision was taken by the Australian Cricket Board of Control against participating in the Memorial Fund [Sir Donald Bradman was not its head that year, he resumed the position in 1969], so I was asked to write to the Rt. Hon. Sir Robert Menzies inviting his intervention because of his keen admiration for Sir Frank as a man and a cricketer. I have not yet had any reply from him. Further, firm replies are being awaited from India, whose High Commissioner in Trinidad [Muni Lal] is now on vacation there, as well as from Ceylon. There has also been no response from New Zealand and Pakistan.'

Sir Hugh agreed that public references to Sir Frank's family were best omitted, 'although I remain firmly convinced of the propriety of coming to their aid.' He wanted to concentrate on two other issues; one being the pavilion at the St. Augustine campus, which he estimated to cost no more than £25,000. The other was the founding of one-year postgraduate scholarships, which he interpreted to be available 'at any of the three campuses of the University of the West Indies open to young men or women from the participating Commonwealth countries outside the West Indies and of like scholarships at any other Commonwealth university open to young men and women from the West Indies.' He estimated that each scholarship would cost £1,000 and that a 'capital sum of £75,000 should ensure the award of four such scholarships annually.' He thought the figure could be reduced, depending on the number of annual scholarships. He summed up his overall estimate of the fund's goal. 'If to these are added a sum of the order of £15,000 to provide an annuity, say, of £1,000 for Sir Frank's family and a further £10,000 for other objects which the Central Committee may agree, the target would be about £100,000.'

After Worrell Month in July, the UK contribution on 30 September, was declared at £8,772.4.3. Donations had come in from a wide swathe of the society. The largest, £350, came from MCC, followed by £100 from William Hill, founder of the UK bookmaking firm of that name. Companies such as Cable & Wireless, Caribbean Packaging Industries, and cricket clubs, Free Foresters and Sussex, contributed £50 each. Members of the British peerage contributed more modest sums, alongside cricketers, clubs and other individuals and organisations. It was more than £8,000 in just the first couple of months, a figure bolstered by £350 collected at the Australia v the Rest of the World match at Lord's shortly after.

In November, Antony Murray wrote to fellow members announcing that they had already obtained from brewers, Courage, Barclay and Simonds, the annual award in Great Britain for the outstanding boy cricketer of the year for the next 20 years. 'We are now seeking to raise sufficient money to carry out the other two,' he wrote, saying they had secured about £10,000 so far. The other two projects were the postgraduate scholarships tenable at the UWI for 'people of this country,' and the sponsorship of schoolboy cricket tours.

Provisions for Velda and Lana were not mentioned, although this was an internal memo, not a public document. In September 1967, Velda had issued a letter authorising Bagenal Harvey, a sports agent who had been a friend of Frank's, to act on her behalf, especially in matters relating to her late husband.

In February 1969, Harvey wrote to Griffith regarding payments to Lady Worrell. He reasserted his right to seek information, reminding him that the Committee, 'for some reason, decided it should be ignored.'

He said that Frank's biggest concern was the welfare of Velda and Lana. 'Frank was a close friend and it would be hypocritical to express sorrow for his death without trying to do something practical in relation to his dependents. Memorial services did not answer the need,' he wrote angrily.

With Velda's approval they had thought to launch a fund for her and Lana, but suspended the idea when the SFWCMF was formed, as it seemed the larger venture could manage the whole matter in a much bigger way. Harvey said that when he saw Velda in Barbados in March 1968 she had not received any kind of payments and 'did not know what was happening on the financial side.'

He spoke with her bank manager and arranged to make a monthly allowance to her for six months, and to pay for Lana's flight to Barbados that July from his personal funds. He thought this would 'carry her through comfortably until payments were made from your fund and would stop her drawing on such modest assets as she had.' It had been six months since his payments had stopped, and he wanted to know the state of affairs. He had been sent a statement, showing £10,851 in the fund and he asked if this was the total raised, if expenses had to be deducted, and what would then be the net figure. His main concern was what proportion would go to Velda. His final query, 'Is the fund going to continue? If so, for how long and what are the future prospects of revenue? What proportion of this future revenue would go to Velda?'

On receipt of this irate correspondence, Griffith dashed off a letter to Antony Murray, who was staying at Prospect Bay in Barbados at the time. Murray replied on 15 February, the day he received it. Griffith used the contents of Murray's letter to respond to Harvey.

He said that Velda knew and approved of the fund's objective, and that neither Antony nor Swanton was aware that Harvey had decided to cancel his appeal fund. At the last committee meeting, 'a figure of £750 was mentioned as a possible figure to send to Velda,' although it depended on the outcome of the appeal to members. They were unaware of what the various committees intended to do in that regard, but assured they would be encouraged to include provisions for her when the fund was closed.

Regarding Velda's finances, Antony had reported that 'his impression is that it is not too bad following conversations with Velda herself and others.'

Harvey was infuriated by this. 'I hardly know how to reply to your letter dated February 21st,' he responded, as he testily proceeded to address its points.

'Yes, Ted Dexter did report to me what was said at your first meeting on October 3rd. In effect it was that the contents of Ted's letter addressed to you dated September 29th and the authority requesting me to act for Velda should be disregarded. I could put it in a cruder way but won't.'

He said it was obvious that the appeal he had intended should be suspended. 'We could only, it seemed, appeal to the same people and to be in competition would have been both stupid and embarrassing.'

As to the £750 being considered for Velda, 'I find that quite staggering. I hesitate to mention my personal contribution again and only do so because it gives me some entitlement to comment on the outcome of the fund since I did produce nearly double this amount.'

He reminded Griffith of cricket's debt to Sir Frank's dependents, 'but points like this are either understood or they are not worth making.'

The committee discussed the disbursement of funds collected so far at its next and final meeting. Antony Murray reported cash in hand was £6,364 but of that figure, £172 was tied to the scholarship account. He said that two tours had been arranged, with West Indies schoolboys visiting the UK in July 1970 for five weeks, and a British team returning the visit in 1971. He estimated the cost of each tour to be £4,000.

After some discussion on the costs of the appeal and efforts to seek reduced rates for services, attention turned to Velda. According to the minutes of 28 July 1969, 'it was reported that although Lady Worrell now had employment which was adequate for her present needs, she had limited financial reserves should an emergency occur.' The Committee decided that as things stood, 'there did not appear to be enough money to make a worthwhile gift to Lady Worrell and to pay for the two cricket tours.' Some effort was made to find additional ways to present her with £1000 and an after-minute note said that they had found the funds.

The committee agreed to try to negotiate with the Winston Churchill Memorial Fund over the possibility of them establishing a scholarship in the name of Sir Frank. Velda's brother, Harold, was there and thanked members on her behalf, and with that, the committee was dissolved and the fund closed. It remains unclear how much Lady Worrell ever received from the UK Fund.

While financial memorials did not seem to have gained substantial traction, other forms of tribute have continued. In 2005, the Centre of Caribbean Studies at the London Metropolitan University launched a Frank Worrell lecture series, with the noted Caribbean poet and writer, Ian McDonald, delivering the inaugural address. Calling it, 'Cricket: A Hunger in the West Indian Soul,' he invoked the spirit of cricket past. 'In our eras of greatness, when West Indies took the field, ghostly presences walked with the players representing commitment to a higher cause, loyalty to the proudest of traditions and attachment to a long line of heroes – and the twelfth man in the team always answered to the name of courage,' he said. Saluting the grace of Sir Frank, he could not resist mentioning that he was unqualified to give the lecture because he had once been given out for 'ugly batting.'

The following year, the former England captain Mike Atherton rendered a less lyrical lecture, cautioning that he was not a man of letters like McDonald, but a cricketer who spoke simply and candidly. He disagreed with McDonald that nobility of purpose was the driver of modern success. The English experience was completely different from the West Indian world that Worrell had inhabited.

'In England, no matter how important we think cricket is to our culture and history it would be a foolish man who said that it played a critical role in the building of the nation state.'

Over the years, there have been several lectures held in Sir Frank's name. The UWI has hosted several. Its Guild of Students across the campuses had agreed to set up a scholarship fund for West Indian students in the social sciences.

In 2007, the Sir Frank Worrell Memorial Committee (SFWMC) was formed in Trinidad and Tobago. It set itself a number of goals; its first event was a panel discussion that March, to coincide with the 40th anniversary of Sir Frank's death. The panel comprised Deryck Murray, Andy Ganteaume, Ian McDonald and the Australian High Commissioner, John Michell. The committee has presented Noble Spirit awards to members of the regional cricket community, and has hosted annual lectures. In 2008, Nari Contractor was invited to launch an annual Frank Worrell Blood Donation Drive in Trinidad & Tobago. In 1980, he had launched a similar one in West Bengal in India. In 2010, another former England captain, Mike Brearley, was the featured speaker at the SFWMC's lecture. His subject: 'C.L.R. James and Frank Worrell: cometh the hour cometh the man.' As McDonald had done in his panel discussion, Brearley invoked the observation from James about Worrell. 'He did not instill into, but drew out of his players.' It is a line that points precisely to the gift that Worrell had of lifting the lagniappe from his team. He encouraged them to be their best selves.

Michael Neville McMorris, an academic and the brother of Easton, constructed a profile of Worrell, 'The Exemplar,' that did not confine itself to laudatory remarks. His was an analysis of the complexity of his character. Saying that he carried elements of the Victorian and the conservative, he noted that, 'In the aggressive sense Worrell did not so much lead; others simply followed. They followed this exemplar, for here was a man of excellence who revealed to his

271

team the possibilities of their "race" and of their art, and released in them a new dignity and a confidence in their ability to exhibit a mature enjoyment of their game.'

McMorris believed that Worrell cared far more about appearances than he let on (the Dandy), and noted that 'it is not too simplistic to point to his always immaculate attire and neatly trimmed moustache to support this judgement.' He felt there was conceit, a reflection of 'a strong belief in his own abilities, a sense of athletic ease and power that only he would know, and it spilled over into an ugly shape which caused embarrassment, dislocation, but not defeat.'

He praised his leadership, his cricket: his batting was a compound of charm and graciousness. 'His genuflection to square leg always seemed to me a gesture of courtesy, and his late-cut a charming after thought. In his most effective drives there was always a hint of persuasion and apology.'

In all of the paeans to Worrell, there is a constant thread: his grace, his charm, his mentoring and his superb leadership. It is a testament to the broadness of the swathe he cut, that Edward Baugh, the Jamaican poet, scolded those who only saw his graceful statesmanship and forgot his graceful cricket. In his 2000 poem, 'The Pulpit-Eulogists of Frank Worrell,' he wrote: 'Any clown can play the gentleman./ But who could time a ball so sweetly/ Or flick a wrist so strong and featly?'

Other poets and calypsonians had been singing his praises long before he was gone. Kamau Brathwaite mentions him, 'The openers out, Tae Worrell out.' In his famous poem, Rites'. In *Cricket's in my Blood*, Faustin Charles declares that 'Every night Worrell's ghost walks/ Through the village/ Delivering inspiration.'

Around the region there are several buildings and monuments in his name. In Barbados, he is depicted on the currency. A life-sized statue of him was commissioned by the government. Scholarships were offered in his name for years. Halls of Fame carry his name proudly.

Given the fickle nature of memory, especially in the Caribbean where so little is done to cultivate archives and museums, Worrell continues to be recognised as the benchmark for the finest West Indian qualities. His name still resonates wherever cricket is played, and whenever discussions arise over Caribbean leadership.

Worrell was a complex individual, barely understood in all his manifestations, but ultimately he shone as an exemplary figure: a man of generosity and grace. It is tempting to speculate about the role Worrell would have played in West Indian development and cricket had his life continued. It can only remain in the realm of wistfulness – that shadowy place of dreams unmade.

ABBREVIATIONS

BCA	Barbados Cricket Association
BCC	Barbados Cricket Committee
BCCI	Board of Control for Cricket in India
BCL	Barbados Cricket League
CCI	Cricket Club of India
F&GPC	Finance & General Purposes Committee
FSSU	Federated Superannuation System for Universities
GSC	Garrison Sports Club
ICTA	Imperial College of Tropical Agriculture
IPL	Indian Premier League
KCC	Kingston Cricket Club
MCC	Marylebone Cricket Club
NAACP	National Association for the Advancement of Colored People
QPCC	Queen's Park Cricket Club
SAC	South African Congress
SACA	South African Cricket Association
SACBOC	South African Cricket Board of Control
SASA	South African Sports Association
SFWCMF	Sir Frank Worrell Commonwealth Memorial Fund
SFWMC	Sir Frank Worrell Memorial Committee
SJOC	Silver Jubilee Overseas Cricket
The UWI	The University of the West Indies
UCWI	University College of the West Indies
WICB	West Indies Cricket Board
WICBC	West Indies Cricket Board of Control

(The capital of Trinidad, Port of Spain, was formerly written as Port-of-Spain. The hyphens have since been dropped but remain in this book where they are part of a quote.)

Notes to Introduction

13 -   'Strokes of exquisite delicacy played so late that one thought he had allowed the ball to go through, when he stroked it imperiously almost out of Evans' hungry gloves. Even the English players applauded his late cuts. It was truly an innings of sheer quality.' (**RC Robertson-Glasgow**, *The Sphere*).

13 -   Australian captain, Richie Benaud said: 'Frank Worrell turned West Indies from being the most magnificent group of individual cricketers in the world into a close-knit team. No one else could have done it.' (**Benaud, Richie**; *On Reflection,* Fontana/Collins, 1985, p.50).

Notes to Prologue

18 -   'People Today' interview, BBC Home Service. Broadcast on June 12, 1963. Interviewer, Rex Alston. Frank Worrell. Transcript.

18 -   **James, C.L.R.**; *Beyond a Boundary*, Hutchinson, 1963.

19 -   **Eytle, Ernest**; *Frank Worrell: The Career of a Great Cricketer*, Hodder and Stoughton, 1963.

23 -   **Wooldridge, Ian**; 'The Gentle Revolutionary,' excerpt from *Cricket, Lovely Cricket: The West Indies Tour*, 1963, Robert Hale Ltd, 1963, in Sport & Pastime, Madras, September 26, 1964. (30-31).

Notes to Part One

Chapter 1 – DUSTY DAYS IN BANK HALL

29 -   Sir Everton Weekes interview, Barbados, June 2016.

32 -   'Mauby women...' (**Maggiolo, Christopher A.**, 'Champagne Taste on a Mauby Pocket: The Socioenvironmental History of Mauby in Barbados' (2010). Undergraduate Honors Theses. Paper 681. scholarworks.wm.edu/honorstheses/681)

37 -   'I contend that the very emergence of blacks in leadership and in near total representation on cricket teams in the Leewards and Windwards had everything to do with these islands being excluded from inter-colonial white-administered cricket, and, therefore from Test match cricket.'   (**Hector, Tim**; "Pan-Africanism, West Indies Cricket, and Viv Richards," in *A Spirit of Dominance: Cricket and Nationalism in the West Indies,* p. 54*)*.

Chapter 2 – THE AGE OF EMPIRE

40 -   'one of the most famous...' (**Sandiford, Keith A.P.**; *Frank Maglinne Worrell, his record innings by innings.* West Bridgford, Notts., Association of Cricket Statisticians & Historians, 1997).
41 -   'We played a lot of cricket...' (Sir Everton Weekes interview.)

Chapter 3 – TRIALS AT COMBERMERE

44 -   'The games master...' (**Sandiford, Keith A.P.**; *Cricket Nurseries of Colonial Barbados: The Elite Schools, 1865-1966,* p. 49).
45 -   'And, strangely enough...' (**Worrell, Frank**; *Cricket Punch,* p. 30).
45 -   'It is an unusually indignant tone...' (That observation is echoed in John Mehaffey's 2018 book, *Dawn of the Golden Weather: When Kiwi cricketers conquered the world,* which chronicles New Zealand's development in the 1980s. Bruce Edgar, who played in that era, is quoted as saying that he always found the English condescending. 'Even if we beat them they were still condescending. They could not accept the fact that we had won. They were certainly not very gracious in defeat. They were poor losers, couldn't acknowledge that we had actually outplayed them, and that carries on today.')

Chapter 5 – THE BREWSTER CLAN

53 -   Michael Walcott interview, Barbados, November 2016.

Chapter 6 – WEEKES AND WALCOTT

56 -   Sir Garfield Sobers interview, Barbados, November, 2016.

56 -   'Everton Weekes was one of the pallbearers. I wasn't asked...' (**Walcott, Clyde; Scovell, Brian**; *Sixty Years on the Back Foot*, Victor Gollancz, Orion Books, 1999, p. 19).

Chapter 7 – EVERYWHERE IS WAR

58 -   "When he came out of school he was selling insurance with a life insurance company. And I think the problem started there. He might not have been able to sell any policies like another person. It hit him pretty hard. That hit him pretty hard. To the point that he went to Trinidad. He left in 1946, in '47 he went to Jamaica and didn't come back. I think he wanted me to do a similar thing, but I was in the army and I couldn't get away. Not that I would have gone, I was not unhappy here. I couldn't see that far. Because I'd gone to school here, a boy without a degree. I was not looking that far ahead. I was just looking to get comfortable but not to the point that I would want to leave anybody behind." (Sir Everton Weekes interview.)

Chapter 8 – HIM LOVE TO BAT

60 -   'I have always loved dancing...' (**Warner, Pelham**; *Long Innings*, Harrap, 1951, p. 53).

60 -   Cricket statistics for Sir Frank Worrell are easily accessible from a variety of sources, both online and in print; thus the primary focus of this biography is on other aspects of Sir Frank's life. Interested readers can consult the thorough accounts of his cricket records in publications like **Keith A.P. Sandiford**'s *Cricket Nurseries of Colonial Barbados: The Elite Schools, 1865-1966;* **Keith A.P. Sandiford** and **Arjun Tan**'s *The Three Ws of West Indian Cricket: A Comparative Batting Analysis,* and **Sandiford**'s *Frank Maglinne Worrell, his record innings by innings.* West Bridgford, Notts, Association of Cricket Statisticians & Historians, 1997

62 -   By the time Worrell left Barbados in 1947, he had played in 15 matches for his country and scored 1,547 runs at an average of almost 74. He had also taken 15 catches and claimed 43 wickets. (*Cricket Nurseries*).

Chapter 9 – JAMMING IN JAMAICA

63 -   'We were so dedicated...' (*Back Foot*, p. 17).

63 -   'One writer calculated...' (**Laurie, Peter**; *The Barbadian Rumshop,* Macmillan Caribbean, 2001).

66 -   'Walcott was amazed...' (**Walcott, Clyde**; *Island Cricketers*, Hodder and Stoughton, 1958, p. 28).

66 -   'I was in the army...' (**Weekes, Everton; Beckles, Hilary**; *Mastering the Craft*, Universities of the Caribbean Press, 2007, p. 80).

68 -   Easton McMorris, a right-handed Jamaican opening batter: (Easton McMorris interview, Jamaica, 2021).

70 -   'Frank and Clyde enjoyed it too...' (Sir Everton Weekes interview, 2016.)

70 -   'We had a lot of fun...' (Sir Everton Weekes interview, 2016.)

Chapter 10 – AFTER THE WAR

72 -   'Stollmeyer attributed this naming of captains according to where the match was to be played, to "the distance between the islands and the difficulty of communication." West Indies cricket "was still in its formative years, and often compromises, of a nature inexplicable in present times, had to be made by the administrators." (**Stollmeyer, J.B.**; *Everything Under the Sun: My Life in West Indies Cricket*, Stanley Paul, 1983, p. 54).

Notes to Part Two

Chapter 11 – 1949-50: INDIA AT LAST

81 -   'It would be idle to pretend...' (*Island Cricketers*, p. 37).

82 -   'players who were either...' (Worrell, in **Eytle**, p. 77).

82 -   'A brochure commemorating...' (*Commonwealth tour to Pakistan, Karachi 1949*).

84 -   'When asked once...' (**Tennant**, p. 27).

Chapter 12 – 1950: THE THREE Ws BEGIN

85 -   British *Pathé* promotional newsreel
youtube.com/watch?v=wN8HaqkRGjw

86 -   'Walcott wrote that at one...' (*Back Foot*, p. 39).

87 -   'In *Cricket Punch*, Worrell did...' (ibid, p. 57).

88 -   **Norman Preston,** *Wisden*:
espncricinfo.com/wisdenalmanack/content/story/155259.html

89 -   'Horace Harragin...' (**Harragin, Horace**; *Sixty Years of Cricket: Australia vs The West Indies,* Paria Publishing Company Limited, 1991, p. 52).

90 -   'This was the match...' (*Cricket Punch*, p. 64).

91 -   'The next day I went out with Frank...' (*Mastering the Craft*, p. 116).

92 -   'Yet, Walcott complained...' (*Back Foot*, p. 34).

92 -   'I have never seen a Test match started...' (*Island Cricketers*, p. 51).

93 -   'There are many...' (**Manley, Michael**; *A History of West Indies Cricket*, (Revised Edition) West Indies Publishing, 1995, p. 86).

93 -   'Stollmeyer's departure:...' (ibid, p. 87).

94 -   Martin Williamson:
espncricinfo.com/magazine/content/story/251196.html

94 -   'There are one or two West Indian characters:...' (**Baxter, Peter; Hayter, Peter**; *England vs West Indies: Highlights since 1948*, BBC Books, 1991, p. 17).

97 -   Sonny Ramadhin was interviewed by journalist, Joshua

Surtees at his home in Lancashire in 2016 and Surtees kindly consented to ask some questions on my behalf.

98 -   'Thousands of our countrymen...' (*Back Foot*, p. 33).

Article on Lord's Test match from Caribbean Beat Nov/Dec 2009
caribbean-beat.com/issue-100/
triumph-calypso-cricket#axzz8H4LpjC4M

Calypsos:
Lord Beginner
1929 – Learie Constantine
1935 – MCC vs West Indies
1940s – All Hail for Constantine
1950 – Victory Test Match
1951 – John Goddard
1952 – Australia vs West Indies
1953 – England regain the Ashes
1954 – Cricket Champions
Lord Kitchener
1950 – 1950 Victory
1951 – Denis Compton
1953 – Alec Bedser
1955 – The Ashes
1967 – Cricket Champions
1976 – Water Lillee
On Frank Worrell
Jackie Opel – 1963, Worrell's Captaincy
Lauren Aitken – 1964 – 3 Cheers for Worrell and the West Indies Cricket Team
All Rounder – 1968 – Sir Frank
24 other calypsoes mention him. (**Khan, Nasser**, *History of West Indies Cricket Through Calypsoes*, Caroni, Safari Publications, 2016).

Chapter 13 – THE COMMONWEALTH BAND

101 -   C.D. Gopinath youtube.com/
watch?v=qC176GoxzRU&t=865s&ab_channel=JaiGalagali

102 - Sir Garfield Sobers interview, 2016.

102 - Bishan Singh Bedi interview, New Delhi, October 2018.

103 - 'There were no personality conflicts...' (**Eytle**, p. 78).

104 - Lalita Phadkar interview, New Delhi, October 2018.

106 - 'Later, I went to the farewell party...' (**Paul Gibb**, 'Gibb in India,' *Wisden Cricket Monthly,* June 1982–March 1983).

107 - 'Allan Rae, Gerry, Jimmy and I...' (**Stollmeyer, Jeffrey**; *The West Indies in India: Jeffrey Stollmeyer's Diary, 1948-1949,* Royards Publishing Company, 2004, p. 115).

Chapter 14 – 1951-52: AUSTRALIA AND NEW ZEALAND

112 - 'The first mistake was...' (*Cricket Punch,* p. 49).

114 - 'On the voyage out to Australia...' (*Island Cricketers,* p. 61).

116 - 'I got my century...' (**Marshall, Roy**; *Test Outcast,* Pelham Books, 1970, p. 49).

116 - 'John Figueroa...' ('West Indians enjoy club cricket in England,' *Beckford's cricket annual*, 1953-54, pp. 35,37,39).

Chapter 15 – 1952-53: A RETURN TO THE CARIBBEAN

118 - 'Sailing by banana boat to face the Three Ws' by G.S. Ramchand espncricinfo.com/story/_/id/23009905/ sailing-banana-boat-face-three-ws

120 - 'I was all too aware...' (*Under the Sun,* p. 134).

121 - 'It was indeed unfortunate...' (ibid, pp. 135-136).

Chapter 16 – 1954: ENGLAND AGAIN, AND HUTTON

127 - 'It was only some time later...' (*Under the Sun,* p. 143).

128 - 'Right from the start..' (*Back Foot,* p. 50).

131 - 'The near riot which...' (**Manley**, p. 104).

132 - 'Frank was in the middle...' (*Island Cricketers,* p. 91).

Chapter 17 – 1954-55: AUSTRALIA AND LEADERSHIP DRAMA

135 -   Correspondence cited between WICBC members during the Fifties was extracted from files donated by Charles Merry from the collection left by his father, Cyril Merry.

135 -   'preposterous in any circumstances...' (*Under the Sun,* p. 151).

140 -   'Atkinson was selected...' (*Back Foot,* p. 74).

Notes to Part Three

Chapter 18 – 1954-67: EMIGRATION AND FREEMASONRY

148 -   Eulogy delivered to the Sussex Lodge, 354 E.C., Jamaica, on the occasion of the death of Sir Frank Worrell by Bro. Carl Jackman, P.M., D.G.J.W., of the D.G. Lodge of Jamaica (undated).

Chapter 19 – 1956-59: MANCHESTER UNIVERSITY

152 -   Monograph: **Mosley, P. and Ingham, B.**; "Fighting discrimination: W. Arthur Lewis and the dual economy of Manchester in the 1950s." Working Paper. Department of Economics, University of Sheffield ISSN 1749-8368, 2013.

155 -   Rodney Norville, another Barbadian living in England who had attended Combermere – he died in 2019 – said that while Worrell was at Manchester, 'he was able to see more of his friend Dr. C.B. Clarke who also played for the West Indies some years before Frank.' Interview with author, London, England, 2017.

Chapter 20 – 1958-59: SOUTH AFRICA –INTEGRATION AND SEGREGATION

159 -   'I was born a Cape Coloured...' (D'Oliveira, Basil; *Time to Declare,* 1982, p. 2).

159 -   'But I never had a hatred...' (ibid, p. 4).

160 -   'As there was no point...' (ibid, p. 5).

160 -   Jonty Winch described the planning in a book chapter called 'Should the West Indies Have Toured South Africa in 1959? C.L.R. James versus Learie Constantine,' in Murray, Bruce; Parry, Richard; Winch, Jonty (eds.); *Cricket and Society in South Africa, 1910-1971: From Union to Isolation,* Palgrave Studies in Sports and Politics, Macmillan, 2018, Chapter 10, pp. 275-306).

162 -   At its March 1959 AGM at the boardroom of Alstons Limited at 69 Marine Square, Port-of-Spain on Wednesday 25 and Thursday 26 March 1959, Sir Errol dos Santos:

164 -   'QPCC members referred to him: as 'The Great White Lord.' (**Lequay, Alloy** (ed.); *A Tale of Three Eras: Cricket Renaissance, Trinidad and Tobago, 1956-2005,* RPL, 2006 (p. 9).

164 -   On 3 April 1959, Edghill wrote the following letter to Worrell at his Radcliffe home as requested.

'I am directed by my Board to bring to your attention certain representations that have been made to my Board by sources in South Africa representing both the white and non white views. In this regard you will find attached copy of a letter from the South Africa Sports Association dated 17.3.59.

'I am also to advise you that my Board has been informed that you have received representations of a similar nature from various other Bodies and persons interested in the advancement and welfare of the non white section of the South African community. I am to quote particularly from a letter received from Mr. G.C. Grant, who has been resident in South Africa for many years.

'I can imagine some saying that by sending a team to South Africa to play against non European teams the W.I. will be doing a service. I desire to suggest that if the W.I. Board sends a team it will be not so much to delight folk as to confirm the declared policy of the Government. Moreover, in sending a team, the W.I. Board will not quicken but delay the breaking down of the barriers which are so part and parcel of the present policy. Again, a visit from a W.I. team is likely to perpetuate colour discrimination, rather than eliminate it. And of course, I am sure that no West Indian will readily welcome being treated at a 2nd class or even 3rd class visitor as far as travel facilities, hotel accommodation, social amenities etc.

are concerned. I strongly advise against the acceptance of the invitation, and you are at liberty to make my point of view known with appropriate discretion.'

'My Board is not disposed to undertake a tour to South Africa so long as the present policy of segregation continues and last year refused an invitation to send a team to South Africa as it was not considered to be in the best interests of either the West Indian or the non white section of the South African community. Our decision was communicated to the South African authority.

'My Board is satisfied, from reports received from parties who view sympathetically the struggle for equity, that you and members of your team will be subjected not only to considerable inconvenience and embarrassment but also to indignities which we are certain are not within your experience.

'Consideration has been given also to the fact that certain players invited by you to tour South Africa may be required to represent the West Indies in the forthcoming tour of the West Indies by the M.C.C. and it is felt that their efficiency may be impaired by the proposed tour to South Africa following as it does the present tour of India and Pakistan, as well as the services or engagements of some of these players.

'In all these circumstances it is the feeling of my Board that any tour of South Africa by a team of West Indian players, at this time with conditions as they are, would be most unwise and they cannot too strongly urge you to give every consideration to the cancellation of the tour."

167 - **Our cricket tour to South Africa** (Constantine, Learie; 'OUR CRICKET TOUR TO SOUTH AFRICA; LEARIE CONSTANTINE SAYS WHY HE OPPOSES,' The *Nation Newspaper*, T&T, 24 April 1959.)

167 - **That Worrell tour**: (James, C.L.R.; 'THAT WORRELL TOUR,' The *Nation Newspaper*, T&T, 15 May 1959.)

170 - 'An excerpt of a letter...' (19 June 1959) 'We have had a long letter from Frank on the South African Tour, the gist of which is that he and the other professionals are left little option but to sell their, what he terms "specialised services" in a market that desires them, and take the chance on the consequence of the Tour. He stresses that the professionals cannot obtain any routine jobs at home during the off season, and are keenly disposed to the idea of earning a

little in South Africa. In this connection, Berkeley says that they have been offered substantial sums, and I believe that he mentioned that Worrell's fee would be £1,000.

'At the same time, and in fairness to Frank, he assures me that late last year he wrote to Cyril Merry notifying him of the Tour in order to prevent a clash of dates with the M.C.C. Tour of West Indies, and he has sent me in support of his statement, the original letter dated 17th November 1958 which Cyril wrote in reply. He says too that he does not wish to offend the West Indies Board in any way, and that he has no intention of jeopardizing our chances against England, as no one wishes to see M.C.C. beaten more than he does. He assures me that he has made arrangements for Sobers, Hunte and Weekes to be back in the West Indies for the Barbados match if their services are required, and that the other players we may want can be back in the West Indies at the end of the year. This all seems fair enough to me, and I am giving him the suggested M.C.C. Itinerary.

'He says that when he spoke to Berkeley in London, he was wavering a bit afterwards, but a few days later, representatives of the South African Board produced some equally impressive arguments which made up his mind for him that he should go through with the Tour.

'As a result of Frank's letter, I am, on the instructions of the President, writing to the key professionals enquiring as to their availability for the M.C.C. Tour, and stating that they are expected to be on hand at the very commencement of the Tour. I shall of course let you know what replies we get from them.'

174 - Internal correspondence suggested that members had become testy with each other. Cecil Marley had written to Wishart on 30 June about the tour, referring to Wishart's letter of the 19th, and his of the 18th.

'This is a matter which was dealt with at some length in my previous letter. I do not see how the contents of your letter can in any way alter our observations on this subject.

'If I know for a fact that Worrell had received the letter from the Board mentioned under the heading Minutes in my letter of the 18th instant I would come to the conclusion, without much trouble, that he was determined to carry through the tour regardless, money being the only consideration. I am quite certain that he has not been

285

properly informed as to the conditions he will meet in South Africa or advised what to expect, and I frankly feel that no good can come from a tour of this nature.

'The reference by Worrell to correspondence with Cyril Merry would seem to indicate that he has received no official communication from the Board; if so, and as a result of our failure to communicate with Worrell at the proper time the Board may once again find itself at the receiving end of the stick. What a difference had the letter been sent in March or early April as was the intention of the Board at the last meeting!'

(The letter he referred to was sent to Worrell after the AGM and was dated 3 April.)

Chapter 22 – END OF THE THREE Ws

182 - Sir Garfield interview, 2016.

184 - **Sobers, Garry; Harris, Bob**; *Garry Sobers, My Autobiography*, Headline Book Publishing, 2002 (p. 44).

185 - 'The marathon Cowdrey-May partnership...' (**Baxter, Peter; Hayter, Peter**; *England vs West Indies, Highlights since 1948*, BBC Books, 1991, p. 31).

185 - Gerry Gomez was part of the commentary team, as a summariser. The first Test at Edgbaston was the first time the BBC was broadcasting ball-by-ball commentary in England.

187 - Dr. Michael Walcott interview 2016.

191 - 'I put my scruples aside...' (*Beyond a Boundary*, p. 232).

192 - In Mike Coward's *Calypso Summer*, Alexander said, 'I had always felt I was only a stand-in for Frank until his studies were completed at Manchester University. Who was I to have an altercation with Frank? I was tremendously delighted when he was finally appointed captain. I thought the great injustice of my appointment against Pakistan in 1957-58 was not primarily to Frank Worrell but to Clyde Walcott and Everton Weekes. When I was made captain Clyde and Everton came to me and said there was a fine set of youngsters who wished to play under me, because they would never let the public say that because Gerry Alexander was captain of the West Indies team they didn't wish to play. They

also said' "Let me tell you, at the end of the Pakistan tour, we will retire." And in fact they did.'

194 - 'I remember we were staying...' (Sir Garfield Sobers interview, 2016).

Notes to Part Four

Chapter 23 – THE CROSSING

197 - 'You like that shot?...' (Sir Garfield Sobers interview, 2016).

197 - 'Although he could be sharp...' (Ainsworth Harewood, interview, Trinidad, 14 October 2016.

198 - 'It calls to mind a profile of the former US President...' (**Gabriel García Márquez**; 'The Mysteries of Bill Clinton', (translated by Alastair Reid) *Cambio*, 1 February 1999.).

198 - Wes Hall interview, Barbados, 2016.

198 - 'Jamican academic...' (**Figueroa, John**; *West Indies in England, The great post-war tours,* Kingswood Press, 1991, p. 71).

199 - 'he was amazed...' (**James, C.L.R.**; in Arlott, John, ed.; *Cricket: The Great Captains,* 1971).

199 - 'In Worrell's obituary...' (**James, C.L.R.**; 'Sir Frank Worrell: The Man Whose Leadership Made History,' in *The Cricketer*, vol. 48, 5 May 1967).

199 - Wes Hall interview, 2016.

Chapter 24 – 1960-61: AUSTRALIA AND THE BEAUTIFUL GAME

203 - 'Out of a muddy pond...' (**David Rudder**: *The Gilded Collection*, 1986-1989, 'Dedication (A Praise Song),' Audio CD 1993).

203 - 'Is nine months...' (**David Rudder**: *The Gilded Collection*, 1986-1989, 'Engine Room,' Audio CD 1993).

204 - 'Recall the Rex Alston complaint...' (*England vs West Indies, Highlights since 1948*, p. 31).

205 - 'As captain in Australia...' (**Coward, Mike**; *Calypso Summer,* ABC Books, December 2000, p. 60).

205 - 'Two books by Australian journalists...' *With the West Indies in Australia* by **Johnny Moyes**, and *Calypso Summer* by **Mike Coward**, offer comprehensive details of the visit.

205 - **Moyes, Johnny**; *With the West Indies in Australia, 1960-61,* Heinemann, 1961.

206 - He told us we were not just flannel(led) fools...' (Conrad Hunte in *Calypso Summer*, p. 27).

206 - 'Frank clearly understood...' (Wes Hall in *Calypso Summer,* p. 27).

207 - 'Coward noted that privately...' (ibid, p. 72).

207 - 'The following day...' (**Moyes**, p. 10).

208 - 'Boundaries were coming regularly: (ibid, p. 20).

208 - 'However, with Sobers...' (ibid, p. 21).

208 - 'His driving was so majestic...' (ibid, p. 23).

209 - 'This impertinent little batsman...' (ibid, p. 32).

209 - 'In the total of 254...' (ibid, p. 41).

209 - 'Although the White Australia Policy...' (*Calypso Summer,* p. 30).

211 - 'Lindsay Kline said...' (ibid, p.35).

211 - 'The West Indies batsmen...' (Moyes, p. 59).

212 - TEST ENDS IN TIE ON SECOND-LAST BALL. Melbourne, Saturday. The fifth Test between Australian and the West Indies at the Melbourne Cricket Ground today broke two world records. The attendance of 90,800 and gate takings of £16,416, were the greatest ever in international cricket. (*The Age*, 15 December 1960).

214 - 'Coward reported that Peter Lashley...' (*Calypso Summer*, p. 160).

214 - Presentation ceremony, post Fifth Test, at Melbourne. youtube.com/watch?v=H8BIzrQX0rc

Chapter 25 – 1961-67: INSIDE ACADEMIA

221 - Alva Anderson interview, Jamaica, 25 May 2018.

221 - Ainsworth Harewood interview, Trinidad, 2016.

223 - Baldwin Mootoo interview, Trinidad, 23 August 2016.

223 - The *Pelican Annual* 1966, 'Editorial,' p. 7.

223 - The *Pelican Annual* 1966, 'The Dean of Students Speaks,' p. 8.
227 - Handwritten letter from Worrell on 25 August, to Hugh Holness.

'I am in possession of your letter of the 18th of August re payment of interest on Mortgage loan. I must confess that I had gained the impression somewhere along the line that repayment was not due until one year after the loan was made, consequently the matter never exercised my mind. I do apologise for my ignorance. You can either deduct the sum from my annuity (if this is constitutional) or from the year's salary whichever is convenient to you. I would rather it be taken from the Annuity if it is possible.' / Letter to Hugh Holness from Worrell, 16 December 1965. 'Dear Hugh, Apologies for this belated reply to your letter re payment of interest and instalment of sinking fund. I was away in St. Lucia for a fortnight and have only recently returned to the desk. I further apologise for the confusion into which I have put you and indeed myself in that I was informed (obviously wrongly) that university loans were interest-free in the first year. So you can appreciate my dismay when I referred to the Rules for Academic and Senior Administrative Staff to find that an annual instalment was due at the end of the first year. To be quite honest, the misunderstanding, the extraordinary expenditure brought about by the secondment in the first place and then the transfer to St. Augustine have played havoc with my budgeting. Things are literally chaotic. I have been trying to find ways and means of borrowing the necessary £600 but it seems to be the wrong time of the year... There are two suggestions I can make (1) sell the house and repay the loan or (2) give you permission to withhold all or any part of my salary that you think necessary. I have burnt up the maximum nervous energy trying to raise the money and failed to do so. The suggestions are desperate ones and I leave it to you to decide what course you think necessary. I had hoped that the superannuation returned by the Trinidad Government on my secondment with them might have been accepted as payment of interest due but I feel this is a bit too optimistic. I am sorry to have to write this sort of letter but the worry I have experienced over the past four months (since I was informed of my debt) has been second to none. I am deeply sorry and await your decision.' / The FSSU mentioned is the Federated

Superannuation System for Universities, of which The UWI is still a participating institution. It is the pension plan for Academic, Senior Administrative and Professional staff.

Chapter 27 – 1963: FAREWELL TO ENGLAND

238 - Naipaul, V.S.; 'The Test,' from *Summer Days: Writers on Cricket,* ed. by Michael Meyer, Eyre Methuen, 1981).
240 - **Ross, Alan**; *The West Indies at Lord's,* Eyre & Spottiswoode, 1963, p. 85.
241 - Letter from Gerry Gomez to Ken Wishart, presented at the WICBC AGM in March.

Feb 20, 1961

Dear Ken,

'The tour has now come to an end, and there are a few days left before we leave Australia on Friday, 24th February.

You are no doubt delighted at the wonderful public response to the Melbourne Test, which attracted 275,000 people and which provided us with a taking of £25,400. This is a record for a visiting team, as was the attendance on the Saturday of the game when 90,800 people attended.

I have asked the newspaper concerned to provide me with copies of an aerial photograph of the ground, which gives an excellent illustration of this great event.

The great experience of the tour, however, was the fantastic public demonstration given to our team by the people of Melbourne. The newspapers reported that 500,000 people took part in this demonstration, and during our parade through the streets to the Town Hall all traffic in that area came to a standstill.

It was quite moving and you can well imagine how emotionally overcome we all were by the wonderful expressions of goodwill and friendliness which these people made to the members of the team; it left us with no doubt that our team has created the greatest impression on the public of Australia, and it was indeed a tribute to the manner in which this team has played its cricket and conducted itself off the field.

Our team has certainly revitalized cricket not only in Australia but throughout the cricket world, and the West Indian contribution to present-day cricket has been the greatest of all time.

The game was losing its interest as a spectator sport and this tour has restored to the minds of cricket enthusiasts throughout the world that cricket is still a worthwhile pastime and a great institution, which has always formed a large part of the British way of life.

This has had the result of considerable financial success and while I told you in my letter of 6th February that I was optimistic about a profit of £A35,000, there is every indication that this figure will get nearer to the £A40,000 mark.

We have started wending our way home by virtue of the fact that the six travellers by ship went off to Perth and this morning I saw Sonny Ramadhin off by air. Tomorrow Gibbs and Solomon are parting company with us ahead of time in order to spend a few days in New York and, as already indicated to you, the rest of leave on Friday 24th.

Gerry Alexander and Cammie Smith will be going to New Zealand to represent Lord Cobham's team against the M.C.C. and it will be noted that Cammie has replaced Frank Worrell whose legs have been troubling him lately.

I have cabled you today regarding the means of travel for various members of the team from New York to their final destinations. In view of our broken itinerary the days of departure from New York do not coincide with B.W.I.A. flights, with the result that we have resorted to the use of other carriers. This is regrettable, and I trust that you will explain these circumstances to anyone from B.W.I.A. commenting on our not using their facilities.

As the tour was coming to an end I had discussions with our Tour Officials with particular regard to the compensation to be awarded to amateurs on this team. It is our understanding that the Board meets on 6th March and this subject will be one of the items on the agenda. In addition, I have no doubt that the matter of a bonus will be raised and I trust that you will bring to the attention of the meeting the views expressed in this letter.

I am taking the liberty, therefore, of submitting this memorandum in the hope that it will provide useful background for deliberation by the Board Members, and produce an ultimate decision in these matters.

The following considerations based on our actual experiences throughout this tour are submitted hereunder:

We are aware that the Board at a previous meeting agreed in principle to compensate the amateurs on this tour to the extent of 50% of any income loss during the period they were on tour. While we do not for a moment wish to appear to be criticizing the Board's decision, it is very evident to us on the spot in Australia that this form of compensation is inadequate and even total compensation of income loss at home would be inadequate, for the reason that home income is in most cases related to standards of living there and cost of items at home. On this tour these same amateurs are required to live in the standard of the environment of the cities and the hotels into which they are booked, and follow a pattern of life customary for the people with whom their touring activities bring them constantly into contact.

In line with the foregoing arguments we would like to make the point that having regard to the evidence on this tour of standards and costs of living, the £7 per week allowance to all members of the party is inadequate to meet the amount of the miscellaneous costs which it is intended to cover. In support of this we have ascertained that each Australian player in a State Game against us received an expense allowance of £A2.10s.0d per day (for some States the figure is greater) plus all travelling, hotel accommodation, laundry, etc. Also, for purposes of comparison, we might add that each Australian player taking part in a Test Match receives an allowance of £85 per Test Match. We mention these facts because they are relevant to our arguments inasmuch as they are payments made to amateur players within the context of standards and costs of living in these cities. We do not wish to insinuate that we consider the West Indies Board in a position to recompense their players at all times at the same level as Australian players. Indeed, the Australian amateur on tour is compensated on a considerably higher basis, but since we are, for this purpose, concerned with our tour in Australia, we regard their allowance for games in Australia to be more relevant.

The evidence of this tour is that every member of the party has had to utilise other funds to meet expenditure which should normally be covered by the weekly out-of-pocket allowance. In many cases we have been able to help the amateurs particularly, by getting for them TV appearances for which they received TV fees. Some of the other amateurs in fact will need to draw on funds from home to meet a deficit. The professionals, of course, have been able to draw on their professional fees.

The Board will be delighted, as we are, that this tour has been an outstanding success. The evidence is glaring that the reputations of the West Indians have been considerably enhanced both as cricketers and as people. It may well be that in the Board's deliberations they will wish to show their appreciation to the members of the party on tour for achieving this state of affairs. It is our view that in any consideration of this matter the amateurs should be first compensated to a level no less than the special allowance granted to the amateurs on the 1951/2 Tour of Australia (i.e. £350 sterling), this, of course, being instead of any broken-time payment allowance. We emphasize the need to compensate the amateurs at this level before awarding bonuses to the professionals, particularly because of the earnings of the amateurs at home, which in most cases are extremely small, whereas the amateur on this tour has played his full part along with the professionals in the tremendous success achieved from all points of view.

It is felt that the above considerations set out clearly what we feel is the entitlement to the amateur and that this allowance should not in any way whatsoever influence to any extent any decisions which the Board intends to make on the matter of bonuses to be awarded to all members of the touring party.

On the subject of bonuses, it is felt that this tour and its great success justifies the award of a bonus the size of which will be dependent on the Board's appreciation of the task carried out by this team.

It has been recorded that this is the greatest Test Series of all time. Our cricketers have set an example of considerable ability, genuine sportsmanship and the spirit of enterprise and enthusiasm which will, for a considerable time, be an example to the rest of the world.

The public relations of this team have been excellent, for many team members proved to be excellent ambassadors by going into sporting organizations, clubs, religious organizations and virtually into the highways and by-ways of Australian life, proving to this country that the West Indian is a good type of human being. This effect on the public has resulted in much popularity accruing to the team and with its high standard of play, the success of this tour was assured.

I make this important point for the fact that our Federated Units are on the verge of self-government, and this team by virtue of its stupendous popularity has shown to the world a very good picture of the West Indian. This is the most important tour that a West Indian team has ever done and for what this band of people have done for the game of cricket should be recognized by the award of a suitable and generous bonus.

In the same context I would like now to strongly recommend that the President should consider making overtures to the right Government quarters to have appropriate honours bestowed on Frank Worrell for the great service which he has done, not only to the West Indies, but to the cricket world in general. He, above all, has had the most profound effect on this team and is easily the greatest single factor in the outstanding success of this tour.

He has had a distinguished career as a cricketer and a gentleman, and apart from gracing all the cricket fields of the world with his majesty and charm plus an exceptional ability, he has now revitalized the game of cricket and has probably made the greatest contribution to the game for very many years.

It is my attention on arrival in Jamaica to obtain an interview with Mr. Norman Manley and put the suggestion to him that Frank Worrell be considered as an outstanding prospect for a knighthood. There is no better way of subscribing to feelings of nationalism than through sport, and here we have one of the outstanding figures of all time in the person of Frank Worrell. Such an honour would have considerable political value, but best of all it would throw the full spotlight on our cricket and give the game in our territories new meaning and importance.

I am very much in the dark regarding the approach to such matters, and I am not certain whether such a matter should be done through the Unit or Federal Government. However, Mr. Norman Manley will no doubt provide me with the proper information, but I felt that a recommendation should also come from our Board as if such a thing does come to pass, it will be of great value to our cricket.

As promised I have enclosed twelve copies of our autographs and trust that they are not too late to be put to the use for which they were required.

Our official picture has now been done and again it is regretted that this had to take place late in the tour. We had taken what was going to be the official picture in Sydney, but the proofs turned out so badly that we eventually had the job carried out in Adelaide – this time to our satisfaction. I will pass out copies to the Australian Board and their affiliated associations, and also to the Caltex and T.A.A. Organisations.

There is little to add except that this tour has been a wonderful and worthwhile experience for every member of the party. This team will take away from Australia many happy memories, the chief of which are the love and admiration of the Australian people who showed in no uncertain manner that they deeply appreciated this team as cricketers and as human beings.

I shall be spending a week in Jamaica and it is hoped that by the time of my return to Trinidad I shall have my report drafted.

I shall obtain from Max a report dealing with the financial affairs of the tour and will include this in my official report to the Board.

Thanks again for all your help and I do hope that you have a successful Board Meeting.

Yours very truly,

(SGD.) Gerry Gomez

P.S. Yesterday on seeing Lance and Joe off it was found that Mr. Menzies the P.M. was travelling on the same plane. He invited Frank and I to have drinks with him in his private rest room and at an appropriate moment I took up with him the matter of having suitable honours bestowed on Frank. As a great admirer of Frank he was most interested and promised me that he would make a point of seeing Mr. McLeod the Colonial Secretary on the matter. I did not specify Knighthood but suggested the highest honours and he waxed quite enthusiastic. This added note comes after dictating this letter yesterday afternoon.'

Notes to Part Five

Chapter 28 – 1964-66: BRINGING IN THE SHEAVES:
Sowing in the Sunshine

245 -   Letters between Ian Turbott, Administrator of Grenada (25 May 1964), and Philip Sherlock, (2 June 1964) and Sherlock's letter to Sir Frank of the same date. ... For two weeks in November, every day was packed with activities. He did coaching sessions with St. Mary's College, Vieux-Fort Secondary, and various clubs at Gros Islet, Victoria Park, Choiseul, Canaries, Anse-La-Raye, Soufrière, Dennery, Micoud, Laborie and Vieux-Fort. He even played for St. Lucia in a festival match against a Combined XI. (Worrell's staff file, The UWI, St. Augustine).

246 -   'He didn't react too good to it...' (Sir Garfield Sobers interview, 2016).

246 -   Correspondence from Worrell's staff files: Mona and St. Augustine campuses, The UWI.

247 -   Link to clip from the 1967 film, *Around the World.* youtube.com/watch?app=desktop&v=-yogeh-y4bY

251 -   Interview with Bryan Davis, Trinidad, 29 August 2016. He had written a newspaper article in 2014, describing the New Year's Day riot in 1967.

Chapter 29 – 1966-67: BRINGING IN THE SHEAVES:
Sowing in the Shadows

250 -   Worrell's newspaper article on Barbados vs a Rest of the World XI is quoted by Tennant (without citation) at pages 93 and 94.

252 -   'He informed the team...' (Bryan Davis interview, 2016).

252 -   'He told me he wasn't feeling well...' (Sir Garfield Sobers interview, 2016.)

253 -   'When I brought the stuff...' (Sir Everton Weekes interview, 2016.)

253 -   'I have looked at the statement sent to you by Mr. Thomas in respect of Lady Worrell's account and certify that all payments

made by me on her behalf are included therein. I expect that you will adjust suitably the money advanced for her air passage since this was subsequently granted to her by the Finance and General Purposes Committee. I would question the item, "£18 to Forte for making suit for the late Sir Frank Worrell," and would think that in Law you would not be on good ground in charging this to Lady Worrell's account. I will take it up with Mr. Thomas, but for the record, wish to advise that Lady Worrell had nothing whatsoever to do with the making of this suit. Sir Frank, who was unaware of his impending death, whilst in hospital here, arranged for a tailor to measure him for two suits. He died on the day that these were completed. We buried him in one of them and the other I was able to sell and reimburse the tailor. The suit in which Sir Frank was buried would seem to be properly chargeable to his estate and not to Lady Worrell's account, since, as far as I know, the payment of six months' salary to the widow of a staff member has no strings whatsoever attached and debts owed by the staff member cannot be deducted from it.' (Memo to Secretary, St. Augustine, from registrar, Carl Jackman, 14 November 1967).

254 - 'My parents had Uncle Frankie...' (Lalita Phadkar interview, 2018.)

Chapter 30 – FAMILY MATTERS

259 - Olwen Cumberbatch interview, November 2016.
260 - Dr. Michael Walcott interview, November 2016.
262 - Online interviews with Tiro Swaby, 2018-2021.

Chapter 31 – ENCOMIUMS

265 - 'He had lived more...' (**Samuel, John**; *Manchester Guardian,* 14 March 1967).
26 - Cardus, Neville; 'Like Hobbs – never a crude or an ungrammatical stroke.' *Manchester Guardian,* 15 March 1967.
265 - 'had already written...' (**C.L.R. James**, *The Cricketer,* 5 May 1967.)

265 - MCC Committee Meeting, 1969, on the Sir Frank Worrell Commonwealth Memorial Fund. MCC Archives.

267 - Letter from Sir Hugh Wooding to S. Griffith (Billy), 16 January 1968. MCC Archives.

268 - Letter from Antony Murray (J.A.J.), SFWCMF committee member, to fellow members. The omission of provisions for Velda and Lana is notable as this is an internal document. (November 1968, MCC archives).

268 - Letter from Bagenal Harvey to S. Griffith, 4 February 1969. MCC Archives.

271 - **McMorris, Dr. Michael Neville**; 'Worrell: The Exemplar' circa 2010. Essay emailed to the author by Dr. McMorris following a conversation in Jamaica in May 2018.

272 - **Baugh, Edward**; 'The Pulpit-Eulogists of Frank Worrell,' in his *It was the Singing*, Sandberry Press (2000).

Appendix

International Conference of Cricket
meeting at Lord's 19 July 1961.
Minutes: Item No. 4. South African Cricket Association.

The Chairman suggested that the Conference might wish to discuss the position confronting the South African Cricket Association arising from the decision of the South African Government to withdraw from the Commonwealth. Mr. R.E. Foster Bowley then suggested that it might facilitate discussion if he were to withdraw.

The Chairman then reminded the meeting that as South Africa were no longer in the British Commonwealth, it was not possible for the South African Cricket Association to be a member of the Imperial Cricket Conference under its present constitution. He said that written representations had been received from Pakistan and enquired whether their representative might care to enlarge on these.

Mr. M. Hussain (Pakistan), expressing the views of his Board of Control, said that any request from South Africa to be associated with the Imperial Cricket Conference, although no longer a member of the Commonwealth, should only be considered if a clear undertaking was given by the South African Cricket Association that they would drop their attitude of exclusiveness and would engage in international contests with all other Commonwealth Countries irrespective of colour. In that case the Conference might consider widening the definition of Associate Membership sufficiently to include a country in the position of South Africa, and making other consequential amendments in the Rules. The question of apartheid inside the teams, which South Africa may select for international contests, might be postponed for later consideration, but until the undertaking and amendments mentioned above are given and made, Pakistan must strongly oppose the admission of South Africa to the Conference in any capacity.

Mr. M.A. Chidambaram (India) said that the views of his Board of Control were similar to those of Pakistan. At the same time, he pointed out that the fact that the South African Government had decided to leave the Commonwealth on 31st May, 1961 had not in any way altered the position in respect of the playing of multi-racial games in South Africa. Nevertheless, he felt that if some understanding along the lines of that proposed by Pakistan were given this would materially help the general situation.

The Chairman then read to the meeting the personal views of Mr. Foster Bowley as stated by him in writing regarding the position of the South African Cricket Association in relation to inter-racial cricket. He felt that this might help to clarify the issues involved.

It was subsequently agreed by Mr. Foster Bowley that this statement should be included in the minutes and it is accordingly set out below:

There is no colour bar in the constitution of the South African Cricket Association and we have no intention of writing one into it.

Although there is, in fact, no law prohibiting inter-racial cricket, we as an Association have not officially promoted such games in deference to stated Government policy.

We have considered promoting inter-racial games, but have for the time being at any rate decided against them, because we feel that if we do we shall only invite the Government to make these games illegal, thereby preventing the unofficial games which presently take place between teams of non-white and white players.

We should gladly accept invitations to tour India, Pakistan and the West Indies. In this connection it must, however, be realised that we could not invite any of these countries to South Africa because the Government, at ministerial level, has stated it will not allow non-white teams into South Africa to play against white teams, and will only permit them to play against non-white teams.

It is not possible to give any undertaking that the South African Cricket Association will take active steps to remedy the existing position, because to do so would be to involve the Association in politics, with, we fear, very disastrous results. The Association has up to now managed to keep out of politics and in the view of the present Board should continue to do so.

Mr. S.G. Webb (Australia) made a plea on behalf of cricket in South Africa, and he agreed that the constitution of the Conference would have to be changed if it was decided that South Africa should be re-admitted as a member. He stated, however, that neither he nor Mr. Macmillan had any authority to express any view which would bind the Australian Board of Control which would consider the matter at its next meeting.

Mr. J.B. Stollmeyer (West Indies) was most concerned that the Conference might be in danger of contributing towards the demise of cricket in South Africa, but he felt that an assurance should be given by the South African Cricket Association that they would direct their efforts towards the playing of multi-racial cricket in South Africa before the West Indies Cricket Board of Control agreed to their re-admission as a member of the Conference. He wondered whether the Conference would declare itself opposed to apartheid in cricket.

Sir Arthur Sims (New Zealand) was anxious to support the interests of cricket. He hoped, therefore, that it would be possible for a bridge to be built to bring South Africa back into the Conference. He felt that their presence was in the best interests of the game, and that the other countries should do everything possible to bring them back.

Mr. G.O. Allen (M.C.C.) pointed out that the South African Cricket Association were willing and anxious to play cricket with all countries in the Conference, but politically this may not be possible for the time being. If it was decided not to re-admit South Africa to the Conference it would only support those in favour of apartheid, and add to the difficulties of those whom we were anxious to help.

Mr. M. Saeed (Pakistan) warned the meeting that the views of Mr. Foster Bowley as read to the meeting showed no change of heart and that in the circumstances, therefore, Pakistan would oppose any move for the re-admission of South Africa into the Conference so long as the situation existed.

It was evident from the views expressed by the delegates that there was a general desire to help the South African Cricket Association in the situation in which they found themselves. Nevertheless, before any question of their re-admission to the Conference should be considered, it would be necessary to revise the constitution. Furthermore, it might well be that for other reasons such a proposal might need consideration.

After this full discussion the following Press Statement was prepared and agreed for immediate release:

Rule 5 of the Rules of the Imperial Cricket Conference provides that membership of the Conference shall cease should a country concerned cease to be part of the British Commonwealth. The agenda for the Conference had to be sent out prior to the South African Government's decision to leave the Commonwealth, with the result that the consequent position of the South African Cricket Association could not be included on the agenda. A long discussion did however take place in order that delegates might be in a position to report back to their respective Boards the general feelings of the Conference on this issue. The whole question will be further considered at the next meeting of the Imperial Cricket Conference.

Acknowledgments

One of the major challenges of writing this biography of Frank Worrell was the paucity of archival material. No collection of his papers exists; whatever was collected has been lost through fires, floods, and the decay of time. While many articles have been written about him, they mostly echo each other, so often repeating misinformation, that they have trickled down as facts.

The only hope of unearthing details was to seek primary sources, people who knew him; but even that was fraught with complications. It was an urgent quest because they were mainly elderly, afflicted with various infirmities, the most common of which was failing memory. During the research, a few of the subjects of my interviews died, some shortly after we had spoken.

Still, most were delighted to share their recollections, however faltering, and willingly allowed me to poke around the cubby holes of their minds.

Luckily, my first encounter was with the late Sir Everton Weekes, with whom I formed a friendship that grew from our initial formal interview in 2016 to regular telephone chats over four years. I cherish my exposure to his remarkable memory and his eventual candour in discussing the early years of the Three Ws, and their experiences. Without those nuggets to guide me, I would have overlooked many of the byways. Sir Everton was my compass.

Perhaps the most serendipitous of meetings took place when I went to the home of Charles Merry on his cocoa estate to interview him about his award-winning beans. Charles is the eldest grandson of Conrad Stollmeyer. Jeffrey and Victor were his cousins, and as we wound up, conversation drifted to cricket. He mentioned that he had recently rediscovered a cardboard box containing documents belonging to his father, Cyril, who had been a member of the WICBC in the Fifties. Charles had emigrated to Venezuela and lived there for 40 years before returning to Trinidad in 2011. The box had remained intact for all that time, and if I wanted, he could let me borrow it. I was excited. My search for WICBC documents had been fruitless – the WICB had lost its archival documents in a fire many years ago, and even individual files from members had been lost over time. In 1961, Gerry Gomez had lost all his papers in a fire at his businessplace. Charles promised to look for the box again and soon, he called to say he had found it and I could come to collect.

These papers, roughly spanning the decade of the Fifties and two years into the Sixties, were in fairly good condition. Cyril Merry was obviously a meticulous secretary, who believed in record-keeping. I carefully pored over those files, gently separating clumps, and removing pins and clips that were deeply encrusted in rust. It was a box of treasure, and for months, I repeatedly went through them, sorting them by date and subject until eventually, I knew the contents, now stored in differently coloured file folders, intimately. Those documents unlocked many mysteries of the period and cleared up several misconceptions. In sharing these documents, Charles Merry has made an invaluable contribution to West Indies cricket history, and his generosity is deeply appreciated.

Despite the general archival sparseness, I consulted often with librarians, and where it was possible, visited to see what I could unearth. The pandemic meant many enquiries were made via email, but despite the limitations, I came away convinced that archivists and librarians must be the most dedicated souls in the world. Without fail, they were accommodating, efficient and enthusiastic, even offering information I had not specifically sought, because they thought it would be relevant.

Thanks to permission granted by the then University registrar, Clement Iton, I was given access to Worrell's personal staff files held at the Mona and St. Augustine campuses of The UWI. When I visited Mona, Stanley Griffin, the assistant archivist then, personally guided me through the holdings of the archives. At St. Augustine, Jo-Anne Georges informed me that the files were in too fragile a condition for me to handle them, but copied and emailed some, a major feat considering she had said they could not be handled. At Cave Hill, I was able to look at the general cricket collection. At the Alma Jordan Library, I was also able to go through newspaper clippings and other material thanks to access granted by Frank Soodeen Jr., the campus librarian. When the pandemic debarred me from entering, Aisha Baptiste, a library assistant for the West Indiana and Special Collections, was a blessing. Not only did she track down my request for obscure clippings, but she contacted other university libraries to see if she could locate them on my behalf.

It was the same at the Heritage Division of the National Library and Information System Authority (NALIS) in Port of Spain. Librarian Camille George ferreted out information, guided me to unknown sources and suggested possible avenues, even when NALIS was closed to the public. I am indebted to her and her colleagues.

Mike Brearley introduced me by email to Adam Chadwick, who was then Curator of Collections at the MCC. In turn, he connected me to Neil Robinson, the Library and Research Manager, and Robert Curphey, then the Archive and Library Manager. They had prepared for my visit by extracting all the material they had pertaining to Worrell, so that I was faced with a practical groaning board of documents, books and photographs: a researcher's feast.

Ramachandra Guha suggested I find the diary of Paul Gibb for an account of one of the Commonwealth tours to India which had been serialised in *Wisden Cricket Monthly*. The MCC did not have it, but fortuitously, at the Kia Oval, a chance remark led me to it. I was talking to Matthew Thacker of Forward Press and mentioned my failed quest. He led me to a bookshelf where bound copies of WCM nestled. He copied and emailed them to me. My thanks.

I am grateful to Martin Cherry, librarian, and Susan Snell, archivist, at the Museum of Freemasonry of UGLE (United Grand Lodge of England), who readily sent me membership records for Worrell and other cricketers.

Anthony Harford (who sadly passed away in December 2021) introduced me to Claire Kilner, who was then Deputy Director of Alumni Relations at the University of Manchester. She arranged for me to meet staff who could help me track down their Worrell records. Dr. James Hopkins, the University Historian, and Dr. James Peters, the Archivist, pulled out everything they could find, including Worrell's exam results. Sue Hall-Smith cheerfully took me around the campus, pointing out where he had attended classes, and the memorial plaques in his honour. It was an enlightening trip, pleasurably enriched by their hospitality.

Joshua Surtees, on an unrelated mission, spoke with Sonny Ramadhin at his home in England in 2016, and asked questions on my behalf; my thanks.

The search for information is one part of the process, but one must distill the information and find a way to present it. It was my great fortune to have been virtually introduced to Professor Arnold Rampersad by the artist, Jackie Hinkson, at precisely the moment of working out the form and structure of the book. We have not physically met, but he was my guide through this process. In the first stages of crafting the material, he read the tentative early chapters, and gently offered ideas. Over the years he and Jackie have been two consistent pillars of support and I cannot fully express the depth of my gratitude.

I had been reluctant to impose on anyone the burden of reviewing the early chapters, but having apprehensively shared with Arnold and Jackie, for their cricket and literary perspectives, I thought I should turn to another kind of reader – one who had no particular interest in cricket. I was delighted when my favourite Caribbean historian, Professor Bridget Brereton, as bemused as she was by my request, agreed to read those same early chapters as well as the chapter relating to Worrell's tenure at The UWI. I wanted her historian's eye and her feedback as a reader who didn't give a hoot about cricket. Reginald Dumas also read those early chapters and his wealth of knowledge brought some crispness to some of the hazy background. I am indebted to Ian McDonald, Scyld Berry, Michael Holding, Sharda Urga and David Woodhouse, for taking the time to read the first draft of the manuscript and offering their insights and helpful comments. Their varied and enlightened perspectives helped me to revisit the material with revised ideas and allowed me to see the events through their collective experience.

Another chance email encounter with Professor John McIlwaine, a retired bibliographer and librarian who has taught librarians and archivists at university, was helpful, as he was the first person to see the entire manuscript and his fastidious eye spotted many errors. His range of skills made him the best possible person to have read it and I feel privileged to have benefitted from his generosity.

I am grateful to Lasana Liburd, who shared his football knowledge generously; to Siddhartha Vaidyanathan, who regularly bailed me out in locating obscure material; to Nasser Khan and Gulu Ezekiel, who are kindred trawlers in their insatiable passion for cricket trivia. They sent me troves of paraphernalia with a diligence that was awesome. Gulu arranged for me to meet with Lalita Phadkar in New Delhi, and gave me a tour of his impressive cricket collection.

My dear friends, Rahul Bhattacharya and Shruti Debi, allowed me to stay at their home in New Delhi, where their hospitality ensured the most memorable visit of my life. Through them I was never at a loss during that first visit to India, and they also enabled me to meet with Bishan Bedi, as well as Nari Contractor, through his son, Horshedar. Renu and Sonali Bhattacharya took me in when I was in Mumbai, and continued the lavish hospitality I had experienced in New Delhi.

To Marlon Rouse, who has helped with the photographic element, I am eternally grateful.

To all the people who graciously allowed me access to their knowledge and memories, I remain beholden. Many friendships were formed along the way. I wish to express my thanks to the people who allowed me to interview them, often repeatedly: Ainsworth Harewood, Alva Anderson, Baldwin Mootoo, Bishan Singh Bedi, Brian Stollmeyer, Bryan Davis, David Woodhouse, Easton McMorris (deceased), Gregory Gomez, Heather Rollock, Ian McDonald, Ivo Tennant, Joseph 'Reds' Perreira, Lalita Phadkar, Lance Gibbs, Marilyn Worrell, Martin Chandler, Michael Walcott, Nari Contractor, Neville McMorris (deceased), Olwen Cumberbatch, Rawle Brancker (deceased), Rodney Norville (deceased), Rudi Webster, Sir Everton Weekes (deceased), Sir Garfield Sobers, Sir Wesley Hall, Tiro Swaby, Tony Becca (deceased), and Tony Cozier (deceased).

Finally, this has been a long and complicated journey that altered my life. Often I faltered, but there was always something or someone to push me along. There are many whose names are not listed here, but you know who you are, and you have my thanks for that support.

Bibliography

Arlott, John, ed.; *Cricket: The Great Captains* (Pelham, 1971).

Barbados Cricket Association; *100 Years of Organised Cricket in Barbados, 1892-1992* (Barbados Cricket Association, 1992).

Baxter, Peter; Hayter, Peter; *England vs West Indies: Highlights since 1948* (BBC Books, 1991).

Benaud, Richie; *On Reflection* (Fontana, 1985).

Best, Tino; Wilson, Jack; *Mind the Windows: The Life and Times of Tino Best* (John Blake, 2016).

Birbalsingh, Frank; *Indian-Caribbean Test Cricketers and the Quest for Identity* (Hansib, 2014).

Birbalsingh, Frank; Shiwcharan (i.e. Seecharan), Clem; *Indo-Westindian Cricket* (Hansib, 1988).

Birbalsingh, Frank; *The Rise of Westindian Cricket: From Colony to Nation* (Hansib, 1997).

Brearley, Mike; *The Art of Captaincy* (30th anniversary edition) (Pan Macmillan, 2005).

Constantine, Learie; (with James, C.L.R.) *Cricket and I* (Philip Allan, 1933).

Constantine, Learie; *Cricket in the Sun* (Stanley Paul, undated, c. 1946).

Coward, Mike; *Calypso Summer* (ABC Books, 2000).

D'Oliveira, Basil; *Time to Declare* (W.H. Allen, 1982).

Eytle, Ernest; *Frank Worrell; The Career of a Great Cricketer* (Hodder and Stoughton, 1963).

Figueroa, John; *West Indies in England: The great post-war tours* (Kingswood Press, 1991).

Ganteaume, Andy; *My Story: The Other Side of the Coin* (Medianet, 2007).

Gilchrist, Roy; *Hit Me for Six* (Stanley Paul, 1963).

Giuseppi, Undine; *Sir Frank Worrell* (Nelson, 1969).

Goble, Ray; Sandiford, A.P. Keith; *75 Years of West Indies Cricket, 1928-2003* (Hansib, 2004).

Gray, Ashley; *The Unforgiven: Missionaries or Mercenaries, The Tragic Story of the Rebel West Indian Cricketers Who Toured Apartheid South Africa* (Pitch Publishing, August 2020).

Grimshaw, Anna (ed.); 'Letter to Berkeley Gaskin,' in *C.L.R. James, Cricket* (Allison & Busby, 1986).

Gupte, Carolyn; *Love without Boundaries: The 49-year partnership of Subhash and Carol Gupte* (Self-published, 2018).

Hall, Wes; *Pace Like Fire* (Pelham Books, 1965).

Harragin, Horace; *Sixty Years of Cricket: Australia vs The West Indies* (Paria Publishing Company Limited, 1991).

James, C.L.R.; *Beyond a Boundary* (Hutchinson, 1963).

Kanhai, Rohan; *Blasting for Runs* (Souvenir Press, 1966).

Kanhai–Gibbs Benefit Committee; *Kanhai, Gibbs: A tribute to two outstanding West Indians* (Victory Commercial Printers, 1974).

Khan, Nasser; *History of West Indies Cricket Through Calypsoes* (Caroni Safari Publications, 2016).

Kumar, Vijay; *Cricket, Lovely Cricket* (Self-published, 2000).

Laurie, Peter; *The Barbadian Rumshop* (Macmillan Caribbean, 2001).

Lequay, Alloy (ed.); *A Tale of Three Eras: Cricket Renaissance, Trinidad and Tobago, 1956-2005* (RPL, 2006).

Manley, Michael; *A History of West Indies Cricket* (Revised Edition) (West Indies Publishing, 1995).

Marshall, Roy; *Test Outcast* (Pelham Books, 1970).

Mehaffey, John; *Dawn of the Golden Weather* (Steele Roberts Aotearoa Publishers, 2018).

Menon, Suresh (ed.); *Pataudi: Nawab of Cricket* (Harper Sport, 2013).

Moyes, A.G. (Johnny); *With the West Indies in Australia, 1960-61* (Heinemann, 1961).

Murray, Bruce; Parry, Richard; Winch, Jonty (eds.); *Cricket and Society in South Africa, 1910-1971: From Union to Isolation* (Palgrave Studies in Sports and Politics, Macmillan, 2018).

Pilgrim, Torrey; *The Sir Frank Worrell Pictorial* (Creativity/Innovation Services, 1992).

Ramchand, Kenneth (ed.); *The West Indies in India: Jeffrey Stollmeyer's Diary, 1948-1949* (Royards Publishing Company, 2004).

Rampersad, Arnold; *Jackie Robinson: A Biography* (Ballantine Books, 1997).

Rampersad, Arnold; *Ralph Ellison: A Biography* (Vintage, 2008).

Roberts, Lawrence Donovan ("Strebor"); *Cricket's Brightest Summer* (Kingston, Jamaica, 1961).

Ross, Alan; *The West Indies at Lord's* (Eyre & Spottiswoode, 1963).

Sandiford, Keith A.P.; *Cricket Nurseries of Colonial Barbados: The Elite Schools, 1865-1966* (The Press University of the West Indies, 1998).

Sandiford, Keith A.P.; *Frank Maglinne Worrell, his record innings by innings* (West Bridgford, Notts, Association of Cricket Statisticians & Historians, 1997).

Sandiford, Keith A.P.; Tan, Arjun; *The Three Ws of West Indian Cricket: A Comparative Batting Analysis* (1st Books, 2001).

Sobers, Garry; Harris, Bob; *Garry Sobers, My Autobiography* (Headline Book Publishing, 2002).

Sobers, Gary (sic); *Cricket Crusader* (Pelham Books, 1966).

Stollmeyer, J.B.; *Everything Under the Sun: My Life in West Indies Cricket* (Stanley Paul, 1983).

Symmonds, Patricia; *Recalling These Things: Memoirs of Patricia Symmonds* (PrintSource, 2009).

Tennant, Ivo; *Frank Worrell: A Biography* (Lutterworth Press, 1987).

Walcott, Clyde; *Island Cricketers* (Hodder and Stoughton, 1958).

Walcott, Clyde; Scovell, Brian; *Sixty Years on the Back Foot* (Victor Gollancz, Orion Books, 1999).

Warner, Pelham; *Long Innings* (Harrap, 1951).

Weekes, Everton; Beckles, Hilary; *Mastering the Craft* (Universities of the Caribbean Press, 2007).

Worrell, Frank; *Cricket Punch* (Stanley Paul, 1959).

Articles cited

Aldred, Tanya; 'Radcliffe Royalty,' in *The Nightwatchman, Barbados Special Edition,* Forward Press, 2016.

Alston, Rex; 'People Today' interview, BBC Home Service. Broadcast on 12 June 1963. Subject: Frank Worrell. Transcript.

Baudelaire, Charles; 'The Painter of Modern Life,' *Le Figaro*, 1863. In *Charles Baudelaire: Selected Writings on Art and Literature* (Penguin Classics, 1993).

Baugh, Edward; 'The Pulpit-Eulogists of Frank Worrell,' in his *It was the Singing* (Sandberry Press, 2000).

Cardus, Neville; "Like Hobbs – never a crude or an ungrammatical stroke.' *Manchester Guardian,* 15 March 1967.

Duckworth, George; 'Commonwealth Cricketers,' in *Commonwealth tour to Pakistan, Karachi 1949*, Tour Brochure, and Tour Report.

García Márquez, Gabriel; 'The Mysteries of Bill Clinton', (translated by Alastair Reid), *Cambio*, 1 February 1999.

Gibb, Paul; 'Gibb in India,' *Wisden Cricket Monthly,* June 1982– March 1983.

Hector, Tim: 'Pan-Africanism, West Indies Cricket, and Viv Richards,' in *A Spirit of Dominance: Cricket and Nationalism in the West Indies,* Hilary Beckles ed. (Canoe Press, 1998).

James, C.L.R.; 'After Frank Worrell, What?', 7 March 1961, previously unpublished paper from the C.L.R. James Collection at the National Library of Trinidad and Tobago, NALIS. It was reproduced in its entirety (with permission) in the MPhil thesis, 'The Journey Towards West Indian Identity Through the Eyes of the Cricketer,' by Vaneisa Baksh, at The University of the West Indies, 2007.

James, C.L.R.; 'Sir Frank Worrell: The Man Whose Leadership Made History,' in *The Cricketer*, vol. 48, 5 May 1967.

Naipaul, V.S.; 'The Test,' from *Summer Days: Writers on Cricket,* Michael Meyer (ed.) (Eyre Methuen, 1981).

Pelican Annual, 1966.

Ramaswami, Cotar; 'Indian tour of West Indies in 1952,' in *Indian Cricketer Annual*, 1954.

Samuel, John; *Manchester Guardian,* 14 March 1967.

'Sport Shorts' in *Sport and Music Cavalcade*, Vol. 1. No. 3. December 1945.

Sydney Morning Herald, 12 February 1961.

'Why Axe Fell on 1959 Cricket Tour,' Johannesburg *Mail & Guardian*, 18 December 2014.

Wooldridge, Ian; 'The Gentle Revolutionary,' excerpt from *Cricket, Lovely Cricket: The West Indies Tour, 1963* (Robert Hale Ltd, 1963) in *Sport & Pastime*, Madras, 26 September 1964.

Newspapers, Magazines and Journals

The Age, Melbourne
Barbados Nation
Bulawayo Chronicle
Jamaica Gleaner
Johannesburg Mail & Guardian, South Africa
The Nation, Trinidad and Tobago
The New York Times
The Sydney Morning Herald
Trinidad Guardian
Wisden Cricketers' Almanack
Wisden Cricket Monthly
Wisden India Almanack

Online Links

Martin Williamson:
  https://www.espncricinfo.com/magazine/content/story/251196.
  html#comments

Garry Steckles:
  The triumph of calypso cricket | Caribbean Beat Magazine
  https://www.caribbean-beat.com/issue-100/
  triumph-calypso-cricket#ixzz6PZMAS5rt

Norman Preston, *Wisden*:
  https://www.espncricinfo.com/wisdenalmanack/content/
  story/155259.html

Link to clip from the 1967 film, *Around the World*:
  https://www.youtube.com/watch?app=desktop&v=-yogeh-y4bY

Presentation ceremony, post Fifth Test, at Melbourne, 1961:
  https://www.youtube.com/watch?v=H8BIzrQX0rc

C.D. Gopinath:
  https://youtu.be/qC176GoxzRU?t=865

One-minute British *Pathé* promotional newsreel:
  https://www.youtube.com/watch?v=wN8HaqkRGjw

Mauby women:
  Maggiolo, Christopher A.; "Champagne Taste on a Mauby
  Pocket: The Socioenvironmental History of Mauby in
  Barbados," (2010). Undergraduate Honors Thesis. Paper 681.
  https://scholarworks.wm.edu/honorstheses/681)

Audio

Rudder, David; *The Gilded Collection*, 1986-1989, "Dedication (A
  Praise Song)," Audio CD 1993.

Rudder, David; *The Gilded Collection*, 1986-1989, "Engine Room,"
  Audio CD 1993.

Primary Sources

West Indies Cricket Board of Control (WICBC) documents from 1950-1961.

Interviews

Anderson, Alva
Becca, Tony
Bedi, Bishan Singh
Brancker, Rawle
Contractor, Nari
Cozier, Tony
Cumberbatch, Olwen
Davis, Bryan
Gibbs, Lance
Hall, Sir Wesley
Harewood, Ainsworth
McMorris, Easton
McMorris, Neville
Mootoo, Baldwin
Norville, Rodney
Perreira, Joseph "Reds"
Phadkar, Lalita
Rollock, Heather
Sobers, Sir Garfield
Swaby, Tiro
Tennant, Ivo
Walcott, Dr. Michael
Weekes, Sir Everton
Worrell, Marilyn

Index

Prabhu, K.N., India visit 1962: 232-233
Prasanna, Erapalli, India visit 1962: 233-234
Preston, Hubert (*Wisden* Cricketers' Almanack editor), 88
Preston, Norman (*Wisden* Cricketers' Almanack editor), England 1950: 88, 89
Princess Alice Appeal Fund, Chancellor, The UWI, 245
Procope, Bruce, 266
Punch, Gordon, 194
Punjabi University, 102, 254, 256

Queen's Park Oval (QPCC), 58, 164
Queens Sports Club, Bulawayo, 179
Queensland, 200

Racial Discrimination Act 1975, Australia, 114
Radcliffe CC, 20, 45, 49, 57, 74-75, 77, 101-102, 105, 153
Radcliffe paper mill, 75
Radcliffe town, 54, 65, 78
Rae, Allan, England 1950: 85-86, 88, 93, 98-100;
in India, 107; 116, 128, 182
Ramadhin, Ramsamooj, England 1950: 97
Ramadhin, Sonny, 72, India: 80-82, 84; England 1950: 88, 92, 95-99;
Commonwealth tour: 103-106;
Wisden Cricketer of the Year: 109;
Australia and New Zealand: 110; 115, 142,
proposed South Africa tour: 162, 171;
apartheid: 179; 185-186, 190, 193, 199, 208
Ramaswami, Cota, India series 1952-53: 122
Ramchand, Gulabrai, India series 1952-53: 118-119, 122-124
Ramdus, Sean, 11
Ramsamooj, Donald, proposed South Africa tour: 162
Randall's Island Stadium, New York, 66
Reynolds Jamaica Mines, Ltd, 67
Rialto Theatre, Jamaica, 67
Richard Taylor (Pa T, headmaster of

Roebuck), 34
Richards, Mervyn, brother of Sir Vivian, 249
Richards, Rolf, 255
Richards, Sir Vivian, 242, 249
Richardson, Peter, 18
Richmond Gap, Barbados, 44
Rickards, Ken, Australia and New Zealand: 110
Ring, Doug, 113
Roberts, Andy, 249
Roberts, L.D.: *Cricket's Brightest Summer*, 213
Roberts, Ron, 179
Robertson, Jack, 73
Rodriguez, Willie, England 1963: 238
Roebuck Boys' Moravian Elementary School, 33
Roebuck Primary, 39
Rollock Reuben, 146
Rollock, Heather (née Brewster) Velda's daughter, 51-54, 260
Rose, Andrew, 265
Rosewall, Ken (Australian tennis player), 46
Ross, Alan, England 1963: 240
Rousseau, Patrick, 176
Rowe, Lawrence, 180
Rudder, David, 203

Samba, 203
Samuel, John, Worrell obituary in *Manchester Guardian*, 265
Sandiford, Keith, 60
Schofield, John, 77
Scott, Michael, 167
Sealy, James Edward Derrick (Derek), 43, 59, 266
Second World War, 56-58, 71, 103, 114
Servol, Trinidad, 201
Shackleton, Derek, England 1950: 99
Sheffield Shield, 200
Sherlock, Hugh, 225
Sherlock, Philip, Vice-Chancellor, The UWI, 225, 244, 247-248, 257-258
Simpson, Bobby, 162, 246
Sir Frank Worrell Commonwealth Memorial Fund (SFWCMF), 265
Sir Frank Worrell Ground, 229

326